Stuart Diver still lives in idyllic Th[...] a ski instructor during winter. Phys[...] priorities for him while he continue[...] his toes, which were frostbitten as a result of the Thredbo landslide. He works on the public speaking circuit and does a considerable amount of charity work while maintaining his involvement in a number of television productions.

Simon Bouda is a Sydney-based journalist and author of 20 years' experience, and is married with two children. He began his career in metropolitan and regional newspapers before moving into television journalism. Currently working for National Nine News, he was part of the Nine Network team assigned to cover the Thredbo tragedy. He was on site within hours of the landslide and provided reports and live coverage until the rescue mission was over.

SURVIVAL

*The inspirational story of the
Thredbo disaster's sole survivor*

Stuart Diver

with Simon Bouda

MACMILLAN
Pan Macmillan Australia

Acknowledgements are due to the following authors and publishers
for permission to quote from:
Poetry by Michael Leunig/*The Age*.
'Winter Grows Colder' by Jodie Young.

Acknowledgements are due to the following photographers and publishers
for permission to reproduce photographs:
Dallas Kilponen, *Sun Herald News*.
Warwick Kidd, Tim Fox, and the New South Wales Fire Brigades.
Bruce Johnston, and the Fire and Rescue Service of Western Australia.

Research sources: *The Daily Telegraph, The Sydney Morning Herald, The Australian,
The Age, The Canberra Times, The Sunday Telegraph, The Sun-Herald, Herald Sun,
The Australian Women's Weekly* and *Australian Associated Press*.

First published 1999 in Macmillan by Pan Macmillan Australia Pty Limited
St Martins Tower, 31 Market Street, Sydney

Reprinted 1999 (four times)

National Library of Australia
cataloguing-in-publication data:

Diver, Stuart.
Survival.
ISBN 0 7329 0981 3.

1. Diver, Stuart. 2. Landslides–New South Wales–Thredbo.
3. Survival skills. 4. Thredbo Landslide, Thredbo, NSW., 1997.
I. Bouda, Simon. II. Title.

994.47

Stuart Diver can be contacted c/o
Harry M. Miller & Company Management Pty Ltd
PO Box 313, Kings Cross NSW 1340 Australia

Typeset in 11/13pt Lucida Bright by Midland Typesetters Pty Ltd
Printed in Australia by McPherson's Printing Group

Poem for Sal

People sing

And people cry

But all I wish

Is that I, oh, I

Could take away

The tears and pain

And put you

Back together again

Stuart Diver, February 18, 1998

Acknowledgements

I would dearly like to personally thank each and every rescuer who braved that freezing week in Thredbo, risking their lives to try to save the lives of those who were trapped. It goes beyond a heroic effort ... it goes beyond a superhuman effort. I'm not only talking about the frontline rescuers; I'm talking about every single person who gave assistance—any assistance at all, no matter how small. And beyond that there are the rescuers' families—they were affected by the Thredbo tragedy in ways only they will ever know and understand.

My dealings with the rescuers that day were, of course, very limited. In fact there are only four names I remember clearly: firefighters Steve Hirst, Geoff Courtney and Warwick Kidd, and paramedic Paul Featherstone. Steve was the first voice, Geoff was the first touch and Warwick was the first face I saw. Feathers simply kept me alive. All four have been crucial to the writing of *Survival*, ensuring the story of the rescue was not just told but told correctly. It was only with the help of these men and countless others, such as Charlie Sanderson and Garry Smith from the New South Wales Police Service, that this was possible.

In writing *Survival*, Simon and I enlisted their aid more times than we can remember. We spent hours with these men, piecing together the story. While my recollection of what happened under the rubble is terribly clear, what happened on the surface was beyond my knowledge ... beyond my imagination. They helped us piece together the jigsaw puzzle of what happened. Our gratitude also goes to the various media relations officers from the emergency services—Kevin Daley, Mark Hargreaves and Scott Willis (New South Wales Police), Graeme Field, Dane Goodwin and Mick Johnson (New South Wales Ambulance) and Ian Krimmer (New South Wales Fire Brigade). Special thanks must go to firefighter Warwick Kidd who provided invaluable technical assistance.

As I sit here writing this the names of those who helped at Thredbo come flooding back. Don Woodland, and Bob and Genness Garven—chaplains who provided the spiritual strength for our families throughout the drama and helped me maintain my sanity afterwards. Doctors Steve Breathour and Richard Morris, and the nurses at the site, the Thredbo Medical Centre and Canberra Hospital, cannot be forgotten. They were there through my highs and lows.

And, of course, there is my family. Mum, Dad and Euan— where would I be without you and your strength? Where would I be without the introduction to the world that you gave me? Where would I be without your love? Sal's parents Margy and Andrew and her sister Anna—your love and support seems boundless and I know you will always be there. We still share the tears and I'm sure we always will.

Then there are my close friends and the people of Thredbo and Jindabyne who, through their understanding and compassion, have helped make it easier for me to continue with my life, sheltering me from the curious and the prying. Beneath their protective wing I feel safe.

For my inner sense of security I must sincerely thank my psychologist Daren Wilson whose pioneering techniques helped me deal with the immense trauma. In his own way he was inspirational to me and was an integral part of my recovery.

So too was my agent Harry M. Miller. It was Harry whose guidance in those early days led me through the public minefield my life had become.

Co-author Simon Bouda was a stranger to me until we

were introduced by the publishers. We immediately clicked and it's his understanding of me, and what happened to me, that enabled us to put it all into words. Over the past year our friendship has grown, with Simon and I spending hours reliving the tragedy in interview upon interview, shedding a tear or two and having an occasional laugh. It was Simon's attention to detail, his dedicated research and his intimate understanding of the rescue operation that resulted in *Survival* being what it is. I know it took him away from his wife, Karin and their young children Erin and Max and for those countless hours I sincerely thank them. And it was Karin who, apart from designing the cover, was often there late into the night providing a testing ground for our ideas.

Of course the mechanics of a book of this nature are complex and it's here where my thanks go to my publisher Amanda Hemmings and editors Cathy Proctor and Vanessa Mickan. Cathy first took on the project but her appointment in the maternity ward was, shall we say, more pressing. Vanessa took over and was able to juggle the reams of manuscript Simon and I provided and, together, we produced the book you are about to read.

Foreword

By Lieut. Colonel Don Woodland OAM
Salvation Army Chaplain

I am deeply honoured to have been asked to write this foreword and to endorse this amazing story of courage, character, determination and above all else love.

As a Salvation Army Chaplain specialising in trauma management, I have been involved in most of the major disasters in Australia over the past 25 years including the Port Arthur and Strathfield massacres, four bus crashes, several major hotel fires and then, in 1997, the tragedy that gave birth to the remarkable story you are about to read.

Prior to July 31st, 1997, thoughts of Thredbo brought to my mind a snow-covered postcard scene, the beauty of nature, fun, entertainment and challenges to be met. 'Bimbadeen' and 'Carinya' were just the names of two lodges in Thredbo village.

Stuart Diver was but one of the many people I had never met, as were the 18 souls whose life's journey ended so tragically on that cold winter's night.

The course of many lives was changed that night, including mine. In the following hours and days my life was entwined with the Diver family's and, in particular, with Stuart's.

The Thredbo landslide took Stuart Diver from a relatively obscure and private life, dragging him through 'The Valley of the Shadow of Death' into a life where the pendulum of his emotions swing madly from one extreme to the other.

I first met and talked with Stuart at the Emergency Department of the Canberra Hospital just a couple of hours after the heroic rescue team extricated him from his secluded, muddy tomb. I discovered a young man with great inner strength and, even in those first few hours, a man who was able to display an amazingly positive outlook despite the extreme circumstances. This was indeed a challenge to those of us who were privileged to be there to encourage and support him and his family.

It was not the tragedy of Thredbo that made Stuart Diver the person he is. It was his self-disciplined, positive character that enabled him to be a survivor of the Thredbo tragedy.

As you read Stuart's story it is his hope, and my prayer, that you will discover an approach to life that makes every single day a day of challenge—a day for which to be thankful. For truly, life is precious.

Stuart has not sought answers as to why the slide 'swept away half of his life'. He does not want to dwell on the 'if onlys', the 'whys' or even the 'maybes', for nothing can turn back the hands of time. Nothing will ever bring back his beloved Sally, but her spirit lives on to encourage and to challenge.

Amidst the joy and the sadness of the path of life Stuart has been called to walk, he has had numerous opportunities to speak to Australians about the power and strength within that enables us to rise above every circumstance of life in a positive way. The purpose of this book is to provide an insight into this miraculous story of survival and to share Stuart's belief that the challenges of life can be met and conquered.

Please take a moment to pause and remember those 18 people who did not survive. Remember too their loved ones, their families and those who, as they read this book, will be taken into areas of thought they would rather not visit.

I can only hope *Survival* will give you a deeper perspective on what really happened in the mountain slide in the deep, cold darkness of night.

May the real life story of one man's survival help you

discover within yourself those characteristics that will change your life and give you the inspiration, the motivation and the wherewithal to be a survivor.

This is the reason Stuart wanted this book not only to be written, but also carefully read.

Don Woodland OAM

Contents

one

Thirty Seconds

I'm fast asleep ... from somewhere in my subconscious comes a rumbling sound. It's growing louder ... louder. It's roaring.

My eyes shoot open. Is this one of those thrilling winds that tear down the valley? No, this is something far more frightening.

A hailstorm? An explosion? A bomb? The thoughts flash through my mind.

My body is shaking, uncontrollably shuddering. Sally awakes. Our flat is moving all around us. Everything's rattling, crashing down.

I hear the window being smashed in. I hear the glass shatter, showering us in our bed. Instinctively I lift my head off the pillow to see what's happening. It's dark. Nothing makes sense. The wall behind us comes crashing down on our bed. My head is forced back down as the roof caves in on top of us.

I can feel the ceiling about three centimetres in front of my face. I'm choking on dust. I can't breathe ... I'm coughing, choking. I can't see a thing.

I've got to get us out ... where? I roll off the bed and try to find the window. I land on broken glass, slashing at my hands and knees. I blindly feel around for a way out but there's no room ... no escape. It's pitch black. I climb back onto the bed.

Sal's screaming and screaming. 'It's OK, Sal. It's OK. We'll be all right.' She's screaming, 'I'm pinned ... I can't feel anything from the waist down'.

'It's all right Sal, we'll be OK.'

I reach out to touch her; she's still under our doona. I run my hand down the shape of her body and find a big concrete beam across her waist. I move my hand up to her face and she's screaming again, 'I can't lift my head. My head is pinned'. Her head's trapped by the bedhead.

There's so much noise. It begins as a rumble and blocks out everything else as it hits—a rush of freezing water. Both of us are screaming—blood curdling, terrifying screams. The water cascades down onto us. It swirls around us ... rising and rising.

I'm holding Sally's face. I can't shift the bedhead off her; it's not budging; I'm trying, Oh God, I'm trying to move it. The water's absolutely freezing—it takes my breath away as it bites into my semi-naked body.

The air is thick with dust; my mouth fills with it. I'm choking.

'Sal, it's OK. We're going to be OK. It's OK ... we're going to be all right.' She's screaming 'Stuart, Stuart' at the top of her voice—'Stuart, Stuart, Stuart' over and over and over again.

The water's flying around us. I put my hand over Sal's mouth. I've got to stop the water getting in. It's rising, rising. It's useless. I can feel the water seeping between my fingers, filling her mouth. I've got to stop the water. Please, I've got to stop the water.

It floods in, I can't stop it. She's gurgling, drowning as her lungs fill up. My hand is still over her mouth. I can feel her face, contorted. The screaming has stopped ... I feel the life drain out of my wife's body ... she goes limp. I can't see her face but I know it's a mask of sheer terror ... I take my hand away.

I feel so useless, helpless—totally, completely and utterly unable to do anything. I feel so small, so insignificant. I'd always thought I had the ability to protect Sal. I can't anymore.

I must survive ... nothing I can do for Sal ... I must try to save myself.

I arch my back, using my elbows to push myself above the water. Mud and water flow around me. My mouth is just out of the water. There's a tiny gap between my mouth and the roof, a tiny air pocket; at least I can breathe. The water laps at my lips. I must keep pushing myself up.

Part of me wants to just drop; the water can take me too. It's taken my wife ... take me too ... I just want to be with Sal.

The walls feel like they're closing in; the roof is getting closer ... get me out of here. No control. I'm constrained. I can hardly move.

The water flows away.

It all took just 30 seconds. Thirty seconds that keep replaying in my mind over and over again, the details as vivid now as the night it happened. Thirty seconds that changed my life forever and took the lives of 18 other people, one of them my reason for living ... my wife Sal.

Thirty seconds earlier we had been safely tucked up in bed. Bimbadeen Lodge had been our home, our haven; it had now become our tomb.

Thredbo has been like a second home, more or less, ever since I was born. I know this place. I know its beauty ... I now know its terror. It was the night of July 30, 1997.

Sal dying in my hands will stay in my mind forever. I'll take that memory to the grave.

Learning to Cry

I met Sally Donald during our first year at the Royal Melbourne Institute of Technology. Sally was like no other girl I'd met before—apart from her natural beauty there was just *something* about her. She had this infectious smile. When she smiled everyone smiled—that was the effect she had. But as far as I was concerned Sal was way beyond my reach, far too beautiful to be on my arm.

My teen years had been plagued with the usual problems and hang-ups. For one I was in a single-sex Catholic College, so I rarely got to speak to girls. And then there was my problem with acne, which put a pretty big dent in my self-confidence. It seemed to run in the family. My older brother Euan got acne before me and I always hoped it wouldn't pass on to me ... no such luck. My whole face, upper body and back were just covered in pimples.

I have never in my entire life asked a girl out, because I'm unbelievably shy. The girls I went out with all asked me. Even Sal asked me to go out. I never had the self-confidence to do it. People say, 'You're not shy, you can talk to anybody about anything'. But I am really an introvert.

I was 17 when I met my first long-term girlfriend. I went out with her for about a year-and-a-half until Sally decided she wanted to go out with me and enticed me away. I sometimes wonder what might have happened if I'd never met Sally— how different my life might have been.

The first phone call I ever made to Sal was when we were doing a major university assignment together. I spoke to her for about an hour. I was the funniest I have ever been in my life during that call. I cracked jokes, I was laughing, she was laughing—she was on the floor laughing. I had never been able to talk on the telephone (I still hate telephones, I like to talk face-to-face with people—it avoids all those uncomfortable silent pauses) but this was the best telephone conversation that I had ever had in my life. I thought: 'This person is really fantastic'. She was so easy to talk to, we could talk about anything. My confidence seemed to turn at this point in my life. I decided this was a person that I would like to get to know.

We started going out at the end of the first year of uni. As usual it wasn't me who made the first move. Finally, Sal said, 'What are you doing? I would like to go out with you'. So I just replied, 'Oh, OK. That sounds good'. Wow! Going out with a slim, beautiful blonde girl!

On our first date we went to the Royal Melbourne Institute of Technology's 'Wild Child Ball' at the Melbourne Town Hall. We kicked on to a dingy nightclub in Toorak and in the end were sitting on a couch down the back in the dark and Sal said 'Are you going to kiss me or do I have to kiss you?' Fumbling along I replied, 'Aah, I think you have to kiss me'. That was the first move and it blossomed from there.

Afterwards I was walking along Toorak Road with a friend of mine, trying to find a taxi. I asked him what I should do—I already had another girlfriend! He said, 'Well, just go with who you want ... you've got to make a decision, you can't hurt Sal's feelings'. The next morning I broke up with the other girl.

Nine weeks after our first date I moved in to Sal's house. We were besotted with each other and it seemed the natural thing to do. Mum wasn't hugely impressed, 'Look, you're only 20, you don't know what you are talking about' and I said 'Mum, this person is unbelievably special and this is the person I want to live with'. She wasn't happy at all. But Dad, who is probably the stricter Catholic, kept telling her, 'It's not a problem. Don't worry about it. There are no dramas. Just let him go. He'll work it out. If it screws up and he comes back, he's the one who is going to get hurt'.

So, off I went. It was the first time I'd had any major disagreement with my mother but considering my 'extensive' life experience I thought that I was the King of the World. It just simply felt like it was the right thing to do. Sal and I had been living in each other's pockets and formed a very strong relationship very quickly.

Sal was still living at home with her sister Anna and mother, Margy. Sal's dad, Andrew, had just moved out so I became the man of the house. I had always had this inbuilt desire to help others that wanted or needed help and perhaps that's the way I viewed Sal's family. So it was Sal, her sister, her mum and I, in a fairly big house out in Research on the outskirts of Melbourne.

I felt at home there. I instantly became very close to the three of them. Sal and I had separate bedrooms, so we had to sneak back and forth in the middle of the night. After eight months I bought Sal a double bed for her 21st birthday and that was the end of separate bedrooms—Sal's mum turned a blind eye.

Moving in with the Donalds probably made me more open than I ever had been. They were a very physical family so there was lots of hugging and kissing. My family was very different. Sure, there was plenty of affection but it was mental rather than physical. Mum and Dad showed their affection verbally with praise, encouragement and support. So moving in with Sal I thought, 'Wow this is pretty good. Warm bodies. This is great'. I was physically and mentally attracted to Sal and our relationship flourished.

Sally gave me my confidence; she made me realise that I wasn't as ugly as I thought I was. She gave me some direction in my life, made me start making decisions. But most important of all Sal taught me how to cry. It was the first time in my life I had ever had any dealings with anyone really outwardly emotional—a person who actually openly cried. We never did that; we were too tough we Divers. We didn't have much outward display of emotion. Sal and her sister cried a lot more than I had ever experienced people crying before. It was just their way of dealing with situations—they'd have a two-minute cry and that would be the end of that. In the beginning it scared me because I'd think, 'I've never seen anyone crying. What are they crying about? I must have done something really bad'. Then I'd realise it had nothing to do with me at all—it was just their way of displaying emotion.

When I moved in with Sal, her family had a black Labrador pup called Pasha. I ended up spending quite a bit of time training her and consequently became very attached to her. One day Pasha got out of the house and was hit by a car and killed. Before now I wouldn't have been too fazed—a dog being run over was not something that would make me cry. But it was different now; here I was openly crying, showing emotion as never before.

Sal was there to give me support when Pasha died and that's how it always was—one partner supporting the other. If Sal was crying because something had happened, then I would support her. Even though I realised it was OK to cry I still preferred to be in the supportive role. It's something that has become even more evident since the landslide—I still find, if someone else is crying, I'll immediately click into the supportive role. Afterwards I might go off on my own and shed a few tears.

Despite Mum's resistance to my moving out of home, my parents quickly came to love and accept Sal. She was bright, intelligent, and always seemed to be smiling and laughing ... and she could control me. Almost. Sal was the sort of person you really couldn't dislike. To list everything about Sal that I loved would take more than just this book—in a nutshell, she was just a beautiful person. She was intelligent, she could hold a good discussion and she made everyone feel comfortable in her presence. Especially me.

Since I lost her I have spent many hours with her parents, Margy and Andrew, remembering everything that we loved so much about her. Right from a little baby she was a beautiful, blonde girl with lovely blue eyes and an ever-present smile. She was extremely popular and charming and always had a lot of friends ... a person who really enjoyed everything that she did, enjoyed the people she was with.

But what most attracted me to her was that she was different from me; she offered a challenge to me in so many ways. That was a crucial part of our relationship. She was a quiet type while I was the original 'noisy boy'. So we complemented each other. Here I was always trying to drag her outdoors and here she was teaching me how to sit down and enjoy reading a book on the lounge. I was a challenge to her and she, in return, presented a challenge to me.

My fondest memories are going away and being outdoors together. But the ordinary, everyday things like going out to dinner or being with friends also meant a lot. Feeling so comfortable in a relationship, even just cooking and working on assignments together, was so special. The simple things, they're the things that have become permanent memories. It was good just to be with her, sharing everything. Having been a loner for most of my youth and then to actually be able to share my life with someone was vital and probably set the foundation of our whole relationship. Those years together in the beginning gave us the basis of trust for the years to come when we were forced to spend time apart because of our work commitments.

Everyone told me Sal wasn't an outdoor sort of person—I proved them wrong. I managed to get Sal and her sister Anna out onto the slopes and taught them both how to ski. I can still picture Sal's face beaming from beneath her beanie and sunglasses. I'm just so glad I got to share so much of my life with her and we packed so much into the short time we had together.

I know I can't ever bring Sal back but my second greatest love can't be taken away from me that easily . . . my love affair with the mountains.

I'd be lying if I told you I could remember the first time I came to Thredbo. But Mum keeps reminding me. I was eight weeks old, perched in a backpack carrier as she carted me to the top of South Rams Head, which is one of the big peaks. I was two-and-a-half when I first walked to the top of Mt Kosciuszko. I was four when I did my first overnight walk out the back of Mt Jagungal, which is also in the Snowy Mountains. I was five when I carried my first overnight pack and did my first three-night walk.

The mountains are in my blood. When I drive into Thredbo I feel so comfortable, like I'm coming home. It's hard for most people to understand that feeling considering how much Thredbo has taken away from me.

My parents Steve and Annette are Scottish. They had it pretty tough growing up. It was the end of the war; they both came from big families and had few luxuries. They lived in Glasgow and used to brave the misty, cold Scottish weather to go walking or skiing in the highlands. Dad drove a scooter, Mum perched on the back carrying the skis as they slid down ice-covered roads. They married in Scotland and honeymooned on the back of a Lambretta scooter touring Switzerland and Austria. A year later they decided to make Australia their home. When they got here it opened a whole new world for them—big open spaces, mountains to climb, fresh air to breathe—and it was warmer. Paradise compared to what they were used to.

They made Melbourne their home. It didn't take long for them to find people with the same interest in the outdoors. They joined the Youth Hostels Association and on Friday afternoons would head off into the hills with other outdoor enthusiasts.

Somewhere along the line they found time to have a family. First they had my brother Euan and two years later, on the 14th of January 1970, I was born at the Holy Cross Hospital in Geelong, Victoria. My mother says it was a difficult birth, a pretty long labour.

From an early age it was always Euan and I against the world. He's always been my *big* brother, always protective. If I got into fights or broke my arm (which I did five times when I was a kid) he was usually the one there to drag me home and make sure I was OK. In many ways he's still always there to get me out of scrapes.

I was a handful as a child. Never sat still. Always running about driving everybody crazy—always trying to do things bigger, better and faster.

I used to have to wear one of those harnesses with a leash on the back when we went to the supermarket because if I didn't I was gone—'see you later!'—down the street. I'm sure everyone used to look at Mum and think: 'Oh, that cruel lady dragging her son around like a dog'. But it wasn't cruel; it was the only way to keep hold of me.

My father was fairly strict. If he didn't pull me up with a smack on the bum every now and then I would have been out of control, especially when I was little. Like most kids I had no trouble finding some sort of mischief to get into—

pulling things off shop shelves when no one was looking, throwing stones off cliffs while we were bushwalking without thinking what might be below, and simply not doing what I was told.

There's little doubt I was accident-prone. Once I started to walk I would constantly fall over, for no apparent reason, and never, ever put my hands out to stop from landing flat on my face. Mum would pick me up and my eyes would be going round in circles in my head. I seemed to have a permanent lump on my forehead. The corners of tables were also a problem. For some reason I never saw them. I've still got scars on my temples from running into them.

My parents are Catholic and that meant we went to church every week no matter where we were—I used to hate it. I couldn't see any point in wasting an hour. It did, I suppose, provide a sense of discipline and probably complemented the upbringing Mum and Dad gave me.

Mum and Dad were very community minded. Dad was on the school council, which made him very involved in the day-to-day running of the school. On Sundays he would do readings at our local church. Mum got involved with groups like Community Aid Abroad. Both Mum and Dad tried to instil in us the importance of being involved in the community and would often take us to visit sick or elderly people in our area. My parents gave us a real sense of caring and compassion, which has never left me.

Even from an early age I had no problem with my own company. I could quite easily go into the backyard and play in the sandpit for three hours by myself. I loved digging holes and building huge monstrosities. If we were up at the snow I would go and build a snowman three times larger than I was. I always had to be doing something and enjoyed spending time by myself. That developed even more as I got older.

A lot of other kids thought we were a little strange—one of the main reasons was that we never had a television. Far from being a deprivation, on reflection, I think it was a blessing. Without a TV we had to create our own entertainment ... and we never had any trouble finding plenty, most of it mischievous. Kids at school would ask, 'What do you do at home? Your dad must have a really big record player and lots of records'. I'd look at them and say, 'Why?' They'd say, 'Well, if you haven't got a television what else can you do? You've got to sit around and listen to music'. What did we do? Well, we just went out. We rode around looking for stormwater drains to explore, hills to ride down or challenges to conquer. Near our house there was a really steep hill with a big bend at the bottom. It was one of our favourite spots for skateboarding—but Euan's skateboard was better than mine. One time we were hurtling down the hill and my skateboard developed the speed wobbles halfway down and I came off, face first, sliding on the bitumen into the gutter. I injured my arm and felt like I had worn my hipbone through the skin. Off I went home, bawling my eyes out. Typically I was cleaned up and told I would be OK. I've still got the scars.

Mum and Dad thought it important to have other adults play a role in our upbringing to broaden our horizons. One of them was a family friend, Irene Morell. Soon after we were born Mum went back to work part-time and Irene looked after us. She and her husband Max gave Euan and me another perspective on life. At their place we were able to watch television. It was a real treat. Uncle Max would always warn us if anything 'rude' came on by telling us to 'cover two eyes'. So we did—Euan covered one of his and I covered one of mine and we therefore got an eyeful of whatever he didn't want us to see. Aunt Irene and Uncle Max were real homebodies, which was a contrast to our lifestyle. Even though they sometimes spoiled us, they were also fairly strict.

My parents were very social within the Scottish community in Geelong and used to have enormous parties with something like 20 kids. My parents would be in their element. Dad would read poetry in his broad Scottish brogue and Mum would cook the haggis outside for three days before. She couldn't cook it in the house because it smelled so awful.

At these parties I was my most accident-prone. I would go ballistic and everyone was too busy to keep me under control. At the age of six I decided to enter stuntman status at one of these parties. I jumped off a four-metre high wall and tried to grab a tree branch to swing off. I thought I would be the life of the party; it was going to be so funny. I jumped, missed the tree, bang, smack, straight on the rocks below. I was screaming in agony—it wasn't very funny at all. Dad took a look at my injuries and declared that I was OK. Off I went to bed. Next morning, when I was unable to get up and my arm was swollen and bruised, it was decided I needed to see a doctor. Sure enough—another broken arm, my second.

I was always having accidents and in some sort of trouble at school, not major trouble, but people were always saying, 'What the hell is Stuart up to today?' Every time I walked through the door of the doctors' surgery nursing some injury from a skateboarding or bike-riding accident the doctor would say, 'OK, what arm is it this time?'.

I've only ever broken bones while doing stupid things. Maybe it was because I was the youngest I took more chances and didn't have to take responsibility. I always knew someone would come, pick me up and put me back together—it was usually Euan.

We were hardly ever allowed to take days off school for being sick. I got sent to school for three days with glandular fever before I was finally taken to the doctor. I had a blood test, fell over and that was the end of that for six weeks. That's how my parents always treated us, with a 'you'll be right' attitude. They were right—I'm still here.

Euan and I joke that it was starvation and beatings that made us the people we are today. But we *were* starved—at least we *thought* we were. Mum used to send us to primary school with just three-quarters of a Vegemite sandwich each. That was our lunch. We never got a whole sandwich. I can't explain why she did it and Mum denies it to this day but I reckon we could go to that school today and they'd still remember the Diver boys with their three-quarter sandwiches.

On the odd occasion Euan and I would get up early in the morning, before Mum and Dad, and make our own breakfast. Then we would wash everything up, clean up the kitchen, head back to bed and get up again when Mum and Dad did and have another breakfast—we'd be so full!

While my parents always made sure they gave us love, attention and anything else we needed, they didn't let us rule their lives. They were always there for us and provided us with opportunities that they never, ever would have dreamt of having themselves. Yet they never lost sight of their own dreams. What they did was include us in those dreams.

My parents were always employed so we always had money but instead of spending it on material assets they took us travelling.

As far back as I can remember the mountains straddling the New South Wales–Victoria border were our backyard. Although we lived in Geelong, and later North Fitzroy, they were simply our addresses—our home was the high country. Every weekend Mum and Dad would pack up the Kombi and off we'd go—it was what they lived for. From my earliest days it created a very, very strong bond.

When I was two-and-a-half we went to Fiji for six weeks to work on a mission, building a house for the Methodist Church. These nice Fijian girls took really good care of Euan and me and introduced us to sugarcane—I think that's where my sugar addiction came from.

It was such a cultural shock for us to go from suburban Melbourne to a Fijian village. For two young boys it was yet another wonderful adventure—mixing with children of completely different backgrounds who spoke another language.

I was three-and-a-half when I first put skis on; it was at Mt Hotham in Victoria. Back then my parents could never see the point of buying lift tickets. So we used to pull up in the Kombi about three kilometres from the main resort. We'd jump out, put our boots on and walk all the way up the hill. At the top we'd strap the skis on and ski down, fall over, do a couple of turns, get up. It didn't matter what the weather was like. Sometimes it was raining and we'd be out skiing. We'd complain: 'Mum, what are we doing skiing in the rain'. She'd answer in her Scottish accent: 'Och, in Scotland it's like this every day'. And that would be it, away we'd go. At the time I thought it was hell on earth but looking back on it now I realise it was a fantastic challenge and learning experience.

I remember my first pair of skis. A family friend, Phil Pilgrim, made them out of wood and I thought they were the hottest things known to man. If it was really icy I had to get the Swiss Army knife out at lunchtime and re-carve the edges because they had become rounded and wouldn't cut through the ice. Phil, his wife Sheila and their daughters Sarah and

Joanne would often come away with us—they had the same love for the outdoors.

Skiing for us was on a shoestring budget. We used to camp out every time. At Falls Creek, Thredbo—wherever we went, we camped out. We used to park the Kombi and set up the tents at the bottom of Crackenback Chairlift in Thredbo, or at the Thredbo Diggings, just down the road. I never had any idea that there were lodges in Thredbo and you could stay in them.

We used to cook in the Kombi and eat in the tents. We would go skiing and if it was raining, at the end of the day we would go to the bistro at Thredbo for a couple of hours, draping our wet ski gear over the heaters. When they had dried out a bit it was back to the Kombi and the tents.

Sometimes, during the school holidays, it would be just Mum, Euan and me because Dad had to work. He couldn't get all the school holidays off like Mum, who was a teacher. Dad would drive up over the mountains and stay for the weekends.

One time Mum, Euan and I were driving on the Alpine Way and a little clip on the accelerator fell off. The Alpine Way was mostly gravel and this little clip had dropped onto the road. In those days very few people used that road in winter. We figured this three-millimetre clip had dropped off somewhere over a 400-metre stretch of road. We walked up and down that road probably for four hours; not a single car came past. There was nothing we could do—we were stranded. We tried to rig up something but there was nothing we could do to get the accelerator working properly. Finally, Euan found it, we put it back on and away we went.

My mum has always been a very strong woman. She's told me stories about being at Dead Horse Gap, near Thredbo, in absolute blizzard conditions with snow bucketing down. There's Mum, Euan and I stuck in the Kombi. I was only a year old and I was screaming, bawling my eyes out while Euan was throwing a tantrum. Dad had gone off to climb Mt Kosciuszko in a blizzard. Imagine it, it's eight o'clock at night and he hasn't come back yet. It was in the days when there were no paths or signposts. I think he finally got back at about 10 o'clock.

Another time, after a weekend of skiing at Falls Creek

we piled into the Kombi for the four-hour drive back to Melbourne. It was in the days when there were no 24-hour service stations. We were happily heading home after a great weekend; but the weather turned nasty, with a blizzard on the mountains and rain down lower. A rock shattered our windscreen. There we were on the Hume Highway, all the service stations were closed and we had no windscreen. So Euan, Mum and I climbed over behind the back seat, on top of the engine, and lay down trying to keep warm and dry. Dad put on his balaclava, goggles and ski suit and kept driving. We were in the back, covered with sleeping bags and clothing and we were getting buffeted. He must have been going through hell. Seven hours later we arrived home in Melbourne. His hands were frozen and he was soaked to the skin.

In summer too we would be out there, no matter what the conditions. But there were times when even Mum had had enough. It would be boiling hot and the flies would be biting and Mum would curse: 'We're selling the van, we're selling the tent, we're selling the packs, we're selling everything. We're going home and we are buying a television. This is the last bloody time we are coming out walking'. She'd come out with this tirade four or five times a year. But by the following Wednesday she'd mellowed and by the Friday we were back out there doing exactly the same thing.

From an early age I had very high pain tolerance. It's an ability that allows me to go through pain barriers onto the next level, and then through the next pain barrier and through the next. I just keep going.

I remember several times when Mum, Dad, Euan and I got lost, we got stuck in big blizzards and amazing storms. I was four years old in one of these blizzards and Mum was hanging onto my hand. She always encouraged us to keep going. She used to say we'd rest 'just around the bend'. Funny, we never seemed to get to that bend.

One time Mum had me by the hand as we climbed up the Carisbrook falls at Cape Otway, on the Victorian coast. She slipped. I let go of her hand. I slid away, careering towards the edge of a 30-metre waterfall. I was scrambling to grab something to stop me sliding away but the flowing water and slippery rocks just swept me away. Somehow Mum managed to grab me just short of the edge.

When I turned six Mum and Dad took us to New Zealand. We did three major walks, each between three and six days long. It was probably the first really serious, hard walking I had done.

One of the walks involved us crossing a river in the Mount Aspiring National Park. It was about a kilometre-and-a-half wide. The locals told us the river was shallow and we could walk across, no worries. Mum and Dad thought this was a great idea so they loaded us all up and away we went. As we got further across, the water gradually got deeper and deeper. Dad was leading the way and we were all holding hands. About halfway Mum decided to turn around and see how I was going, as I hadn't said anything. I couldn't have said anything—I was submerged. Still holding Mum's hand, pack on my back and I'm under the water. I just kept walking, thinking if Mum, Dad and Euan are walking I've got to keep going because we're going to come out somewhere. Holding my breath. That was the trust I had in my parents. And the commitment to get through and come out the other side.

As I've said, Mum and Dad spent most of their money on taking us travelling. We had this money jar on the top of the cupboard—Dad used to shove $50 bills into it instead of taking us to the footy, or buying a bottle of Scotch or a few bottles of wine.

That jar took us to Nepal when I was nine—it had always been Dad's dream to see the 'biggest and best mountains in the world'. My parents organised a 27-day trek to the Everest base camp. But that wasn't enough—then we did another 'little' nine-day walk in Annapurna Sanctuary. We carried all our own gear; Mum ended up hurting her knee and Euan, Dad and I had to carry her gear as well. Typically, for us, it rained most of the time. Mum called it the 'Wet Hell of Annapurna' and that was going to be the end—the absolute end—of her trekking career. She vowed never to go again—but we had heard it all before. Since then she has been back to Nepal twice. She'll never, ever stop trekking. She'll always be drawn back.

In Nepal we had to write a diary of events; that was our English lesson. And we had to do our times tables every night until we knew them back to front, upside down and inside out. To just sit down and write, especially about your own experiences, at the age of nine, in such a foreign country, was a great thing to do. My parents felt that sort of experience was an equally good education to staying at home and going to school. While schooling played an important role there was so much more to do, so much more to experience.

My parents' determination, especially Mum's, was passed on to us. If Mum was forced to stay at home for a weekend she just went mad. Sure, she'd go to the theatre and enjoy a meal in a restaurant, but if there were three hours in the middle of the day where nothing was planned she'd head down to the beach or get out into the bush. She just couldn't stand being cooped up and still can't. I can't stand being idle either.

Those early experiences gave us adventure and a certain adrenaline rush—I think that has carried on through my life. I suppose if you start skiing or doing overnight walks when you're three-and-a-half or four and you're doing things like going to Everest base camp when you're nine, where do you go from there? You've got to keep challenging yourself and taking more and more risks. It either set me up for a really big fall or gave me a fantastic base from which to grow—I think it gave me a fantastic base. Through travel and adventure my parents gave me the opportunity to expand my mind and my knowledge of the world, world events, and what was going on around me.

When we weren't off skiing or climbing mountains, we lived in Geelong in a modest four-bedroom home. Mum and Dad could have saved their money and put it into a big, flash house or flash cars but we would have missed out on so much. You could never put a price on the experiences we had as kids.

I went to St Joseph's Marist Brothers College in North Fitzroy. Ninety-three per cent of the students were Italian, Turkish, Greek or Lebanese. That had a fairly big impact on me because here I was living in Australia but we were the minority, we were the skips, we were on the bottom rung of the ladder at school. On my first day I stood in the playground and bawled my eyes out.

Going to that school helped Euan and I develop survival skills. While we were always at the bottom of the social pile we were near the top of the academic pile. We nearly always achieved high grades and so that put extra pressures on us— it created tension because all these other guys were below us. I don't see that tension as necessarily negative. It just added a bit more of a challenge.

From the time I was about halfway through primary school my dream was to become a ski instructor. That's all I wanted to do. The teachers and other kids couldn't understand it, but I couldn't see any better lifestyle in the world than being a ski instructor. Towards the end of high school I got pressure from Mum about it; she wanted me to study information technology. She wanted me to become a computer programmer, sitting inside at a desk, which is really funny coming from the woman who dragged me through the outdoors for most of my early life.

What my upbringing gave me was a feeling for the big picture in life. With their preference for travel and adventure over material possessions, my parents gave me a sense that there was more to life. That the little things, the peripheral, day-to-day things, aren't so important.

When I left school I decided to do a degree in hospitality studies because it was a really broad degree—cooking, bar work, as well as business law, accounting, economics and management. It gave me a good general grounding. But ski instructing was never far from my mind; that was my ambition.

My time at RMIT was great. For the first time in my life I spent a lot of time with one group of people. There was a core group of eight of us; we would all do combined assignments and homework together ... Sal was part of that group.

The eight of us were pretty close (we still are ... they've been crucial in getting me through since the disaster). It seemed like we did everything together. We had a favourite lake on the South Australian–Victorian border called Lake Monibeong and we would go there and fish. Or, we would go skiing or windsurfing. It was the first time I had ever had friends that I could actually go away with and share my love for the outdoors. Up until then I had only ever shared those experiences with my family.

Yet I still needed my time to myself. I didn't join the university ski club, or the mountaineering club or the bush-walking club—I just wasn't a club sort of person. I enjoyed going away and doing those things by myself.

It was about then that my confidence started to build because I realised that I could show people how to ski and take people into the bush and go camping, and show them how to windsurf. It's probably when, in a way, I started to break away from Euan. Being the younger brother, the younger sibling, meant that I had always been in Euan's shadow. Now I'd started to break out, to branch out on my own.

During uni I got a job at the Loaded Dog pub in North Fitzroy and slowly worked my way up to be trainee manager. I never had a drink until I started working at the Loaded Dog. I used to hate the taste of beer but I started to enjoy the occasional brew. I left there and became assistant manager at the Station Tavern in Prahran, a boutique pub brewery. I didn't mind working there because it was something I hadn't done before so it was an adventure, a challenge. As long as I was challenging myself I was fine. When I got bored, after a year or so, I left.

It was about this time that I followed the trends and decided to grow my hair. Dad wasn't too impressed; he thought I looked like an English sheepdog. One night he armed himself with a pair of scissors, grabbed me and gave me an ultimatum: 'cut it or I'm going to cut it for you'. It didn't get cut.

In the third year of uni, as part of our course, Sal and I went to Hamilton Island in the Whitsundays to work in the hospitality industry. It was the first time we'd moved out on our own so it was a turning point in our lives. We worked there over Christmas and it was just us without any outside influence from either Sal's or my family.

We had quite a hard time on Hamilton Island. The work was ordinary and the boss wasn't the nicest. We were supposed to stay there for a year but we had no money and we couldn't even make enough to pay the rent so after about six weeks we headed back to Melbourne. Even so, it had been good for us to face the challenge together.

This was when I came to the realisation that Sal was the person I wanted to spend the rest of my life with. I was only 22 and it was a fairly monumental decision given my philosophy on long-term relationships. I was very anti-marriage in my teen years and into my twenties. I'd always thought great relationships were meant to end so new ones could start. I believed that marriages were only meant to last ten years and then you had to marry someone else because there's no way you can keep a relationship going past ten years. Even once Sal and I started going out I still had that attitude—I couldn't see any point in long-term relationships. But after Hamilton Island things changed; I decided that it was the way to go. I wasn't ready to propose, but I was heading in that direction.

The next year, 1992, Euan and I went travelling for three months—Canada, Britain and Europe. Sally stayed home. That was the first long break that we'd had. We'd basically been together for four years, in each other's pockets, and then I said 'I'm going on holiday, do you want to come?' Sal didn't want to come on a skiing holiday with us because her skiing wasn't up to par and she didn't want to spend that sort of money. So, I said, 'All right, no worries, I'll go with Euan'. So, I jumped on a plane and away I went.

Even though my love for Sal was really, really strong I still wanted to do what I wanted to do. It was a hard decision to make. I missed Sal like I'd never missed anyone before. It was a very difficult time. I guess it was a test of our relationship—a test we passed. When I came back she threatened to kill me if I did it again.

It was a turning point in our relationship; we realised we needed each other but could be separated and come back together again—the trust was there.

Back in Melbourne Mum suggested it was time for me to do something constructive with my life. Despite her desire that I enter the cyber world she found out about a traineeship with a company called The Outdoor Activities Group, based in Eildon in Victoria. It was a 12-month traineeship where you went away for six weeks training in rafting, six weeks in rock climbing, six weeks in all the other disciplines, 12 weeks taking kids on an outdoor program and work experience with other companies.

21

It was pretty hard to get into and cost about eight-and-a-half thousand dollars. Obviously I had no money. Mum and Dad came to the rescue. I think there were about 150 applicants and they only took eight—I was lucky enough to be one of them.

It was January 1993 and yet another turning point for Sally and me. We realised that we both had ambitions and wanted to fulfil them. We both knew how much we loved one another but we also understood that we were still going to be our own, separate characters.

Sal really wanted to climb the corporate ladder in five-star hotels. She'd always wanted to have a good career and enough money in the superannuation fund. But I, on the other hand, was more interested in outdoor adventures than a full-time job. The beauty of our relationship was that we understood each other's dreams and respected them.

My course took me away every week but I would come back on weekends. Sometimes I'd get a week off and I'd spend time with Sal but there were also times when I would use that week to go rock climbing. Sal would say, 'What are you thinking Stu, you've got a week off, what are you doing going rock climbing?' Obviously it put strain on our relationship. But by the end of the year everyone, including Sal, could see I was changing and evolving. I really started to show some leadership. I'd always had that trait but it hadn't emerged—now I was starting to use it. Everyone close to me saw the benefits. I was coming further out of my introverted shell. By the end of the year I had achieved guiding instructing qualifications in all disciplines as well as a wilderness first aid qualification.

It was during the course that I met Iain 'Grovesy' Groves, a friend who today still shares my dreams. He was a like mind. Like me, he'd travelled, been to Nepal. He'd had a similar upbringing to mine. We shared the attitude of 'let's show the world what we can do'. We had our own program and we were both very, very strong headed. During that year we formed an unbelievably close friendship and Grovesy is still one of my best mates.

The course taught me a lot about survival. I realised you could survive a fair bit of pain—although my accident-prone childhood had begun teaching me that long ago. Again I grew in self-confidence. I was on a roll, releasing things from my mind and forming new ideas. Letting go of the past and planning for the future. Grovesy and I hatched a plan to set up an outdoor adventure company. He would concentrate on rock climbing and rafting while I would handle the skiing, bush walking and the management side. It was going to involve Sal and Grovesy's partner at the time. We were all going to get together and set up this great company. Grovesy and I still are.

The Outdoor Activities Group employed me as a group leader the following year. So again I was away on five- or 10-day programs. Out with a group, back for two days, quick turn around, always away. I began to really miss being in Melbourne with Sal. But I had this passion for the outdoors. I was torn between the two. Eventually we decided that I should pursue that path and so I headed for Thredbo. Sal and I agreed it would be the perfect place to one day set up our outdoor adventure company.

I'd always wanted to be a ski instructor and I'd become a cross-country instructor during the course. So we decided I should get my downhill skiing qualifications in Thredbo. We knew that I needed as many qualifications as possible to make the outdoor adventure company work. At about the same time Sal decided to move to Sydney where she got a job at the Hyatt Hotel.

There was never any doubt we could keep the relationship going—we never even questioned it. We were so close by then that it didn't matter where we lived—'absence makes the heart grow fonder'. It truly did. The more time we spent apart the stronger we became. Of course it was hard being away. It was the worst at night, all I could think of was being with Sal ... it's still like that now.

I'd go up to Sydney for weekends or Sal would come down to Thredbo. It was the 'alternate weekend relationship'. But it was OK—it made the time we were together all the more special. Halfway through winter '94 I decided it was time to ask Sal if she would be my wife.

three

Engaging Adventures

T he sun was setting on Bondi Beach; the waves were rolling up the sand; a few surfers were out the back waiting for the next wave and there we were—Sal and I—sitting on the esplanade wall. We had just bought some fish and chips and in my pocket I carried the corkscrew which would open the bottle of red we'd brought along.

It was no candle-lit dinner but it had all the romance of one—it was the celebration of our engagement. I had been living in Thredbo and Sal was in Sydney. I telephoned her and said I was coming up. I had the plan already in my mind. When I got there it was pretty simple, almost inevitable.

I met Sal after work. We were parked in my car at Kings Cross about to head back to her flat at Randwick. I looked across at her and she looked as beautiful as ever, her blonde hair pulled back in a ponytail, dressed casually in jeans and a t-shirt. I was nervous but somehow mumbled the words.

'Why don't we get engaged, Sal?'

She seemed a little surprised but smiled as she looked into my eyes.

'Oh ... yeah ... I'm into that as well, let's do it.'

The next question was the ring. We drove straight into the city and looked at a few shops until we found one we both liked. It featured an emerald surrounded by diamonds. It was simple in design but that's what we wanted.

'I can't just give you the ring here in the shop,' I told her.

But then I thought 'Why not?' So I did. With the shop assistant looking on I slipped it onto Sal's finger.

Back in the car we headed to Bondi Beach to celebrate. It had been less than four hours since I'd arrived in Sydney.

As we fought off the marauding seagulls we got on the mobile phone and rang everyone we knew and told them we were engaged. Like us, I think most knew it was inevitable. Both our parents were over the moon—they couldn't have been happier for us.

Once we'd finished telling the world we just sat there holding hands, looking out to sea. Words had always been unnecessary between us and now was no different. It just felt so *right*.

Because ours was a mutual back and forth relationship, after I bought Sal the ring Sal bought me a new pair of ski boots. Sal got the ring—I got the boots. Typical. That was my idea.

By now Sal was becoming more adventurous. I had started taking her rock climbing and abseiling. It was terrifyingly scary for her the first few times but after a while she really started to get into it. Here I was sharing my love for the outdoors with the woman I loved. Sal had the confidence and trust in me that I would never place her in danger. Rock climbing and mountaineering are relatively safe sports with the proper training, which by now I had had plenty of.

They say it's always the hardest thing to teach a spouse and I don't deny there were lots of tears. I always pushed Sal. Growing up in the outdoors it was hard for me to understand why she couldn't get over her in-built fears as quickly as I could. So we had our tiffs when I pushed her out of her comfort zone. I soon came to realise that of course Sal would be scared and apprehensive about abseiling down a 100-metre cliff. But as her confidence grew and she came to enjoy the adventure it became unbelievably rewarding for the two of us and seemed to draw us even closer together.

Helping Sal push beyond her boundaries was one of the huge positives in our relationship, as I look back on it now. Although she obviously found it hard sometimes, the joy of our adventures together far surpasses anything I could have ever wished.

It's like an addiction, the love for the outdoors—an addiction that has only developed and become stronger as I've grown older. It's something I have always wanted to pass on to others—to share the enjoyment my family experienced. With Sal it was no different—she was always eager to learn or experience more.

The snow drew me like a magnet; I always wanted to be where it was and it wasn't long after Sal and I got engaged that I decided I wanted to go to Canada to work as a ski instructor for six months. In the long run it would help us in our plans to start the adventure company but obviously it posed a dilemma for Sal, who had work commitments to think of. We decided to make a firm date for the wedding so that if we were again to be separated we would at least have something definite to aim for—our marriage on 12 November 1995.

Then Sal surprised me. She decided that it was time to briefly put her career on hold and to join me in Canada. She was willing to postpone her career to come with me, for which I am forever indebted. She left her job at the Hyatt Hotel, we got our working holiday visas, and away we went.

When we arrived in Canada we stayed with a family friend for four weeks while we looked for work. Both of us found jobs in Silver Star, British Columbia—Sal as a restaurant manager and I in the ski school. It was another step in our relationship; we had to find our own place to live, we had to buy a car, we had to fend for ourselves and survive as a couple. Apart from our short stint on Hamilton Island we'd both been living at home and now we had to find our own way in life. We both got pretty homesick but it didn't take long for us to meet some new friends and feel more at home.

Both Sal and I really changed a lot during the six months we were there, I suppose you could say we matured. We began to rely more on each other and that helped us grow within ourselves and made us take responsibility for the decisions we made.

While we were in Canada Sal's skiing ability improved out of sight and she developed a real love for life in the snowfields.

Sal's camping experience was very limited; she'd only ever gone camping once in her entire life. At the end of the season my mate Grovesy came to visit and the three of us headed off on a big trip into the Wapta Icefield, an eight-day, eight-night trip. This was serious adventuring; we had avalanche transceivers and avalanche probes, and had to cross crevasses with fully roped-up harnesses and big packs on our backs. It was no picnic. Sal had never done any ski touring before and the icefield was nothing like I'd ever experienced so we were both on a steep learning curve. We had an absolute ball. The only thing Sal didn't like was not being able to wash for eight days.

Then we graduated to the next challenge, the Columbia Icefield, one of the biggest icefields in North America. Sal and I, Grovesy and another friend, Greg Beanland, walked and skied for days, sometimes under huge ice seracs, big ice blocks liable to crack and fall at any time. The idea was that Grovesy, Greg and I were going to climb Mt Columbia. We set up a base camp, dug in and pitched the tents. The day we were doing the alpine ascent we got up at 2.30am and set off. We climbed up and summitted out at the top of Mt Columbia at about 10.00am. We'd told Sal that if we weren't back by the following morning, she had to ski out and get help. What were we thinking? We'd left her on a massive glacier 20 kilometres by 20 kilometres with these big ice blocks just falling off the landscape. Sal's skiing ability was good but it was by no means up to that. We had just told her to ski out and get help—simple! At the time I really didn't realise what we were asking of her. We left Sal stranded on a glacier; you can imagine how lonely it was out there on her own.

Every so often I'd look back towards the camp and all I could see was this tiny little pinpoint. This little black dot in the middle of an expanse of snow—that was my fiancée.

It was a warm day by the time we reached the top of Mt Columbia. We knew the warmer it became the greater the risk of avalanche and that we couldn't rest long before we started back down. We had a bite to eat for about 20 minutes and then we saw this plane circling around Sal. I had no idea what was going on and there wasn't much I could do about it anyway because I was miles away. The plane landed and taxied right up to our campsite. Then it took off again, circled around us a few times, and landed again near our campsite. So we started rushing back and all the way I'm thinking: 'These bastards, they've stolen Sal'. We arrived at about 6 o'clock that night—

exhausted—it had been a 20-kilometre day. We'd done a two-day climb in just one.

Sal was still there ... safe. The plane had been full of Japanese businessmen on a tour of the Columbia icefields. They'd flown in, saw our tents, saw Sal. It must have been a sight; there's Sal stripped off, sitting in her undies getting a tan. Beautiful. Photos of this blonde girl in the middle of a glacier—their minds must have just blown. Two tents. No one else and she's trying to explain to them 'My boyfriend and his two mates are climbing over there'.

What the hell was I thinking taking Sal there and then leaving her on her own? Anything could have happened. A massive whiteout could have come in. We knew what we were doing and where we were going but forgot about Sal. I look back on that day and shake my head with disbelief but Sal later told me it was a tremendous experience. She told me she knew I would be back; she seemed to have the same faith in me that I had in my parents when they took me on some adventure. It was so rewarding because Sal was trying things she'd never have dreamed of before we met.

I'm so glad Sal enjoyed the adventures we shared. Sure, she was often apprehensive to start with but afterwards would rave about how much fun she'd had. I'd always wanted to take her to Nepal. Euan and I had enjoyed it so much as boys I thought she would too. We were planning to go in October 1998. I know she would have loved it.

After our six months in Canada Sal decided she was going to live and work in Thredbo. I couldn't have been happier. She worked out that she could have the same job in Thredbo as she had in the cities. But Thredbo provided something else—lifestyle. She figured she could have financial stability, a quality job and a tremendous lifestyle in Thredbo. Sal lined up work at the Thredbo Alpine Hotel and I was going to do my second season as a ski school instructor.

That winter Sal gained the respect of everyone she was working with and quickly became very popular. She earned the praise of her superiors because she was so focused and diligent in her work. She was working in the reception and reservations area and loved it because she was dealing with people, helping them. Committed—that's an appropriate description of Sal's character, both personally and professionally.

I always felt that as long as Sal and I had enough money to survive, had a roof over our heads and a car, plus a bit extra to go travelling overseas and to go skiing, that's all we needed. Sal obviously had other ideas because she really enjoyed her material possessions. Clothes and shoes. She had the biggest shoe collection in the world. She liked going out and loved getting her hair done, a facial and a manicure. It provided a balance, it was another integral part of our relationship.

Our relatives would come up and visit and they just saw how happy we were. Sal grew to love the Thredbo environment as much as I did; she really started to have a passion for it.

By the time we were living in Thredbo I'd shed my shyness and developed a bit of a reputation as a 'noisy boy'— that quickly became my nickname. But Sal had a calming influence over me. There was one occasion, though, when Sal came out with an uncharacteristically crude joke. Everyone was shocked—she was quickly dubbed 'noisy girl'.

That winter we spent a lot of time travelling up and down to Melbourne on weekends, visiting the folks and organising things for the wedding. I used to tell Sal about driving up the road into Thredbo and feeling that I was coming home—and she quickly felt that way as well. We were coming home to the mountains we both loved so much, the valleys and hills covered with snow gums, black sallees, alpine ash, and the pretty silver snow daisy. Sometimes you would even see wombats and emus on the Alpine Way or wedge-tailed eagles floating on the updraughts or crimson rosellas darting between the gum trees ... this was home.

I think the trust we had in each other really grew from those years of being apart. That builds up an amazing strength in a relationship. Sal was different from any other woman I have ever known and I think that was because of her ability to communicate and be one with me.

There was a jacket with a sunflower pattern on it that was pulled out after the landslide. It was Sal's. It really summed up her character—bright, cheerful and warm. I bought it for her when we were in Banff, Canada. It was so her. Black with big yellow sunflowers on it.

It was hard not to like Sal. She just had that personality. I don't think she ever hurt anyone in her life. She had patience for everyone. She would come home from work and tell me about some of the abuse she got on the telephone while working at the hotel. I wouldn't have been able to put up with it but she just accepted it, dealt with it in her way and because she was so accepting you couldn't dislike her. That was her beauty.

With the majority of people you meet there's always one or two things that annoy you. You might be 90 per cent attracted but there is still that 10 per cent you're not sure about. With Sal everything worked so well. She was unbelievably special. There was no difficulty in anything between us. It was too easy. It all sounds unbelievably rosy but it's true, we were just so close. We were lovers and best friends. I would have been happy to have no other friends in the world, never have done anything, just spent all my time with Sal. We were always so comfortable in each other's company. That's what I really miss now.

four | One and One
Makes Three

Sal and I had a theory about relationships and I think it's about right. On your own you are a 'one'. If you are a really special person and have achieved something that sets you apart from the crowd then you are a 'one-and-a-half'.

When you meet with another 'one' you join together but you don't just make a 'two'—what grows out of the relationship makes a 'three'. Now, if over time, you, as a couple, go out and do things in your lives that number grows and gets bigger.

Even if you split up or are forced apart you don't revert to being a 'one' again because of what you have already achieved in the relationship. You've learned so much from the relationship that you go away a 'two' or at least a 'one-and-a-half'. And then if you meet someone else and share that point system you can continue to grow for the rest of your life.

That theory is something Sal taught me and it makes so much sense. Sal and I were probably both 'ones' when we joined together but by the end I feel we were 'fours' or 'fives'— we'd done and achieved so much together.

We made our 'three' on November 12, 1995. It was our wedding day.

We wanted it kept as simple as possible. Even though marriage is a big step and a life-long commitment, we saw it as just another development in the growth of our relationship.

I had always wanted our wedding to be a little bit different to the norm. We didn't want to destroy traditions just for the sake of being anarchists, but we wanted it to be subtly different. A wedding that was very personal to both Sal and me, something our friends and family would always remember.

About four weeks or so beforehand Sal and I sat down and sorted out exactly what we wanted to happen on the day; we didn't want to be restricted by what was 'expected' or by what society dictated. I had been to a lot of weddings that were so formal and religious that it seemed like the couple was so involved in the pomp and ceremony of the situation that they didn't actually *say* anything to each other.

We wanted to make it really personal—about family and friends—things that meant a lot to us. We wrote our own vows—we had only one piece of religious verse in there. Neither Sal nor I were religious. I think Sal was basically an atheist. She never went to church in her life. Her mum and her sister were the same. But in saying that, I believe the three of them were probably the most Christian-living people you could ever meet—very caring and sharing.

We had one meeting with the celebrant beforehand to sign the official forms and to take care of the legal requirements. Afterwards, as we drove back up from Melbourne to Thredbo, we sorted out what we wanted to say—Sal wrote out our ideas and that's the way they stayed. None of the traditional words were going to be said; we wanted our wedding to be more personal and less formal, using words like 'friend' and 'lover'. Words came so easily between us so there was no difficulty in deciding what we wanted to say to each other on the day.

I wanted Dad to read one of Robbie Burns' scandalous poems. Burns was the classic Scottish poet with a reputation as a womaniser and a drinker. Sal and I thought it would be a laugh but Dad wouldn't be in it: 'No, I won't. I draw the line. I'm going to read a romantic soliloquy from Shakespeare'. So that's what he ended up doing.

Sal was responsible for the invitations. There were none of the usual problems deciding who should be there—the people we really wanted to be there were there and that was that, there was no argument from either side of the family.

Sal's Uncle Pete and Aunt Judy said we could have it at their house; they had a big mudbrick home out in Eltham. So we decided on a garden wedding. Pete and Judy were so meticulous with their garden and bent over backwards making it just right. Pete chose the spot where the ceremony would take place—a section of beautifully manicured lawn surrounded by rose bushes, just the perfect place. The day before the wedding they were putting the final touches to the garden and decided to paint the window frames. Judy shook the brush out on the lawn right on the spot Pete had chosen for us to stand—almost instantly the grass turned brown—he was beside himself. Sal and I turned up to see how things were going and there was Pete, shovel in hand, madly trying to fix it up. Luckily Judy's brother was the greenkeeper at the local golf course so Pete asked him to get some of the best pieces of turf from the course. The next day you couldn't tell the difference—the grass was once again super green—I reckon they must have been up most of the night making it just right.

I have always disliked big groups and formal occasions so it was a very informal, low-key sort of thing but nevertheless, Dad, Euan and I decided to wear traditional Scottish dress— kilts, sporrans, the lot.

We set up the marquee out the back, just in case it rained, and opened the bar at noon. I was there serving drinks. Everyone helped out—relatives, neighbours and our friends from uni organised all the food and serving.

It was a sensational spring afternoon—there wasn't a cloud in the sky. Sal arrived at about one o'clock ... she was just so radiant. I greeted her as she climbed out of a Rolls Royce with her bridesmaid and flower girls. My heart was racing; the butterflies in my stomach felt more like ele- phants. A myriad of thoughts went through my mind, but above all else I had an overwhelming feeling that I was the luckiest man alive. Sal just looked absolutely gorgeous—her white dress was simple in design but absolutely stunning. A string of pearls around her neck and a bouquet of white and pink roses highlighted her beaming smile. Every reason I had for marrying Sal filled my mind. It was sunny and it was just perfect.

I took her arm and we began to walk into the garden to the sounds of a trumpeter. We took our places on the 'golfing green' and the service began. My best man Euan stood beside me; alongside Sal were her sister, Anna, and the two flower girls wearing pink dresses, with tiaras of pink and white roses decorating their hair. The lump in my throat almost choked back the words as the celebrant asked Euan to give me the wedding ring. As I placed it on Sal's finger she looked into my eyes as I recited my simple, but heartfelt, vows.

'I, Stuart, take you Sally to be my wife. With this ring I thee wed and I promise to share the rest of my life with you as your husband; as your lover; as your very best friend.'

We kept the bar open the whole time because I wanted people standing around drinking champagne during the service. That's what our marriage was all about—a celebration. It was all over in about 15 minutes; as we posed for the photographs we were showered with confetti and flower petals.

I remember glancing over to where Mum, Dad and Sal's parents were standing and you could see the pride in their eyes and their smiles. You couldn't wipe the smile off my face. I remember there was a fleeting moment when there was just Sal and I standing there, waiting for the next photo to be taken and we looked into each other's eyes ... we didn't need to say anything.

As we were signing the legal documents someone in the crowd who doubted my writing skills called out 'Just put a cross, Stu'. Someone else shouted: 'You have to sign your life away'. I replied with a laugh, 'No one said anything about this part'. It was all just so relaxed, exactly the way Sal and I had wanted it to be. The celebrant then introduced us to the crowd as the 'newly married couple Sally and Stuart' and someone started singing 'For they are jolly good fellows' and gave us three cheers.

Then we partied. We danced to a bush band and had a barbecue. Sal and I had made all the salads the day before. One of Sal's relatives made the desserts and the rest of the family and friends chipped in with even more food—it was an enormous feast.

Many of our friends came from different parts of our lives and didn't really know each other and here they were sitting around in circles on the grass chatting. People I would never, ever have expected to get on. Any tension or problems, which exist in all families and friendships, were put aside for that day and that's what really made it.

After cutting the cake I made a marathon 30-second speech (I used to hate making speeches). Then everyone just had a good time. Everyone who came to our wedding said that it was the best wedding they'd ever been to. Of course I'm always going to say my wedding was the best I've ever been to—it was just unbelievably wonderful—nothing could go wrong.

It was five years into our relationship. We were so consolidated; we knew where we were going and what we were doing. It wasn't like 'I've taken this huge step', it was simply 'Look, I'm here. Isn't this fantastic?' I truly felt I was the luckiest man in the world. I'd made the commitment. I'd spent the previous ten years of my life professing that marriage was the most ridiculous institution in the world but at 25 I'd realised that marriage is a great thing.

But I still think that even if Sal and I had never married it would have made no difference to our relationship. It was just a public display of our commitment to each other, a commitment that we were hoping to carry on for the rest of our lives. Our wedding was obviously an important day that meant a lot to both of us but it was only as important as every other day had been in our relationship.

We had planned to leave the next day for our honeymoon at Surfers Paradise in Queensland, but hadn't made any plans about where to spend our first night as a married couple; we thought we'd just go with the mood of the night. By the end of the day we were absolutely exhausted. We'd been given a tent as a gift so we figured we'd pitch it in Uncle Pete's front yard and that's where we'd spend our wedding night. I was pretty tired so I wasn't exactly thinking straight. I pitched the tent and then we decided, 'What the hell—let's drive to Queensland'. We jumped in the car and took off, driving in four-hour shifts. Seventeen-and-a-half hours later we arrived in Surfers.

We checked into the hotel and slept for two days straight. It was a big penthouse suite overlooking the Gold Coast, it was something really special. We had all the luxuries—spas, an enormous bed and the best of everything. We'd booked for a week. It rained the whole time—did we care?

Marriage did little to change our lives, it just added a new dimension. Instead of tying us down it seemed to give us extra freedom, more freedom in our relationship than we'd ever had. It upped the trust, it upped the ante. That came out of knowing each other so well and understanding each other's needs, likes and dislikes. I was only married for two years after going out with Sal for five so I am not, and don't pretend to be, the world's authority on marriage. But I was intending to stay married for the rest of my life and I think it would have worked. I say that because we saw our wedding as just that little extra step. We weren't plunging into some frightening crevasse of marriage—we knew what we were doing and we knew that, if anything, marriage was going to add to our lives. Maybe I'm a little old-fashioned but I think it's important if you ever want to have kids that they can say 'Yeah, this is my mummy and this is my daddy. Yes, they're married. They're Mr and Mrs Diver'.

After we got married I knew that our trust was heightened. We were committed to one another. We'd signed that bit of paper and now society viewed our relationship as permanent. But I still had a hangover from my early 'anti-marriage' days— it took me a long time, probably 12 months, to call Sal 'my wife'. So I referred to her as 'my partner'.

Everyone seemed to view us as a single entity, one unit— 'Stu and Sal'. You couldn't refer to one of us without referring to the other. I guess that was because we complemented each other so well. While maintaining our own personalities, together we formed a joint personality. But, like me, Sal wanted a certain amount of independence as well; she needed her own time. Yet the best times were those we shared together; it's what I now miss so much, being able to share my life experiences with Sal.

Sometimes I go to the top of Mt Kosciuszko and sit up there and simply gaze out over the horizon, I can be there for hours. It's peaceful, beautiful, to look out over the seemingly endless hilltops of the Snowies. There are some beautiful big granite boulders up there, hundreds of them. I sit on a big rock by myself in the sun, reading a book, snoozing or solving the world's problems. That's my pinnacle. I enjoy being by myself. I believe you can share a lot with yourself and you can grow within yourself. But Sal's never far from my thoughts, I'd much rather walk up there with her. We wouldn't have to say a word to each other, just enjoy each other's company.

One of the things that survived the landslide was the video of our wedding. It's still got some mud caked on it. I haven't sat down and tried to watch it yet so I don't know if it's ruined. When I do I think I'll want to have Euan with me.

five

The Never-ending Honeymoon

Although Sal and I never sat down and formally made plans or laid out our lives, we always knew where we were going. We had the adventure business idea that we had developed with Iain Groves—we always knew that was going to happen and it was going to happen in Thredbo. Sal and I decided to aim to buy some land somewhere around Thredbo, on which to build our home. From there we were going to run the business. We often talked of those plans.

We'd talked about kids; we knew one day we would like to have them but we decided that we were still too young. There was plenty of time for that in the future. We had always lived on a fairly tight budget and to have kids we decided we should be more financially secure. We agreed that we should only have children when we had enough money to bring them up and give them a lifestyle full of adventure and travel. And that obviously costs a lot of money these days. So until we had the business and started making some decent money we weren't even going to consider having kids.

We were finally settling down. Sal was getting what she wanted out of her career; it was working out really well. I must admit I wasn't that ecstatic about my early employment situation in Thredbo. I was a village worker—not exactly a plum job, a jack-of-all-trades. But I wanted to be in Thredbo with Sal, I'd had enough of being away from her. I could have gone back and worked for the Outdoor Adventure Group— they'd offered me a job—but I decided I just didn't want to be away from Sal anymore.

I had made a commitment to her and it was time for me

to start making a few sacrifices. What goes around, comes around. So I came to Thredbo and worked as a labourer for Euan. He was in a pretty senior position with village management by this stage. I did that for a whole summer, pretty ordinary work; but as I said, it kept me in Thredbo and close to Sal. If it was possible, we became even closer to Euan and his girlfriend, Susie Rowland.

Part of my job was garbage collection. Working the compactor was absolutely disgusting because I was always getting splattered as the food bags broke open, showering me with stinking, rotting garbage. So much for the glamorous lifestyle in a mountain resort. I did that for six weeks or so and Sal put up with all my grumpy moods.

When we weren't working we spent a lot of time together. We were getting back into bushwalking; going up over the high country. When it was warm we drove down to the beach at Merimbula and surfed. We got out of Thredbo a lot on weekends to explore what was around. But at the same time we had really started to get into the Thredbo community. Sal had her friends and her own interests—she had earned enormous respect from just about everyone she came into contact with. We had really started to feel a bond with the village.

We were looking at setting up our company in 1998. We'd drive down the mountain and look at land and inquire at the council about rates and zoning, we were starting to put the plan into motion. Our dreams centred on the business, on buying the land and building our own house. It was Sal's ultimate dream I suppose—to get out, to get our own place and get out of the rental bind. She had lots of little plans and ways of getting there but, although she was pretty focused, she didn't let it drive her to distraction. If we never got our own home I don't think it would have really mattered.

We spoke about that dream quite often. We would hike up the mountain and across to Mt Kosciuszko where we would just sit and talk about where we were going to be in ten years.

I'm a great dreamer. That's probably what has got me where I am today. I dream and fantasise all the time about where I am going to be and what I am going to do. I always believed that something big was going to happen in my life. I didn't know if it was going to be good or bad, but it was definitely going to be big. It was a feeling I had from about the age of ten.

I can remember when I was in primary school I told one of my classmate's mothers that one day I was going to own a mountain in Canada and it was going to be a ski resort. I promised to invite her to the opening. She thought I was crazy. As time went on and as my plans got bigger and grander I always knew something even bigger and grander was going to have to happen.

I've always believed that if you are determined you will achieve your ambitions. In 1994, I wanted to be a fully certified ski instructor, an instructor trainer. At the time that seemed completely out of my reach. But three years later I was there— a supervising ski instructor. It normally takes people five to 10 years to reach that stage; I did it in three. That, in a lot of ways, sums up my whole focus on life—if you dream and commit yourself to something you'll get there.

People have always called me lucky. But I think that 'luck' comes from my ability to dream, to see where the future lies and to map it out in such a far out way that no one else could conceive that I would reach my goal. For instance if I had said in 1994, 'OK I am going to complete my full level three instructors in three years', everyone would have said 'Stu, you can't even put in a proper turn. What are you talking about?'. I just scraped through by a mark in Level 1. I topped my Level 2 and my Level 3. I had the top marks in Australia. My dream had come true.

We were really focused and driven. We were saving as much as we could. We cancelled any plans for an overseas skiing trip because we wanted to save $20,000. At least that would enable us to get a loan and buy that block of land. Even if we couldn't build a house immediately, it would be the start of the dream. I always knew there was going to be a way of doing it.

If we had set up our company, I'm sure we would have thought of even bigger and better schemes. Grovesy, Sal and I sat around and talked about it. The next thing we wanted to do was climb Mt Everest and clean it up—get rid of all the rubbish climbers have left there over the years. We were going to parachute all the garbage off the mountain down to base camp and ship it out. Funny—I think someone else is doing that now.

Sal never, ever ridiculed my plans but occasionally Grovesy and I would come up with some crazy idea and then she might pull me up. Every dream I've ever had has come true so far. Obviously now some of my dreams have had to change. I used to dream about Sal and me getting old together, looked forward to the day Sal was 40 and I was 40. I couldn't wait for the day when Sal was 60 and I was 60. I was looking forward to that time so much because I knew that some of our dreams would have come true by then and so we'd be at a different level in our lives. I used to fantasise about growing old together and how great that would be. Every day I was with Sal she got more and more beautiful, in my eyes anyway. I just couldn't foresee anything bad happening to either of us. I could never picture it.

Death is not something we discussed in great detail, because I never expected either of us to die. I thought we were both invincible. I have never really been scared about dying, although it has crossed my mind a couple of times when I was in hairy rock-climbing situations. I've thought, 'Gee, it would be really bad for Sal to have to come and bury me'.

I was actually pretty adamant that I was going to die first. I spoke to Sal about it once: 'What about when we are both 90 or 100 and one of us dies first? What are we going to do then? Who is going to survive the last four or five years? How are we going to survive without each other?' I used to play around with these little notions. It was a scary thought— 'how would I ever live without Sal?'

At the time I didn't think I would be able to continue without her. But I have. If someone had said the day before the landslide that Sal was going to be dead the next day I could never have considered living without her, we just couldn't live apart. If someone had told me the afternoon before the landslide, 'Tomorrow you are going to wake up and Sal is not going to be there. What are you going to do?' I would have said, 'I could never survive through that. I couldn't deal with it'. But when you have to, your mind takes over the emotion and deals with it.

In a lot of ways Sally was shy, like me, a little bit introverted. We had to try to help each other out. Together. She gave me so much confidence in everything I did. She gave me confidence to survive the landslide; she still gives me confidence to survive today.

We became almost telepathic. In the end we could sit around, not say anything to each other for half an hour and get up and feel as though we had discussed a few things and worked a few things out. We often felt as though we knew what the other was thinking. We would finish off each other's sentences because we knew exactly what the other was going to say. It was the same with our train of thought. In the end we could make decisions on the other person's behalf and know, with full confidence, that it was exactly the decision the other person wanted to make.

I always wanted her to be more adventurous, to take more risks, but she always held back. There were times when I would try to encourage Sal to come out and do something adventurous, but Sal was strong-willed, if she didn't want to do something there was no way anyone would convince her otherwise. You could pay her a million dollars, promise anything, she wouldn't budge.

But if it was something she wanted to do, Sal was incredibly driven. This did cause some conflict. I would want to go outside and climb a mountain and Sal would want to do something that meant staying indoors. At the end of the day you look back at those little differences and just laugh.

I guess we did come from two different poles and I think that made our union so much stronger. We could teach each other things. I have always loved a challenge and in the beginning it probably was just that, a challenge. Here was someone who was so different to me so I had to try and adapt to her lifestyle and she also adapted to mine. It took us four-and-a-bit years to find that middle ground and then it was all taken away from us.

I guess couples with identical characters to one another could have just as strong a bond. Whether they get bored after five years and that's the end of that, I don't know. Whether Sal and I would have been bored with each other in ten or 20 years I can't tell. I like to think not because we had so many interests and things to keep challenging ourselves with.

Like everyone else Sal and I had our ups and downs. One of my biggest mistakes was trying to fool her one afternoon after I'd been drinking with a couple of mates. It was Jazz Weekend 1996. A big weekend in Thredbo. People came from all over the country and there was a real party atmosphere. On this particular day I woke up with a pretty bad hangover after consuming one or 20 beers the night before. By 11 o'clock in the morning I was ready to punish myself again and was straight back into it. I'd told Sal I would meet her in the Kosciuszko Room at the Alpine Hotel at one o'clock. Anyway I was with my mate Lizard, also known as Steve Lyster, and his then girlfriend, who was a flight attendant. She'd just got back from a trip with a whole lot of miniature bottles of grog. So we decided to play soldiers with them. We lined them up; they were the enemy and we were defending the lodge. So every time a soldier came to the front we all had to drink and he'd go down the back. We emptied all the bottles.

We were plastered and I knew I would be in some strife as by now it was nearly six o'clock—I was five hours late! So I decided to ring home and leave a message on our answering machine, 'I'm in the Kosciuszko Room, it's 20 past one and I can't find you, Sal. I'll catch up with you at home at about six'. Sal was at home but hadn't picked up the phone and had just listened to my slurred tale. So I rocked in thinking I was King of the World. I'd had an absolute skinful and thought I had conned Sal. You can imagine what happened. It wasn't very pretty.

I had really let Sal down. We went out to dinner. It was the worst meal we'd ever had. Everything was burnt—it was just a shocker. But we talked. Even though I probably was unable to talk very coherently by then. I talked to the best of my ability; I knew I was wrong and I had deceived her and I told her so. We talked it through. Within an hour my deceit had been, if not forgotten, at least forgiven. It was a classic example of Sal's ability to accept me for who I am.

I paint a rosy picture of what Sal and I were like because it *was* rosy ... 98 per cent of the time. There was obviously tension sometimes and things that happened that hurt that we had to work through. Marriage doesn't necessarily mean that you are going to be happy all the time. The truth is that you're not going to be happy all the time, you are going to disagree with your partner sometimes. I was the one that created the most havoc because of my personality. Sal was a lot more relaxed and calm. I can honestly say we never had a serious argument, shouting at each other, and storming out. Maybe that might have come in the next ten years of marriage.

But that was the future, for now Sal and I were cruising along so well. We were happy and content in our marriage and we were feeling more and more a part of the Thredbo community. Both our jobs were going well. I was promoted to supervising the top end of the ski school. Sal was conference reservations manager at the hotel. Our dreams were coming true.

six

Welcome to Bimbadeen

By April 1997, Sal was well and truly on her career path at the Alpine Hotel. She had a really good job. She'd been promoted and we moved into Bimbadeen Lodge because accommodation was part of her package. With the rent we'd been paying at the Riverside Cabins in Thredbo, we were never going to be able to save enough to buy our land. So when the offer of Bimbadeen came up it was too good to pass up and we moved in.

Bimbadeen Lodge was good. It may have been cramped and small, but it really felt like home. The Riverside Cabins had never really felt like home because we knew we weren't permanently there. But at Bimbadeen, even though it was staff accommodation, we had our own space, which is very hard to get in Thredbo. It was a ground-floor bedsitter flat. The main room was the size of a normal lounge room with an adjoining bathroom, kitchen and small laundry. It was comfortable.

After we moved in we decorated the apartment to suit us. We had the whole back wall covered in photos and pictures of us—little frames, big frames and no frames. Pictures of Sal and me all over the world. Photos of our friends. Sal's mum had given us a painting for our wedding and that was on one wall.

Buying a washing machine was a highlight—having your own washing machine in Thredbo is pretty special because not many people have one. Sal always used to get stuck into me because I was washing mad. Every day she would come home and I would have done another load of washing. I would constantly have washing all over the apartment.

Strange how you remember the smallest things but I recall the heating was fantastic ... it was always beautifully warm.

The front wall was virtually all glass. We had a fantastic view of the whole mountain from there. You could look out at the scenery for hours on end. Waking up together, lying in bed and looking out that window across the valley to the ski fields was one of our favourite pastimes.

I have fond memories of Sal and me just living simple, normal lives. I have pictures in my mind of Sal reading a book on the bed, or doing her nails at the table in front of the window, or me hanging out the washing.

We got on well with everyone in Bimbadeen. It was like its own little community. We used to have progressive dinner parties, organised by Wendy O'Donohue, Thredbo's Marketing Manager. We'd have entrée in one apartment, the main meal in another, drinks in another, dessert in another and so forth. Everyone knew everyone. Because the walls were so thick you couldn't hear the people around or above you, but you knew they were there—it was like one big extended family.

The night before the landslide we had dinner at our place with Mike and Mim Sodergren, who were also living in Bimbadeen. As they walked in the front door they both said our place was just great and we could tell they meant it. We had squeezed in a little table with a couple of candles on it and had a great night with them. Sure, we couldn't have huge dinner parties or anything like that, but it was enough for us. We had been meaning to have Mike and Mim around to dinner for a season and a half, so that dinner is a precious memory because they too were buried in the landslide.

Winters at Thredbo were just so busy, so hectic. Ski resorts start to get you down after a while—it's a pretty frenetic lifestyle—so you have to get out occasionally. At the time of the landslide we were six weeks into the season; the school holidays had just finished and we were preparing for the busiest time of the season during August. We were tired of the whiteness, the snow, and we had to see some green. There was a great place, Crackenback Cottage, halfway down the road to Jindabyne. We'd really enjoy looking out over the green valley and watching the horses graze while we relaxed and had a bottle of Chardonnay. You've got to be able to escape. Even though we were in Thredbo for the escapism we still had to escape the escapism sometimes.

Many people think living in a ski resort means using every spare moment you've got to go skiing. I skied every day, all week and Sal was getting a couple of hours' skiing in the mornings before she went to work during the week. So when we had a day off spending time together was more important than going skiing. The only day off we had together was Sunday.

We'd usually go out skiing for a couple of hours then leave Thredbo and go have lunch somewhere. Quite often, unless it was a really nice, sunny day, we wouldn't even bother going skiing at all. We'd just stay at home and do things around the flat. But at least once a week we would try to get away from Thredbo.

The day of the landslide was a stock, standard normal day, just like the entire winter had been. Sal had gone to work at the hotel and I had gone to work as a rookie trainer on an instructor trainers' course for the APSI, which is the professional body for Australian Professional Ski Instructors. That had gone well and I was due to do that the following day too.

I gave Sal a call when I got home from work at about 4.30pm and she said we should go down to Jindabyne to do some shopping. So when she finished work, at about 5.30pm, we jumped in the car and headed off. We bought some takeaway noodles from the noodle shop at the back of Nugget's Crossing shopping centre and then thought about going to see a movie but decided we were both too tired and headed home. During the drive we spoke about the mundane, day-to-day things a husband and wife do. We spent a lot of time talking about my rookie trainers' course because I wanted to become a trainer. I thought I had done really well that day so I was planning what I was going to do the next day. Sal said work was getting her down a bit because it was getting so busy. We didn't really talk about any major, groundbreaking issues.

We got home at about 7.30pm. After heating up the

noodles we ate and then had an early night, we were watching a little bit of television in bed and I started to nod off. Life in Bimbadeen was good. It was special. It was our home. Sleepily I turned to my wife ... 'Goodnight ... see you in the morning'.

seven

No Goodbyes

F irst reports were frightening—up to 100 people trapped, buried or dead in a landslide. At least two lodges, Bimbadeen and Carinya, were gone. Another was in danger of toppling. Witnesses told of an explosion immediately before the slide. Thredbo, one of Australia's most popular ski resorts, was the scene of shocking devastation.

Nestled at the foot of Australia's high country, the home of the nation's highest mountain, Kosciuszko, Thredbo resembles a small European ski village, with lodges, restaurants and shops terraced into the steep hillside facing the ski fields. Through the middle runs the Thredbo River. About 200 kilometres south-west of Canberra, Thredbo is popular all year round—snow sports in winter, bushwalking and a range of sports in summer. Its reputation is world-renowned. Some three million people visit the Kosciuszko National Park yearly.

It was just after 11.30pm on July 30, 1997. A whoosh of air, what sounded like a sonic boom and trees cracking, splitting the still, cold night air like gunfire. Alarm bells started ringing across the nation. Calls for help went out to all emergency services. No one could really believe the nature of the appeal; no one ever imagined a catastrophe like this could happen.

The disaster struck as many in Thredbo were heading home to their lodges after a night out in one of the resort's many bars and restaurants. Wednesday is normally payday in the village so there were plenty of people out enjoying the alpine atmosphere. The mercury had plummeted to minus 11 degrees Celsius as the steady drone of the snow-making machines echoed through the valley. Walking along Bobuck Lane most were blissfully ignorant of what had happened just seconds before . . . until they discovered debris scattered across their path and saw only darkness where the two lodges once stood. Dozens of people staying in neighbouring lodges swarmed outside within seconds. Their feet sank in wet, sticky mud. Forming a human chain they immediately began trying to remove the rubble, all the while hearing the muffled screams of those buried beneath.

A journalist from Canberra's Network Seven, Glenn Milne, had been staying with his young family at Leatherbarrel Lodge, next door to Bimbadeen. Their lodge shook and their windows rattled as the landslide swept past their room, which was just a metre-and-a-half from where Bimbadeen Lodge stood. The roar woke him and his wife, Karyn. As car alarms began wailing Karyn rushed onto the balcony to see what had happened while Glenn wrapped their two daughters, aged seven and nine, in doonas. Fearing their lodge could also collapse they ran outside and down to the road, down to safety. Making sure his family was safe Glenn ran back up to the site—from beneath the rubble he could hear three voices.

Thredbo ski patroller David Kuhn was also one of the first there. He knew everyone living in Bimbadeen Lodge. He was trained in snow avalanche rescue and treated the landslide as such. Gingerly he took a couple of steps across the sea of mud and debris. The ground under his feet started to give way and he almost fell into a cavity. As he scrambled for a hold a concrete besser block came tumbling down, missing him by centimetres. He too could hear voices. Mike Sodergren had been a good friend and now Kuhn could hear Mike's distinctive American accent calling 'Get me out of here, get me out of here'. The voice was strong and sounded close but Kuhn couldn't see his friend.

The stench of gas from ruptured underground pipes was overwhelming; the fear of explosion very real. But with the cries for help ringing in their ears those on the scene frantically tugged and dragged debris away. Although it wasn't snowing sub-zero temperatures hampered their efforts.

Thredbo engineer and part-time firefighter Euan Diver had been asleep in his unit in Bobuck Apartments, immediately below the landslide. He'd heard the whoosh and initially thought it was a tornado. Rushing outside he saw the devastation in the cloud of dust that was still rolling down the hill. Immediately he thought of the threat of a gas explosion. He could see people roaming around the site but showing no signs of panic, no signs of urgency—perhaps it was the stunned disbelief before the reality set in.

Throwing on his uniform he rushed back outside. Running down the steps of his apartment block he reached the bottom and looked back up the hillside, back up to where Bimbadeen should have been—instead he just stared at a black, dark hole. It just wasn't there. His thoughts switched to his brother and sister-in-law who lived on the ground floor of the lodge. He whispered a prayer that they weren't home—their car wasn't parked where it normally would have been so there was a glimmer of hope that they had been out.

'You bastards. Look what you've done. What the fuck have you done to me, to us?' I screamed. My abuse came in a torrent. I was abusing the world. I had to blame somebody for what had happened. There I was buried, cold, barely able to breathe through the dust, plunged into a world of pitch darkness and I was fucking angry. Furious at the world in general for taking away my wife and for causing me so much intense pain when all I wanted to do was enjoy life.

What really hurt was there were no goodbyes. If Sal had a terminal disease and was told she had six months to live then at least we would have had a chance to say goodbye. That is one of the hardest things to deal with. The last memory I have of Sal is a blood-curdling scream.

I had two options, neither of them good. The first was to die along with Sal. What use was there living when you have lost the thing you most cherished in your entire life? It was a very good option and a part of my mind wanted to do it but another part wouldn't physically let me. There was no fear of death, no fear of dying. It was a fantastic option. What better place to be than with my wife? Why bother living? The other option was to live and be thankful that I did. That was the option I took. There are a number of reasons why. Rational thoughts had started to enter my head. I was thinking of Sal's mum, her sister, my parents and my brother. I had to get out to see them. This thought spread and I began to think of all our friends. Suddenly I had 200 people to live for. Sal was dead but I had to live—for each and every one of them—I had to live.

Jindabyne policeman Paul Hoyer had been off duty, visiting friends in Thredbo. He'd heard the gust of wind that accompanied the slide. He'd felt the lodge he was in vibrate as if it had been hit by a small earth tremor. Before this, the night had been still—cold, but still—there had been no wind at all. So from where had this massive gust suddenly come? The fire station siren that echoed around the village alerted Hoyer to the fact that something had happened. He ran outside and up the narrow Bobuck Lane and saw a fire engine blocking the road. Past the truck he could see the wall of dirt, mud and trees that had crossed Bobuck Lane. It was about two metres high. The whole area seemed to be engulfed in a cloud of gas. Frantic witnesses rushed at the policeman telling him they had heard voices—he must do something!

Ambulance officers Ron Carey and John Bartley had pulled up on the Alpine Way after the 36-kilometre dash from Jindabyne. Driving, Bartley turned to Carey: 'My God, look at this. The whole mountain has gone'. Carey, Bartley and Hoyer carefully made their way onto the site, clambering over toppled trees, at stages knee-deep in mud, struggling through water flowing down the site like a stream. Hoyer could also hear voices beneath the rubble, a man and a woman's. They were faint—but they were there: 'Help'. The voices became fainter and fainter. Nearby Carey too heard three distinct voices— they sounded like the groans of dying men. He also heard the word 'Help'.

Bartley crawled into a hole in the rubble from where the voices could be heard. Two metres in he could still hear them and guessed he was probably only a metre away, but to go any further meant removing some of the debris, which could have caused a further collapse. Carey, holding Bartley by the ankle, asked if he could see anyone—he couldn't. They decided to back out because the rubble was still moving beneath their feet.

Most of those missing were well known in Thredbo. Kosciusko Thredbo Pty Ltd owned the four-storey lodge Bimbadeen. Built from reinforced concrete blocks, it had 13 units with 28 beds. It housed staff members holding senior positions within the company. They came from resort management, ski school, the ski patrol, snow grooming and the Thredbo Alpine Hotel. Bimbadeen was near full. The two-storey Carinya Lodge, mostly of timber construction, had the capacity to sleep 23 people. It wasn't clear how many had been staying there at the time.

Thredbo media spokeswoman Susie Rowland fielded calls from around the country. In a trembling voice she revealed up to 33 people might have been booked into the lodges. The reporters couldn't know just how traumatic this was for Susie— her boyfriend, Euan Diver, was the first on the scene. His brother and sister-in-law, Stuart and Sally Diver, were believed to be trapped in the wreckage.

Luckily a team of elite police from the New South Wales State Protection Group had been undergoing a 'Cold Climate Operation' training program in Thredbo. They were on the scene within minutes arranging the initial evacuation of surrounding lodges. Four were emptied, their residents ushered to safer accommodation.

Deputy Fire Captain Euan Diver had a job to do, despite his fears about Stuart and Sally. His adrenaline was racing. The smell of gas was becoming overwhelming so he grabbed one of the other firefighters and rushed back to the station to get the keys needed to isolate the supply. By the time they got back all hell had broken loose. There were people everywhere. Lights had been set up and, for the first time, Euan got a good look at the mess. He hadn't expected what he saw but he knew immediately what it was—a bloody disaster.

Civilians were scrambling all over the muddied hillside and the emergency service personnel knew how dangerous and precarious the site was. They began asking people to get off, get out of the way, get away from the danger. It was procedure. The first rule of first aid is to ensure safety at the site. They realised, even at that early stage, that to jump in boots and all could be disastrous. Part-time firefighter Stephen Ryan—known as 'Feral'—was one of Stuart Diver's closest friends. He helped remove locals—some physically, and some of them friends—who were trying to dig for survivors. His mind too was racing—he knew his good mate could be entombed, but there was also the fear, the very real fear, the site could give way at any time.

After the initial panic had passed, Euan and his fellow rescuers began to realise the enormity of the task ahead. The mountainside had gone strangely quiet. The decision was made to wait until dawn because there was nothing they could do. The lights that had been set up provided some illumination but the rescuers just couldn't feel confident enough because of the ever-present danger of further slippage. For Euan it was a torturous time but he realised it was the correct decision—it wasn't as if they could simply lift the concrete slabs off and pull people out, the scope of the job was just too big.

Thredbo village had been sealed off. Roads were blocked. A lodge near the landslide site was hastily set up as the triage post; anyone with medical expertise was asked to go there and attend to any casualties. Rescue crews from all over New South Wales, and some from the Australian Capital Territory and Victoria, were speeding to the alpine resort. They were arriving by the truckload. But darkness prevented any rescue attempt. Those there first recall hearing the site moan and shift for hours after the event. Any rash decision could have led to more deaths. Any sudden movement could have triggered another landslide and killed any survivors trapped underneath and possibly rescuers as well.

Senior Constable Warren Denham, from Jindabyne, initially assumed the role of Forward Police Commander. It was his job to call the shots, make the early, crucial decisions until someone more senior took over. He asked ambulance officer Ron Carey to take him to where the voices had been heard. They climbed over the mass of debris that littered the site—trees, building materials, broken concrete slabs and various household items. Denham could hear grating noises coming from beneath his feet and he could see wreckage still moving down the slope. A large amount of water was running through the debris and over it. The mud covered large areas. Carey yelled out 'Can you hear me? Can you hear me?' Denham heard a low-pitched distant groaning sound coming from below them. The sound was muffled by the layers of debris. Carey yelled again, 'Can you hear me? It's the ambulance'. The groan intensified—it was deep pitched, probably a man's. There were no clear words to indicate who it was or what their injuries were.

Denham decided the whole site was extremely unstable and that it could be life-threatening for any rescue personnel to enter because there could probably be further movement of the debris. It was a decision initially supported by John Kite, a senior environmental health and building surveyor with the National Parks and Wildlife Service, based on the steepness of the site. He told the police constable that he was very concerned about the stability of certain areas of the landslide site and several lodges in the immediate vicinity. Kite continued to assess the site and surrounding structures to ascertain if there was any evidence of problems that could result in further instability.

Police Superintendent Charlie Sanderson had only recently been appointed the Local Area Commander of the Monaro area, which takes in Thredbo. He was living in temporary accommodation at the police academy at Goulburn, north of Canberra, and was woken by the phone ringing next to his bed. It was a police officer from nearby Queanbeyan breaking the news that two lodges had been destroyed and there was a possibility a number of people had been killed.

After telephoning his boss in Sydney, Chief Superintendent Bruce Johnston, and implementing other emergency procedures required during such a disaster, Sanderson jumped in his car and joined the convoy of emergency vehicles heading south to the ski resort. He agreed with the decision to keep people off the site but also realised just how frustrating it would be for those on site. It would be a heroic effort to stand back and wait. They just had to; there was no other choice.

It was a decision not made lightly. Johnston later told a tearful meeting of the village's surviving residents: 'We might have taken wrong decisions ... I hope we haven't'. It obviously frustrated the 55-year-old veteran police officer too. 'Clearly the chance of survival is going to be minimised but we have to be careful. It may well be that something we do could cause further slippage—may indeed take a life that may be saved in a day or so.'

Euan's responsibilities in the village didn't give him much time to think about whether Stuart and Sally were buried under the slide. As a firefighter he had to consider the gas leaks, as the village manager he had to supervise the water being cut, as a brother he had to endure the terrible thought that two people he loved were buried in the slide.

A geophysicist was summoned from Sydney; his opinion would be crucial to assessing the risk of further landslides. It would take hours before he arrived; anxious, tense hours for those desperate to do something to help.

At first I pulled together everything I had learnt in my entire life to survive. Every little thing I had ever done. I questioned my strength and ability: 'Can I get through this? Do I have the inner strength and the power? Am I physically fit enough to get through this? I'm not superhuman'. It came down to the question: did I have the right level of physical fitness and enough mental stamina or mental fortitude or robustness? That was the key for that first hour.

I was stuck in a situation where I had absolutely no control and that sparked a real disbelief in myself and went against everything I believed in, my upbringing, Sal's confidence in me, everything. It felt like I was driving down a freeway with a brick on the accelerator and my hands and feet tied. Totally out of control. I started feeling I wasn't able to believe in myself any more.

The slide had started on the lower side of the Alpine Way, a 108-kilometre tar and gravel road that sits at the top of the village and links New South Wales to Victoria through the Snowy Mountains. The Snowy Mountains Hydro-Electric Authority had originally built the road in 1956. From Jindabyne to Khancoban it had a reputation for breathtaking views of the Snowy Mountains—its reputation had now horribly changed.

A wall of earth, travelling at an estimated 30 kilometres an hour, had slammed into Carinya Lodge which in turn hurtled down the slope, across Bobuck Lane, and wiped out

Bimbadeen Lodge—it probably took less than ten seconds from start to finish. The thunder of the slide was replaced by an eerie silence that hung over the valley like a low cloud. It didn't take long for a simple, if premature, explanation for the landslide to emerge. Underground water, its source undetermined, had loosened soil beneath the Alpine Way causing a slip that sent the 4,000 tonnes of earth rumbling down the hill like a steamroller, flattening everything in its path.

There was water everywhere. As the water poured down I began talking to myself, talking myself through it. I just kept coaxing myself, 'Buddy hold yourself out. Hold yourself out'. I was arching my back, using my elbows, trying to keep my head above the water level.

The first flood lasted for about ten minutes. 'I can't get through this'. I wanted to let myself back down into the water and just drown. But my body simply wouldn't let me do it. So I kept holding myself out of the icy water. Breathing, still choking, with my mouth so close to the concrete above me I was breathing in more concrete dust than air.

The water just kept flowing down; I thought it was never going to stop. And with it came the mud and debris, which slowly pushed me up off the bed. I was getting even more squashed against the roof as the mud filled all the cavities around me. Somehow my lips stayed about a centimetre above the water line. I could feel the freezing water cover the rest of my face, it was so icy that it took my breath away. That was how close it was—that was the fine line—one solitary centimetre.

After ten minutes or so the water started to trickle away and I thought 'Thank Christ it's gone. I may be able to hang in'.

How long was I going to be stuck here? I expected I would be out within 20 minutes. That was all I was thinking. Sure it was bitterly cold, but I had been cold before—I should be able to survive for 20 minutes.

My mind reverted to Sal. I had to try to help her. I felt around to her side of the bed, to where she should have been . . . she wasn't there . . . all I could feel was the slimy, cold mud. I frantically tried to sweep my hand across where she should have been but all I felt was a piece of our doona poking up out of the mud. I couldn't find her head; she was buried in the mud. Not being able to touch her sparked renewed anger. It wasn't sadness; it was just pure anger. I was shouting. You fucking this and you fucking that. It was directed at no one in particular but just out-and-out anger. It seemed to give me an immense feeling of strength, an amazing feeling of power. 'You bastards, you've taken my wife. You've taken the only thing in the world that I care for, the only thing I love that much, and you've taken it.' I went through a whole range of emotions—swinging from one end of the spectrum to the other—sadness, anger and fear. Bugger this, I'm not going to bother living—but in the next breath I vowed I was going to survive, I would show these bastards and live.

Two minutes later the water came back and for the next hour it came down five more times for periods of between five and ten minutes. Each time pushing me to the absolute limit of my endurance, mentally and physically. Every time I had to arch my back and tilt my head so my nose and mouth were above the water level. No matter how hard I squeezed them shut the water got into my eyes. It was putrid, laced with diesel and who knows what else—my eyes were stinging. I knew I mustn't let any get into my mouth.

Then the water would subside again and I could lower my back. Minutes later I heard it again. It came with a roar, 'Bloody hell, here we go again'. Where I got the strength to repeatedly arch my back for those lengths of time I'll never know. And then the water would stop flowing again, then it would start again and stop and start again. It was torture and really started to drive me over the edge. The noise of the approaching water instilled absolute terror in me. How could I go through another drenching in this freezing, stinking water? After the fifth time I was beginning to think that there was no way I was going to survive. At the end of that first hour I didn't think I had a hope in hell. My body was convulsing, shaking because of the cold.

I had done shouting and cursing. I didn't have the energy. Once the water had finally slowed down to a trickle I could hear people above me starting to work, I could hear the fire truck arrive, and I could hear people roaming around. I knew people were there and that something was happening above me—that gave me renewed hope.

Sal's death became my impetus to live. After my initial feelings of despair and wanting to die so I could be with my wife, I made a promise to her that I was going to get out. I would show the world—it might have taken one of us but there was no way it was going to get us both.

On the surface frustration grew to near hysteria as friends of those buried tried desperately to begin the rescue. They were held back by authorities. Tempers flared, there was a lot of shouting and screaming. The situation was not helped by the darkness and cold, making assessment of the situation all the more difficult. And with the water and gas supplies cut off the village had been thrown into chaos.

I began to assess my situation. I was completely horizontal. I could put my arms out to the side and feel around. I could feel the slab above me. I could feel the mud below. I could feel the bent wrought iron bedhead and, with my feet, I could feel where the couch was at the end of our bed. If I strained I could just reach my knees with my hands. My head had been forced forward by a concrete block which acted as a pillow. And underneath my back there was a rock jabbing into me. I wasn't buried in the mud but lying on top of it. There was glass all around me. The smell of gas and diesel was almost overpowering. There was also the smell of burning concrete, like when you hit concrete with a hammer, a really pungent, burning smell.

Surviving the first hour was my priority. I didn't think I would need to survive past that because I would either be rescued or dead. It was so cold. But I was confident the rescuers were going to get to me before I died—surely it wouldn't take them much longer.

The cold was my biggest problem. My survival training told me I had to keep my torso warm so I hugged myself to maintain what little warmth I had left. I put my hands under my armpits to protect my fingers and then just basically hugged myself. I knew if I kept my torso warm my head would be OK. But my legs and feet were another proposition altogether. I couldn't touch them, couldn't do anything with them, so they were just going to have to fend for themselves. All I could do was wiggle my toes, so that's what I did.

From doing a first aid course I knew about hypothermia, what the signs were and what you have to do to try to avoid it. I knew that if I could keep my vital organs warm then I was going to be OK or, at least, I would have a better chance of getting out of here alive.

An icy draft was blowing through all the time. On my wet and freezing body it felt like I was being pricked by thousands of needles. Every time it blew it cooled me down that little bit more. It was just so bitterly, bitterly cold there wasn't anything that I really thought I could do. It was purely basic survival. I had to just hug myself, hang on and see how long I could go for.

By 3.00am police had begun to activate the Snowy River Shire Local Disaster Plan. An office located at the National Parks and Wildlife Service headquarters at Jindabyne was converted into the emergency operations centre. The disaster plan outlined the resources available in the area—trucks, earth-moving machines, buses, medical workers and evacuation centres. Cooma Hospital was put on standby for the arrival of survivors.

At the same time, at the Sydney command post, arrangements were made to have a navy Sea King helicopter fly a Mines Rescue Service team, including Grant Douglas and Con Stromer, from the south coast. Both were seen to be vital additions to the team as both had vast experience in underground rescue missions.

At Bankstown Airport, in south-western Sydney, a team of eight crack paramedics from the Special Casualty Access Team was loading extra blood supplies onto a light aircraft. The team included SCAT instructor Paul Featherstone. He had no real idea what they were heading into. His first concern was for his team and to ensure they had the right equipment to deal with the alpine conditions.

Inspector John Denny and Station Officer Warwick Kidd, elite firefighters trained by the internationally recognised Urban Search and Rescue team, were also airlifted out of

Bankstown. They were on site before dawn. Kidd knew Thredbo well—he'd been here in happier times. As he gazed at the landslide, which had been illuminated with floodlights, he puzzled over what the hell he was looking at. He turned to Thredbo fire captain Dave Milliken who gave him a brief description of what lay before them and what had been done by the rescuers so far.

Kidd clambered onto the roof of the precariously perched Schuss Lodge, which overlooked the devastation. He scanned the site with an Argus thermal imaging camera, a piece of equipment used by firefighters to locate body heat through smoke. It was still dark. But it didn't matter if it was dark or light; the camera would have picked up people's exposed limbs as white heat blooms. There were no blooms.

A damp mist hung over the valley. Sunrise seemed an eternity away, an eternity to wait before emergency workers would hopefully begin to do their job of trying to find anyone alive in the mud, twisted metal and smashed concrete. It was probably futile but there wasn't one rescuer there without some hope, no matter how small. Thredbo chaplain, Reverend Harvey Sloane, joined the 70 frustrated rescuers at the top of the site looking down at what had once been two ski lodges. Together they waited and offered a prayer.

Police now had a rough idea of the numbers of those missing—20 people were unaccounted for. No names had been released.

I could still hear people wandering around and I could hear trucks starting to move. I started to wonder what had actually happened but those thoughts were quickly pushed out of my mind by thoughts of what I had to do to keep myself alive.

Time was the key and as each minute passed I kept convincing myself that it wouldn't be long before they got me out ... it couldn't be long before they got me out. I still had this idea that it was only going to take an hour at the most; after the first hour passed I thought OK maybe it'll take another hour or so. I wasn't setting myself up for a big long wait because I don't think my mind would have coped with that prospect.

I could hear muffled voices; if someone yelled I could hear it. I couldn't make out any real conversations, but I definitely knew people were out there. I could hear them moving around on the site. I never, ever heard anyone yelling for help. I never heard anyone call out. I never heard any other survivors.

'The chances of anyone being alive in there are very, very negligible,' police chief Charlie Sanderson sadly admitted to a crowded news conference.

Collective Grief

eight

Australia woke to news of the tragedy. Pictures of the devastation were beamed around the world. Emotional and graphic accounts from witnesses took the breath away.

'I looked out my window as it was going past and it was just like someone had emptied a giant vacuum cleaner bag.'

'It sounded like an express train or a jet fighter taking off.'

'It's like someone drove a great big bulldozer over the lodges.'

'There was just silence. It was just so eerie because it was total silence—it was like a silent evolution of panic.'

It was a clear, crisp night and Manos Ellard could see clearly the drama unfold from across the valley; from his vantage point he saw the whole terrifying disaster. Manos had been with friends for dinner and at about 11.30pm stepped out the front door to head home. Saying goodbye they heard a loud cracking noise, like a tree splitting.

'I immediately looked towards Bimbadeen and I saw the trees above Carinya falling, coming down the hill with a dark shadow of land sliding ... The bottom floor of Carinya Lodge was pushed out by the impact of the landslide. I saw the two upper floors of Carinya begin to fall, collapse and spread out. The top floors rolled forward with the momentum. As they hit solid things, like trees, they broke up into pieces. It was like a slow, gradual thing.

'I then saw the slide with parts of Carinya, slide down the hill and hit Bimbadeen Lodge. Bimbadeen was forced forward and then slid and collapsed with one big movement.

I saw Bimbadeen collapse to the ground, underneath the landslide. There was a huge cracking as the landslide stopped. There was a big puff of white-coloured dust ... then, there was silence.'

At Sally's mother's Melbourne home the early morning silence was shattered by the shrill ringing of the telephone just after 6.30am. Margy Donald picked it up. It was Sally's uncle: 'There's been a terrible accident in Thredbo'. He'd heard it on a radio news bulletin. Shell-shocked, she hung up and punched in the number of Stuart and Sally's apartment. The phone rang and rang—there was no answer. Comforted by the ringing, Margy felt they must both be safe and were probably out helping with the rescue effort. She needed to know for sure so she dialled the hotel where her eldest daughter worked. She identified herself and asked for Sally. All she was told was that Bimbadeen had come down. Numbed and confused, Margy couldn't even remember the name of the lodge Stuart and Sally were living in. She rang Stuart's parents.

Annette and Steve Diver too had been asleep. Dazed by the early morning call, Steve told Margy the name of Stuart and Sally's lodge—Bimbadeen. There was dead silence on the phone ... it was a nightmare.

Sleepily, Annette Diver sensed her husband's tension. She'd woken up thinking he'd been talking in his sleep—then she realised he was on the phone. He hung up and told her the news ... her heart sank. Believing one son was buried in the rubble the Divers desperately tried to contact the other, but caught up in the rescue operation Euan was unreachable. What followed was an agonising wait for news.

For 17 other families the news was just as grim. In the dead of night their lives had been changed irrevocably. Hotlines were hastily set up by the Red Cross for family and friends but the information was still very sketchy. Twenty-one surrounding lodges had been checked for safety and more than 220 people evacuated.

A disaster recovery centre was set up in the Thredbo Alpine Hotel. Coordinated by the Department of Community Services, or DoCS, it provided for personal needs, including accommodation, transport and counselling. As well as the

DoCS workers, more than a dozen Department of Health counsellors and at least six Red Cross workers were there to help.

The dark night sky turned a ghostly purple as the sun started to rise and the temperature struggled above zero. Around the mud and rubble that now scarred the landscape rescuers were still arriving, briefings were being held, decisions were being made. Heavy machinery was being hauled in from surrounding towns. Whether it would be needed wasn't yet known. The request was simple: 'Just get it here . . . and fast'.

Daylight allowed most in the village to take their first look at the catastrophe. Stunned, tired and dazed, some simply burst into tears. Others stood staring, unable to believe their own eyes. What was once a picturesque mountainside was now scarred forever. It reminded everyone that this was snow country, in many ways untamed country.

As light snow began falling on the village the nation's leaders offered their condolences. Prime Minister John Howard issued a statement from his hospital bed where he was recovering from pneumonia: 'The thoughts and prayers of the entire nation are with those people unaccounted for and their families and friends. The hopes of all Australians are also with the rescue teams as they carry out the dangerous task of searching for any survivors beneath the devastation caused by the land slippage. The horrifying pictures of the scene at Thredbo are a reminder to all of the fragility of life and reinforce the strength which can be gained from a sense of community in times of tragedy'.

Daylight confirmed Euan Diver's worst fears. As the mist began to lift out of the valley he spotted Stuart and Sally's car parked in the overnight carpark. At that moment he realised there was a high chance they were buried in the devastation. But he still held out some hope that they had survived. He knew Bimbadeen Lodge well and knew that, because their flat was on the ground floor, there was a chance a void had been formed in the rubble. They may have made it.

He also realised for the first time just how close he and his girlfriend Susie had come to being buried. It was a wonder the slide hadn't swallowed their apartment block and its neighbour Tombarra Apartments. Both were unscathed; the wall of earth had lost momentum just metres short of claiming more lives.

Daylight didn't hasten the rescue efforts. The site of the slip was still so dangerous no one was allowed on it. Frustration reached new heights, many spectators and villagers again questioned the delay. But it was a delay that had to be. If the wrong piece of rubble was moved it could cause another slide and more devastation. Weather was also a concern; it had been drizzling on the site and more rain was expected. It was going to be a protracted and obviously dangerous rescue. The site was still too unstable for the rescue machinery so an anxious silence again fell over the resort. Everyone silently prayed for some miracle as a human conveyor belt cleared away felled trees on the edge of the landslide.

'I have been saying the best prayers I can say and I hope we will cap this off by having some survivors out there,' Charlie Sanderson told reporters.

If the slab above me moved in any way I knew I would die because I had such a small gap above me. What the hell was going to happen if either the bed, which I assumed was holding the slab up, collapsed or the rescuers started moving things around at a rapid rate of knots, knocking the slab around? The margins for me to move in were very, very small ... if they rushed in and started belting things around, I was going to be in a fair bit of trouble.

When the water stopped flowing, and I didn't have to hold myself up to breathe, I yelled. For all I was worth I yelled. Why could I hear them so clearly and yet they couldn't hear me? I was screaming out and no one seemed to notice.

After the initial noise above it went strangely quiet. I started to think that whatever had happened was big. Maybe it wasn't just our building but the whole of Thredbo! My mind was beginning to fill with all sorts of wild thoughts. Had a bomb hit the village destroying everything? No it couldn't have because I'd heard trucks and people up above. Maybe only 20 lodges had fallen down.

When it was quiet I began fearing the rescuers had left our building because they thought no one was alive so they had moved on to the next building and they would just keep moving through the village.

'I'm here. I'm down here.' Why can't they hear me?

Several hours passed. I decided I had to do something. I couldn't just lie there and let this beat me. I needed something to cover me so I started feeling around. I could feel the couch that we had at the foot of the bed and on it was a cotton cover, a throw rug. It wasn't much but it was better than nothing. It was out to the side. The bed must have twisted because there was no way I could have reached it if it was still at the end of the bed. It was quite strange because I found it on my right side, where Sal should have been. Whether I had rotated a little bit I couldn't tell, but technically speaking, I could have been lying in the mud on top of Sal, without even realising she was underneath me.

Somehow I managed to grab the cotton cover and started to pull. It was snagged on something. If I could just get a bit of this cover off, it would be good. I pulled and I pulled and I pulled. Between one and two hours later I finally managed to tear off a strip. It was only about 40 centimetres wide and about a metre long. I dragged it up and put it over my torso, trying to push it down over my feet as much as I could. My feet were getting colder. I was still wiggling them and trying to move them around as much as I could. I knew if I got this cover over me, even though it was only a thin piece of cotton, it would make me feel just that little bit warmer.

Once I had it over me it did actually deflect a lot of the drafts that were hitting my body through the rubble. Of course it wasn't warm but it was better than nothing. Up until that point all I had on were my boxer shorts. The struggle to tear the cover off the couch also helped warm me a little and take my mind off the pain of my body slowly freezing.

I really don't know how I managed to get that cover because there was so much mud, it was pitch black and I had become very disorientated. It was total cave darkness, totally devoid of light.

Apart from the physical benefits of the cover it was a tremendous boost, mentally. I still couldn't hear a hell of a lot of digging up above. I could hear occasional noises and voices but not a real lot of digging. So, getting hold of that cover gave

*me a little bit more belief in myself again. Maybe, just maybe,
I could survive. I was still looking hour to hour.*

*As time progressed I thought 'Well, we'll make the ten-
hour mark and away we'll go'. I was shivering uncontrollably.
It felt as though the blood in my veins was being frozen solid—
my skin was so frigid I thought it would just crack open.*

While initially fearing up to 100 people were caught in the
slip, police were now able to narrow down exactly who was
missing. There were between 18 and 20 people unaccounted
for—11 men and seven women from Bimbadeen Lodge and
one man who had been in Carinya.

Included in that figure was a woman who was thought
to have been swept away in the rush of earth and rubble as
she walked along Bobuck Lane with her husband. His story
was heartbreaking. Police revealed he and his wife had been
walking back to their lodge after a night out when the woman
was swept away. Her husband had been a few paces in front,
police said, and had managed to get clear ... she hadn't. It
was to be the first of many heartbreaking tales of those lost.

Luckier though were Werner and Madonna Siegenthaler,
and their two-year-old daughter Lillie. They occupied a top-
floor apartment of Bimbadeen Lodge. Werner had Thursdays
off from his position as mountain manager so his usual practice
was to pack up his family on the Wednesday night and head
off to their house at Jindabyne where they would spend the
following day. Their apartment had been empty when the slide
hit. It was, so far, the one and only piece of good news.

*I started trying to focus on what the rescuers were doing, picture
exactly what stage they were at. Although I couldn't hear
anyone on the site I knew they were somewhere out there—
they must be! I could hear trucks and vehicles. Even though
they weren't on the site, they were near the site, around the
site. I knew Euan would be out there, Feral too, they'd be there—
if only they could hear me.*

*I'd hoped that I would be out in the first hour; I had now
been here for around eight hours. I started to fear that no one
was coming and maybe the problem was really much bigger
than I'd imagined. Surely they wouldn't just give up.*

Chief Superintendent Bruce Johnston offered this description: 'It's like a pack of cards ... like a set of dominoes. If you move something you have to be quite sure that something else isn't going to fall. We can hope there will be life but we have no sign of life'.

A clearly distressed Thredbo Alpine Resort managing director, David Osborn, told a crowded media conference he didn't believe the village was at fault: 'Those lodges have been in place for over 25 years and there's been no indication that there's been any problems with them'.

The opinion of the geophysicist was now all the more important. Roads and Traffic Authority geotechnical engineer David Warren-Gash had been woken early; a police helicopter collected him from a football oval near his home in Sydney's northern suburbs. It was an anxious and tense flight; a fly-over of the site on arrival confirmed the seriousness of the situation.

The officer in charge of the Police Rescue Squad, Inspector Garry Smith, was also on board; his role was to coordinate the rescue operation. He was a realist, a respected rescuer with years of experience to back his decisions. It was his resolve to continue a deliberate, controlled and coordinated rescue effort until everyone that had been reported missing was accounted for.

Warren-Gash was also considered an expert in his field. He'd had experience in this environment and his advice regarding the stability of the site was essential before the operation could swing into the next phase. After inspecting the scene he told rescuers he couldn't be sure whether there could be another major slippage.

In the opinion of the District Engineering Services Functional Area Coordinator, Glenn Vardy, the whole area was in an extremely precarious state. The landslide site immediately below the Alpine Way was standing at a 60-degree slope with dangerous overhangs on top. The base of that area was a quagmire of liquefied soil, which was being kept saturated by the continuous flow from an underground spring at the base of the slide. Most of the superstructure of Carinya had been removed by the slide, and the remaining foundations covered with two large concrete slabs and filled with a mass of liquefied soil. The eastern side of Bimbadeen revealed a series of sloping concrete slabs and debris overlaid by a 60-tonne concrete parking bay slab with four motor vehicles still perched on it. Below Bimbadeen was a steeply sloped area of building debris including another motor vehicle.

Inspector Smith had set up office in the forward command post, from which the rescue mission would be coordinated, in the nearby Christiana Lodge. After discovering some of the people missing may have had mobiles it was decided to try dialling the numbers. It was a long shot but worth trying; anything was worth trying. No one answered the calls and the ringing of the telephones couldn't be heard by the rescuers.

In consultation with the team of geophysical engineers from the National Parks and Wildlife Service and the Snowy Mountains Engineering Corporation, who were already on site, it was finally deemed safe to begin the rescue operation. Carefully. There was still the possibility—and probability—of a further slide.

By 10.30am, 11 hours after the slip, rescuers were allowed, albeit tentatively, onto the edges of the site which covered an area about 150 metres down the slope and 50 metres across the face. On Bobuck Lane a small front-end loader had begun picking away at the rubble spread across the narrow roadway.

Firefighter Warwick Kidd and a policeman carefully checked the rubble as it was moved by the loader. The pair had the grisly task of seeing if the loader uncovered a body, specifically that of the woman who was reported to have been swept away as she walked along Bobuck Lane.

Australian Federal Police rescue squad officers, Sergeant Warren Williamson and Senior Constable Mick Travers, set up a trapped person locator on the site. The size of a shoebox, the device had small seismic and acoustic sensors that were capable of picking up movements or noises and amplifying them 20 times through the operator's headphones. As Travers put the headphones on, Williamson tested the device's sensitivity by throwing a pebble onto one of the slabs. It almost blew out Travers' eardrums. Satisfied it was functioning correctly Williamson used a loudhailer to make a plea to any survivors; he asked anyone who could hear him to make the smallest movement, the slightest sound. Travers heard nothing through the headphones.

Under the shadow of the wrecked cars teetering on the edge of Bimbadeen's carpark, rescuers formed a human chain to remove the rubble piece by painstaking piece, all the while fearing their next move might be their last.

I searched my soul for strength. Sal and I both had the ability to overcome fear and that would be crucial to my survival. But this was just sheer terror. Fear beyond the imagination. Fear of the unknown. It's amazing what you can overcome. I had this overpowering fear of the water coming again. And the water coming again ... and again. That drove me so close to the edge. When I talk about the edge I'm talking about death, wanting to die. Getting pushed to the wall. I'm the sort of person who never, ever would have thought that I'd consider taking my own life. I'd always believed that someone would have to be driven to the absolute depths to try to take their life. I was now reaching those depths.

The pain was becoming unbearable. That physical pain. On top of that, the emotional pain of having just lost my wife and lying in mud and cold water in pitch blackness, with no idea of how the hell I was going to get out—if I was going to get out.

How I got through it I don't know but the mind just has an amazing ability to take control, to say, 'No, I'm going to keep going. You can worry about the fear and you can deal with the loss later, but at the moment you are in survival mode and this is what you have got to do'. Here I was afraid of dark places, afraid of small places; everything that absolutely terrified me but still my mind pushed me on ... made me survive.

Furniture, bedding, clothing, bricks and wood slowly snaked their way along the human chain, hand to hand, up the slope to waiting trucks. An eerie silence enveloped the valley, broken only occasionally by rescuers' distant voices encouraging one another. Sometimes a single word passed up the line—'Personal' simply meant an item belonging to one of the victims was being passed up the chain of men and women, stark against the muddy rubble in their orange overalls—the men and women of the State Emergency Service.

The Urban Search and Rescue teams, dubbed the 'tunnel rats', began their job burrowing into the quagmire. Using seismic sensing equipment, flexi search cameras and thermal imaging cameras they edged forward—millimetre by millimetre—looking for any sign of life.

When Bimbadeen Lodge and its adjoining carpark collapsed five concrete slabs came crashing down. The four-storey building had been originally connected to Bobuck Lane by a suspended concrete parking bay, which joined the building just below the top storey. The impact of the carpark into the building had cannoned the top floor through the air and down the slope. The 60-tonne parking bay ended up on top of the collapsed structure. The top-floor slab flew through the air, landed and split in half with one half flipping over and the other wedging into the ground and splitting in half again.

In places there was just a few centimetres' space between the slabs. Items such as refrigerators, washing machines, dryers, wardrobes, beds, mattresses, filing cabinets and computers were flattened. Charlie Sanderson was standing on the edge of the slide watching: 'I saw a full-size refrigerator being removed from the rubble which was 60 centimetres high—wardrobes filled with clothing were reduced to the same height'.

A police helicopter had arrived just after dawn, bringing with it more seismic listening devices and thermal imaging cameras. The equipment was quickly put to use. Every time a piece of rubble was removed the thermal imaging cameras were used to check for any body heat blooms ... there still weren't any. It was a technique mastered by rescuers at the 1995 bombing of the US federal government building in Oklahoma City, which claimed more than 170 lives. After that blast firefighters from across Australia underwent specialist training in Urban Search and Rescue techniques.

Oklahoma Fire Chief John Hanson knew how valuable patience was. 'One thing that your citizens will have to be is extremely patient, as our citizens were. It's something you can't hurry up because of the danger of injuring further victims that you've located and bringing firefighters and rescuers in harm's way,' he told reporters.

As time went on my hearing became more acute. Once the water stopped flowing there was silence all around me, complete silence. That silence and the pitch darkness heightened my hearing. I guess, like a blind person, I began to rely on my hearing for my survival. There was no use smelling because the cavity smelled putrid—a mixture of mud, gas, diesel and sewage. My taste was useless because there was nothing, but the dust, to taste.

I felt I was yelling at the top of my voice. But was I really yelling that loudly? My throat hurt so much I must have been yelling. Or was my hearing so much more acute that I wasn't actually shouting as loudly as I thought I was? I never, ever yelled, 'Help'. I made a conscious decision that if I yelled 'Help' I was just going to scare myself more because that would heighten the reality of the situation I was in. I was terrified enough as it was and that terror seemed to magnify as time went on. Instead of yelling 'Help' I was calling out 'Hellooooo', because it was more prolonged and I could start off quietly and yell as loudly and for as long as I could rather than just a short, sharp 'Help'. 'Hellooooo' seemed a lot more comforting as well. I didn't want to scare all the others who had survived in our building.

My throat was unbelievably parched because of the dust. Sucking in concrete dust and yelling on top of that didn't do a lot for my throat. Whenever I heard the rescuers come close I would let loose, shouting and screaming as loudly as I could. I did everything I could to try to get their attention. I found a little metal pipe and I was banging it against the wrought iron of the bedhead. I thought I was belting it pretty hard but obviously not hard enough—there was still no recognition from the people up above.

As well as focusing on getting their attention I also focused internally, on myself. I started to realise that I wasn't in the world's greatest situation and the likelihood of me getting out was not all that great. That was the reality of it—there was no point lying to myself.

Those hours gave me a lot of time to think about what

was going on around me. I was still willing to just lie there and wait—I didn't have much choice. I was talking to myself, 'You'll be all right, mate. You'll get through. Keep going, keep going, keep going'. In my mind I begged Sal for her support to try to get me through it. To give me strength.

Above, not a murmur was heard.

By now more than 200 emergency workers were involved in the operation. As the members of the human chain continued to shift what they could, others began shoring up the site to prevent further slippage. The rescue strategies being used emphasised the need for teamwork. Multi-agency teams made up of police, firefighters, ambulance and State Emergency Service personnel abandoned any inter-agency rivalry and adopted a single-minded effort to locate and rescue survivors.

The initial plan called for loose rubble to be removed from Bobuck Lane by an excavator. This was critical to the entire operation as it would give heavy machinery access to remove the mountains of rubble burying the two lodges. Drainage was another priority. Water constantly flowing over the site had to be dammed and drained away.

Four-hourly briefings were being held at site control. At these briefings the current situation was reported, engineering advice discussed, future plans laid and agencies assigned to carry out those plans.

A meeting between engineers, geologists, geophysicists and soil specialists decided it was still too dangerous to begin work on the centre of the site. The on-site engineers told the rescue chiefs there were no guarantees there wouldn't be another slide. 'We can't be positive that whatever triggered the event is not still active,' Glenn Vardy said.

The blocked Bobuck Lane became a priority. Rescuers felt that once it was cleared of rubble it would be a safe base to begin using the heavy machinery to remove the larger slabs. But it was so narrow it was going to be difficult to manoeuvre the machinery into place ... if possible at all.

That afternoon, 17 hours after the disaster, the rotors of a twin-engine Squirrel helicopter could be heard coming up the valley. The police chopper gingerly hovered over the ugly gash in the mountain. A policeman was slowly winched down to survey the site from above. Of most concern were mangled cars caught in the slide—rescuers feared people might have been trapped inside them. It was an extremely dangerous exercise. If the cable had snagged on a tree or a piece of rubble the chopper crew would have had to cut the officer loose; there would have been no safe way of getting him out. It was yet another heroic effort. The operation was over quickly, the brave officer able to confirm the car wrecks were empty. But the down thrust of the rotor blade had sent lighter pieces of rubble flying around the site; it was the last time a helicopter was brought so close.

I heard the chopper coming down. I could feel the wind blowing through so I knew there was air circulating. That was comforting in a way because it meant I wasn't going to suffocate. I could hear the helicopter's rotors as they got closer and closer and it began to really get to me because it was blowing more icy air over my body. I could hear the slab above me vibrating.

I thought that maybe they were winching people out, so I told myself, 'No problem, it's OK Stu, put up with the cold air, put up with it, because they'll be down to get you in 20 minutes. There goes another person being airlifted to hospital. Fantastic'. In my mind I had actually planned the whole rescue. I knew where I was and I knew the layout of the building, I knew there were 12 other apartments. I tried to picture how the building had collapsed—if the building fell down one way they'd be rescuing these people—if it fell down another way they'd be rescuing others. They're just progressively working down the site towards me. I figured our bedhead was holding up the slab above me so I was planning to tell them how to cut the slab so that it would break in half and split over the bedhead, then I would just stand up in the sunshine and walk out. That would be it—it would be that simple.

But the down draught caused by the chopper's rotors posed another problem. Vibrations shook the loose soil, causing renewed fears that the operation would trigger further land slippage.

As the overhead reconnaissance was under way Australians prayed. At St Andrew's Anglican and St Mary's Catholic

Cathedrals, in Sydney, those who had loved ones missing and those involved in the rescue operation were remembered. Soon those prayers were being echoed around the world as news spread of the disaster.

At the site a bobcat carefully began moving tonnes of boulders and dirt that threatened to tumble down onto the rescue area. Rescuers equipped with chainsaws and jackhammers were busy cutting away tree branches and beams. The operation seemed frustratingly slow, still hampered by slippery mud and pooling water.

I had an overwhelming temptation to drink the water around me. I was as thirsty as thirsty could be. I was so dry. But sanity prevailed and I didn't. I didn't know exactly what the water contained but that it was contaminated with at least sewage and diesel. I probably would have been very sick if I had drunk it.

I began realising that it was possible others in Bimbadeen had died. I thought that half the people had been rescued by this stage. That was a critical thing that kept me going—the confidence that I too would be rescued. Why should I die if others had made it?

I just had to bide my time. I would wait as long as I could and I'd keep warm enough to stay alive ... they'd get to me in the end. I knew I was at the bottom of the pile so it was going to take a long time to get to me. They'd get everyone else out first and then it would be my turn. I had started formulating pictures in my mind of what it would look like on the outside.

For the 300 permanent residents of Thredbo the grief was communal. Everyone knew somebody lost in the rubble. It was collective despair. All through the village they hugged and comforted each other in small clusters. The '12-monthers', as they were known, because they spent all year in the resort, were enveloped in tragedy. Tears flowed freely, along with words of hope.

'Thredbo is like a family, everybody knows everybody else and some of the firefighters have family or friends in there,' Salvation Army chaplain Colonel Don Woodland said.

Euan had to ring his parents. It was something he'd been

Above: Adventure has always been a part of my life. Here's me, Euan and Mum on one of our adventures in New Zealand.

Right: Euan and me beneath the towering Himalayas. I was nine years old.

Left: Sal and me carving the turns in Canada.

Below: Iain 'Grovesy' Groves, Sal and me at Lake Louise, Canada. Another great day's skiing.

Right: Sal Pal on our wedding day.

Below: The family together on our wedding day — Sal's mum, Margy, my dad, Steve, me, Sal, my mum, Annette, and Sal's dad, Andrew.

Looking towards Bimbadeen and Carinya Lodges (arrowed) in idyllic Thredbo.

After the landslide.

Looking into what became known as the 'A frame'.

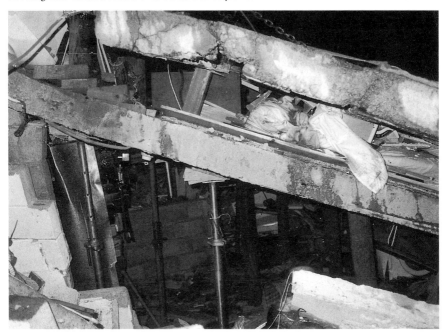

Concrete slabs of Bimbadeen with furniture sandwiched in between. Rescuers shored up the slabs from below.

They've heard me. All hands on deck.

The hole the rescuers dug. On the right you can see the mattress the rescuers had to cut through, and the monitor of the closed-circuit TV.

Above: Our bedroom after much of the mud and debris had been cleared out.

Right: Sixty-five hours of freezing temperatures took their toll on my feet. This photo was taken at Canberra Hospital after I'd been rescued.

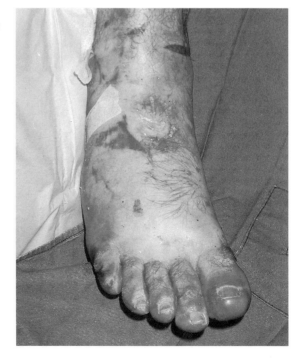

I'm free at last. The rescuers carry me up the slope on a stretcher to an ambulance.

Here I am in Scotland a few months after the landslide with my friend Grovesy, competing to build the world's biggest snowball.

trying to avoid. He didn't actually tell them Stuart and Sally were under the rubble—he felt his mum and dad already knew that—there was no need for words. Although both were absolutely devastated the conversation was very matter of fact. Perhaps shock had taken hold. Euan tried to explain the extent of the damage.

As Steve listened to his eldest son's account of the disaster he looked into his wife's eyes. For Annette Diver that look spelled everything out. A pessimistic cloud descended on her.

Steve asked if they should come up—could they help? But Euan gave some noncommittal answer ... no one really knew what was going on. 'Don't bother at this stage but I'll call you back.' But 'back' never came so Steve and Annette made the obvious choice to make their way to Thredbo—if not for Stuart then as support for Euan.

I refused to cry about what had happened. There was too much to do to survive, mentally and physically.

I made a promise to Sal—I was going to get out. I knew that I was physically OK. I knew after the first few hours that the only thing that might kill me was the cold and I had a rough idea how to survive in the cold. Physically I should be able to survive, what would happen mentally was anyone's guess. So I promised. That was what drove me. I promised Sal that I was going to get out and tell her mum what had happened.

nine

Stacked Decks

Sally's father, Andrew, organised a private plane for the mad dash from Melbourne. On board were Margy and her partner Colin, and Andrew and his wife Carol. Television screens in the arrival hall at the Snowy Mountains airport in Cooma gave Margy her first glimpse of the disaster that had buried her daughter.

Margy couldn't believe her eyes: 'Oh God, there's no way they are going to get them out of this alive'. Although she refused to give up hope she concluded that if Stuart and Sally were to die then at least they had gone together. They were inseparable alive, they will still be together. In a way it was a comforting thought ... if anything could be comforting.

Rushing by car from Cooma to Thredbo they, along with hundreds of other people, were stopped at police roadblocks. Confusion reigned and they were forced to turn back, heading for a friend's home in Canberra until they could get clearance to enter the village. It wouldn't be until the next day.

On the scene emotions were running high.

Urban Search and Rescue firefighter, Steve Hirst, was part of a team burrowing into what was left of the top flat of Bimbadeen Lodge. They hadn't found any bodies there, but as they burrowed into the wreckage they started to uncover something almost as chilling—babies clothes and nappies. The lump in Hirst's throat was almost choking him as they found 'Bananas in Pyjamas' clothing, nappies, parts of cots.

It shattered an already delicate morale, and senior USAR instructor Warwick Kidd knew the danger of that. He watched as the mood of everybody plummeted. The next thing they expected to uncover was a baby's body. Furiously they dug. For three hours they tunnelled into what appeared to be a baby's room ... digging, digging, digging. It wasn't until they went to the debriefing at the end of their shift that they were told there had been a family living in that apartment but they had left before the landslide—it was Werner and Madonna Siegenthaler's flat.

Kidd was furious—why hadn't his team been told the family had long gone? For three hours they had to face a horrible possibility; their spirits, already dented by the tragedy of the slide, had been further battered. Kidd later realised that in the early confusion the information had simply not been passed on to his team.

It was an example of some of the teething problems of the rescue operation. The police had to treat the site like a crime scene and try to limit the public release of information as they would eventually have to investigate what had caused the collapse, but the overwhelming desire of everybody on the site was to find any survivors and keep them alive.

While the cold, in the beginning, was painful, by now it was indescribable. It was eating away at me. I was soaking wet and I had no way of drying myself.

I calculated that I'd been trapped for about 15 hours or so and I knew I had to do something or I wouldn't last much longer. Suddenly I remembered there'd been a polar fleece jumper at the end of the bed when we'd gone to sleep. Why hadn't I remembered it before?

I frantically felt around for it where I thought it would've ended up. Sure enough it was there, but it was a monumental effort to get hold of it. Time was hard to gauge but it must have taken about two hours. It was jammed under rocks and rubble and I just couldn't free it. I pulled and pulled as hard as I could, with one hand first and then the other. In the end I finally managed to drag it out.

I would do anything to keep warm. I had even started trying to urinate on my feet, which is almost impossible when you're horizontal. But I had also been urinating where the polar fleece had been so it was absolutely soaked in diesel, mud and urine. Should I even bother with it? 'Why the hell are you putting this on. Is this really going to do anything?' Then I remembered the polar fleece had similar properties to wool so it didn't matter how wet it got, it would still warm me up.

But pulling it free from the rubble was just the start of the battle. It took me another three hours to get it on—I probably put it on incorrectly about 12 times. I couldn't, for the life of me, find the sleeves. When I finally rotated it around the right way and managed to get one hand through a sleeve I then had about a three-centimetre gap underneath my body to try to feed it through to get the other sleeve on. For a long time I couldn't get it far enough under my body to pull it through to the other side. I was totally exhausted—I'd try to squeeze it through, fail and then have a rest before starting all over again. A couple of times I would get it all the way under, but I had twisted it on the way through and so then I couldn't find the sleeve. Then I would have to pull it all the way back out and try again.

Ironically it was probably good for me because the effort kept me occupied for a long while. I was determined that it was what I had to do and it was going to make me survive. My determination paid off. I finally got the polar fleece on. Just doing the zip up took me half an hour because I couldn't get my frozen fingers to function properly. But after all that, the fleece was so muddy and wet initially it just seemed to make me colder.

It was muddy, wet and cold on the surface as well. Despite the intensity of the work, the rescuers were also freezing, so frigid their bones seemed to rattle. The heart of the site was still bare of rescuers. Instead they carefully tried to shore up the sides of the slide.

Across the valley surveyors had set up camp and were carefully monitoring the rubble for the slightest movement. Any hint of movement brought an immediate halt to the search efforts. A siren system was instituted: one blast to cease work, two to resume and three for immediate evacuation of the site.

The rescue efforts had taken on a military-like precision. It was precisely the job the USAR firefighters had been trained for, according to Warwick Kidd, who had helped establish the New South Wales unit:

'When a structure collapses, at some stage, it reaches what we call equilibrium ... that's when it can't collapse any further. But with 50 to 100 people clambering on it, the next thing it's going to do is move past its equilibrium and start to collapse again. We had to stop that.

'We did that by shoring up, that's one of the technical specialities of a USAR team, to crib up and build impromptu little barricades and guards to stop things falling any further.

'USAR provides very disciplined teams. I think every one of the rescuers—firies, police, ambos, SES—on the site adopted the same discipline. When the sirens went off and called for an evacuation, the discipline had to be there. Everyone had to leave, follow those commands. We were there to carry out rescues and if the rescuers got injured who was going to rescue the rescuers? It was a very hard thing to do at times but it showed how much dedication and professionalism there was in all our emergency services.'

It wasn't long before I figured out what the sirens meant—and they began to terrify me. I started riding an emotional roller-coaster. I knew the rescuers were close to me and I thought, 'It's been a long time. I know it's been a long time so they must be nearly down to me'. They must've been digging like fury—I could hear them. Then the sirens would go and there would be silence again. I can't explain how frustrating and scary that was. Once again, alone in this mess, this dark, cold wet tomb. Those silent periods seemed to stretch forever ... until finally I would hear the familiar sound of digging. Finally there was renewed hope. It was playing havoc with my mind and the faith I had in the rescuers.

I could hear the rescuers when they were working below where I was and that made me think that they must be getting other people out. But why weren't they coming to get me out? That's when doubts started to creep into my mind: were they going to come and get me at all? And then I would hear them come closer and I'd shout again.

I felt panic and terror and disbelief in myself. Could I actually survive for much longer in this cold and this pain? When they came close it gave me hope that I could carry on ...

then when they went away again I hit the wall. Negative thoughts returned.

At one stage there was a flash of light—the power had suddenly come back on for a split second. There must be a light bulb somewhere nearby. If I could just find it I could break it and end it all right here and now. Stop the pain. Be back with Sal. I felt along the slab that was on top of me but I couldn't find the bulb. I didn't even think about the shattered glass all around me—I guess it was just as well.

There was no room for negative thoughts a few metres above but it was a tremendous battle to quell feelings of despair. Personal effects, photographs, golf clubs—simple things that make up people's lives—were being dragged from the rubble. For every rescuer it was emotional turmoil—they were touching the lives of people who, in all likelihood, were now dead.

But still they continued in the hope of finding survivors. Kidd too was hopeful: 'In every single collapse there is a potential for survival. It's a bit like an iceberg. What you see on the surface is only ten per cent, everything else is underground. The way buildings collapse in some cases, the potential for voids to be formed around furniture is enormous.

'All we were concerned about was finding survivors. As rescuers, if we had gone to Thredbo with the attitude that everybody was dead our level of enthusiasm and our demeanour would have been straight away shot. So we had to have a very, very positive attitude.'

I was running out of energy. All the effort of getting the piece of cotton and the fleece seemed to have drained what little energy I had left. It took a lot out of me physically. I had been wiggling my feet for about 20 hours and I didn't even have the energy to keep doing that anymore.

So, finally I had this fleece on but I was colder than I had ever been, and that's when I thought, 'Well, this is it. You're gone now. You've put this wet fleece on and it is not going to work. It's not going to warm you up one little bit'. But eventually it started to dry out a little; the mud started to dry and went hard. That posed another painful problem that just heightened my already highly irrational state. I was still hugging myself, trying to keep my torso warm but my strength was fading and my arms kept falling off to the side. My elbows, which were covered in cuts, would end up in the mud, and the blood from the cuts would stick to the fleece. When I managed to move my arms back up, across my chest, the scabs that had bonded with the fleece would rip and tear, adding to my myriad of pains.

Then the water would come down again, though not as much as in the early stages. It seemed as though every time the rescuers moved something above, it released another flow of freezing water.

At 4.30 that afternoon a USAR team found the first body. Rescuers pulling back a mattress and some bedding revealed the slide's first confirmed victim, Sydney carpenter John Cameron. He'd been on holidays at Carinya Lodge. Kidd glanced up and saw a young State Emergency Service girl standing just above him. The look on her face is not something he'll easily forget—it was clearly the first dead body she had ever seen.

The young girl's presence on the 'front line' embodied the enthusiasm and dedication of the rescuers—everyone was willing to do their bit, regardless of personal hardship.

As the sun set on the mountain hamlet, Kosciusko-Thredbo Pty Ltd chairman Alan Rydge asked Charlie Sanderson to address some of Thredbo's staff to explain to them the intricacies of the delicate rescue mission.

Sanderson expected a small gathering. When he walked into the Thredbo Alpine Hotel bistro he was met by a sea of faces—several hundred locals had shown up. It was one of the hardest duties the police officer, who had more than 25 years' experience, had ever had to perform.

'I can't tell you how sorry I am—I can see your sorrow on your faces,' he told them from his perch on a table. 'The chances of anyone being alive in there is very, very negligible.'

Explaining the decision to wait until daylight to commence the rescue operation, Sanderson, who had only four weeks earlier been appointed Local Area Commander, said: 'The risk of future catastrophe and of injuring or killing our own people had to be weighed against the sensible way of tackling the problem'.

With darkness falling, the floodlights once again cast their eerie glow over the site, creating hazardous and dangerous shadows, shadows that could have easily spelled disaster if a rescuer made a mistake with their footing. Most felt safer using their own torches. However the dark and the plummeting temperatures did nothing to quell their enthusiasm.

Chief Superintendent Bruce Johnston was the most senior police officer in the south-east region of New South Wales, which covers 45,000 square kilometres. It was on his shoulders that the ultimate success or failure of this delicate operation rested. 'There is still concern [about] walking over the rubble itself—it really is a volatile area,' he said. 'The mood is one of frustration ... it's been frustration all day.'

It was several more hours, and almost 24 hours after the slide, before John Cameron's body was finally released from the rubble and carried by a sombre group of pallbearers up the steep embankment to a temporary morgue. Everyone feared it would be full before too long.

Police rescue squad veteran Sergeant Mark Powderly arrived by car that night, rendezvousing with Superintendent Charlie Sanderson and Inspector Garry Smith by the side of the road between Jindabyne and Thredbo. Briefed as to what was happening, he climbed back into his four-wheel drive with their parting words echoing in his head: 'It's all yours'.

Arriving in Thredbo a short time later, Powderly saw what he had inherited. 'Oh shit,' he thought, 'we're here for the long run on this one.' From that point on it became Powderly's job to oversee the rescue by night, while Smith ran the operation during the daylight hours.

While Smith and Powderly supervised the operation they constantly sought advice from Mines Rescue and the on-site engineers. At any one time up to five multi-agency rescue teams targeted areas where it was anticipated victims would be found. But that involved a certain amount of guesswork as there was no way of knowing exactly where the victims would be. Each team had up to 12 accredited rescue operators along with an ambulance paramedic. The paramedics were there to treat any injured survivors but it was also their task to prevent injuries occurring to the rescuers by ensuring appropriate safety precautions were followed.

Logistics were a priority. Clothing, food and sleeping arrangements all had to be taken care of. Thredbo had been besieged by hundreds of rescue personnel, stretching sleeping arrangements to the limit. Initially they worked in four-hour shifts—four on, four off.

A dormitory had been set up in a conference room near the bistro restaurant. Inside were more than 100 mattresses strewn across the floor, covered by a sea of blankets and pillows. They were never empty. Their sleeping arrangement was called 'hot bedding'—as one weary rescuer arrived for his sleep another would awake and they'd swap, the sheets still warm from the previous occupant.

Many of the rescuers had been sent to Thredbo with next to no notice. So the essentials were a problem. Local supplies of even the most basic necessities had been exhausted. But it provided a lighter moment amongst so much gloom. Warwick Kidd had to organise underwear for a group of 50 men and all that was left in the village was ten pairs of women's underpants.

'Consequently these also went. The individuals wearing this underwear never made themselves known, however I did receive a request for a matching bra and garter belt. The request was unsigned!'

Sleep seemed the easiest option. I was just so tired, I really, really wanted to sleep. Twenty hours in and I felt it was well and truly over. My will to live was at its lowest point. Even better than sleep, suicide again took over my thoughts. Everything was way out of control. You can only lose so much control before you feel that there is nothing left. I was so far out of it there was no use being there.

I wanted to die. Sal was there, why couldn't I be with her? I was in total despair. I'd hit the wall and there was no way that I could see to get through that wall. I'd been in this tomb for at least 20, probably up to 24 hours now. I'd hit that wall over and over again. Up till now I had managed to get through the barrier. Keep going. Hit the wall. Keep going. Hit the wall. My body felt like a battering ram.

But finally I had started to warm up. The polar fleece was drying out a little and this gave me a new reason to keep going.

When I'm talking warmth, though, I'm not talking real warmth, I'm not talking 'under the doona' warmth. I'm talking warmer than absolutely freezing. I was still wet. The water continued to flow through intermittently. It was around zero degrees and I still only had cotton boxer shorts on my bottom half. This caused the most excruciating pain in my groin. My feet were getting colder. My head was uncovered and you lose a lot of heat from your head. To say I warmed up with the polar fleece is probably not the correct term. I just stopped cooling as quickly. But it still eased my mind.

You can't sleep in pain. Even if I tried I couldn't fall asleep. I still had that sharp rock in my back. I was scared I was going to black out if the pain got too much and then I would become unconscious. If I lapsed into unconsciousness I would die. I knew about hypothermia; I knew that my body would give up the fight if I became unconscious.

I really started to wonder just how long it was going to take and whether I had the internal strength to get through it. Doubt again crept into my mind. Could I physically survive this cold? The agony was excruciating. I was slowly, but surely, freezing to death—what made it all the more frightening was that I knew it.

Medical staff knew it was possible for someone to have survived. Paramedic Graeme Field raised everyone's hopes: 'There is a possibility someone could be alive. If they were in their beds, wrapped up, that's a help. If they were not traumatised or injured in the landslide, it is possible they could still be alive'.

While the warmth would help, so too could the cold by slowing down the body's metabolism and heart rate, meaning that survivors would need less oxygen than normal. But the cold was a doubled-edged sword. While hypothermia could protect someone against trauma it could also kill them. The risk of 'crush syndrome'—where damaged muscles release toxins into the bloodstream, causing kidney failure—was great.

Feelings of frustration and anger returned every time the rescuers deserted the site. I heard the sirens go off. I knew they weren't blowing them because they were having a big party. I feared the sirens sounding and the rescuers leaving me. I wondered how long my internal strength could last. Could I go on?

But I also had an amazing determination to live. I swung between two, totally opposite, ends of the spectrum. At one end I was racked by great doubt, great fear, and at the other end I experienced a strange calmness and a feeling that I could conquer anything. I was fluctuating between the two, back and forth like a pendulum until in the end something told me, 'Well, we can go on, we can get through this'.

Psychologists and military survival experts say the body clock usually keeps working for the first 24 hours. So I reckon that my memory of the first 24 hours is pretty accurate even though it was as dark as a cave, no light whatsoever. In a way that desperate feeling of helplessness, the confined space and the inability to do anything wasn't as bad as it could have been simply because I was just so helpless. My tension and fear would have escalated if I had been able to do something to try to get out. Because my situation was so desperate there was just this feeling of nothing. It almost had a calming effect.

I had been angry, tormented, terribly depressed and abusive and now I had this amazing sense of calmness. It was all so out of my control I thought, 'Well, bugger it. I am just going to lie here and let them come and get me'.

I still thought others in the building would have survived and this gave me an impetus to survive. I felt I had to get out and see all the others. I thought they must have all been airlifted, otherwise why the hell was it taking so long? I knew the rescuers wouldn't just be hanging around worrying about dead people; they would be getting living people out.

It seemed to be one hurdle after another for the rescuers; if their hands weren't tied by the precarious nature of the site they had to deal with other problems. In the early hours of the morning they had finally managed to dam and seal a diesel leak from one of many tanks in the rubble. Then work was once again forced to a halt as a boulder the size of a small truck, and poised on the upper section of the site, was seen to shift. If it came down it could crush dozens of rescuers working down lower.

By now there were hundreds of emergency workers on site—police, fire brigade personnel, ambulance staff, State Emergency Service members and National Parks and Wildlife Service officers.

Chief Superintendent Johnston said: 'We have got some of the best rescue brains in Australia here. Everyone is totally committed from all the combat agencies and other areas. And yet everyone has to stand around frustrated, to pick at the edges'.

The headlines screamed 'No Hope', 'We have no sign of life', 'No heartbeat from icy ruins' and 'Buried'. Despite the brave and determined faces of the rescuers hope was fast dwindling of finding anyone alive. Twenty-four hours after the disaster only one body had been recovered.

Life or Death

ten

$\mathbf{A}$t Stuart's family home in Melbourne his parents tried to come to terms with what had happened as they packed to head up to Thredbo. Long-time family friend Phil Pilgrim, an engineer, had come around first thing and together they assessed the possibilities of Stuart and Sally surviving.

They pored over a newspaper featuring a photograph of the slide on the front page. They figured that if Carinya had come down and wiped out the top floors of Bimbadeen there was a chance, a small chance, that Stuart and Sally would be OK. It gave Steve Diver renewed hope and a positive attitude but did nothing to shake his wife's doubts—she couldn't believe there would be a survivor.

Phil helped the Divers pack and prepare for the trip. It gave the three of them the chance to go over old times, remembering the early days as their two families grew up together, until it was time to head for Thredbo.

It was the same route that had, over the years, led Steve, Annette, Euan and Stuart Diver on so many joyous adventures ... this time it was leading them to a living hell. As they were heading north their mobile phone started ringing. Annette picked it up and said hello ... it was Euan. She started crying ... it was the first time she'd heard Euan's voice since the disaster. She was unable to speak and handed the phone to her husband.

'We're on the way,' said Steve. He could tell by Euan's tone that he was beginning to hit an emotional wall; he was one of the first there and had to cope with the trauma of what was happening around him. He needed their support.

The Divers arrived almost 24 hours after the disaster; the tears flowed freely as they were reunited with their eldest son.

'I've lost my best friend, I've lost my best friend,' Euan repeated over and over again as he hugged his dad.

'It's OK son, it's OK,' Steve tried hard to keep a brave face.

'All we can do is hope that by some chance one, or both, of them are OK,' Annette said as she tried to comfort him. They were courageous words from a woman whose hope was all but gone. Instead of rushing to the site, the Divers decided it was best to wait until daylight to take a look.

As the family consoled each other, the landslide site continued to be a hive of activity. The 4.5-metre boulder that had halted work was secured with slings. Parts of Bobuck Lane were cleared, allowing a crane to drag a vehicle out.

I could hear everything they were doing. I could hear trucks driving around and moving things in and around the site. When they brought the excavators in and started to dig I could tell exactly what they were doing. I could tell if they were going right or going left. I could even hear when they drove the excavator off to refuel. I could recognise the sound of low-loader trucks driving in along the bottom road. I could hear when they got the mini-excavator down the side because everything started to shake and I thought 'You bastards, what are you doing?' I could even hear when the excavator lost one of its tracks. I could hear the operator swearing. I could hear conversations. When the rescuers came close I could hear them speaking. And then they would go away again and I'd think 'Bloody hell, when are you guys going to come?'

Early the next morning Steve held his wife's hand as they laid eyes on the landslide that had swallowed their youngest son and his wife. It hammered his optimism and heightened his wife's negative thoughts. Everything was just flattened.

They watched as body bags were carried up the steep face of the slide.

Because I could hear so much happening I formulated this plan in my mind about how they were coming to get me. It helped increase my hope. Constantly reassuring myself that I would be rescued added to the calmness that had seemed to overtake all other emotions. I started focusing on what was happening, my family and friends and the rescuers. I figured there were probably about 20 blokes out there, having a shot at it.

I also began asking 'Why?' What had happened? Was it a bomb? Was it me? Did I do something on my way in the door that I couldn't quite remember that had knocked the building down? Crazy ideas went through my head. The day before, I had drilled a hole in the wall to hang a picture—did that cause the building to fall down? Buildings don't just fall down, especially all the way to the bottom. I was at the bottom so I felt the collapse had to have something to do with me. I began to believe that perhaps it was just our building that had fallen down because it sounded like so much activity was happening above me. But I couldn't figure out how. It looked pretty sturdy when I got home. It was a solid brick building, why had it fallen down? But there was no point agonising over it. It was down and that was it. What was important now was solving the problem of getting out.

So there I was cold, but very much alive, waiting for the rescuers to reach me. And then silence returned above me. I thought the rescuers had finished and were now deserting me. Again I collapsed into depression, plagued with self-doubt, fear and terror.

A lot of the other families were now in Thredbo. The names of those affected by the landslide were made public:

John Cameron, 45, Sydney carpenter
Michael Sodergren, 46, senior ski instructor from the US
Mariam Sodergren, 41, Mike's wife, also a ski instructor
from the US
Wendy O'Donohue, 38, marketing and summer
business manager
Colin Warren, 47, Kosciusko Thredbo property manager
Mary Phillips, 31, ski instructor and cafe waitress from
New Zealand
Steven Urosevic, 32, front office manager at
Thredbo Alpine Hotel

Dianne Ainsworth, 33, Thredbo Accommodation Services
head housekeeper
Barry Decker, 35, Dianne's partner, assistant accountant
Anthony Weaver, 47, Thredbo Ski Patrol director
Oscar Luhn, 56, maintenance personnel
Aino Senbruns, 58, Oscar's partner
David Watson, 36, restaurant manager at
Thredbo Alpine Hotel
Stephen Moss, 30, restaurant manager, Friday Flat
Dianne Hoffman, 34, Thredbo Alpine Hotel head
housekeeper
Andrew McArthur, 25, building maintenance
Werner Jecklin, 42, slopes manager
Stuart Diver, 27, ski instructor and summer activities leader
Sally Diver, 27, Stuart's wife, Thredbo Alpine Hotel
reservations manager and conference bookings

Also listed as missing was the woman thought to have been
swept away by the slide as she walked home with her
husband ... her name had not been released.

For every relative it was the waiting, the not knowing
and the climbing death toll that was gnawing at them.

*I was really, really scared of talking to Sal. I had this terrifying
fear that she would reply. I became truly terrified that she
would reply if I spoke to her. So I didn't. I spoke to her in my
mind but I never, ever said anything out loud. My yelling
'hellooooo' instead of 'help' was also partly because I didn't
want to scare Sal into thinking we were in such a dire
predicament.*

*Of course, I knew Sal was dead. I knew that after the first
30 seconds. But my mind started doing funny things to me. I
didn't want to scare myself either. If I had scared myself any
more than I already was, what depths could I drive myself to
then? There are only so many places you can go within yourself—
by now I had been to most of them.*

Given the instability of the site, and the extremely cold weather,
the further the fragile rescue operation proceeded the more
frustrating it became. Charlie Sanderson admitted the chances

of finding anyone alive were 'infinitesimally small'. The mud and debris were several metres deep—the rescuers faced a mammoth task.

As one weary firefighter wandered off his shift, wiping the mud from his eyes, he told reporters: 'You have to think that there could be someone who just happened to get caught in their sleeping bag, in a pocket, in the right place, one of the lucky ones, that they'll be the one we find. That's the main thing that drives you on—the hope that you're going to find someone alive, that we're not just here as a body recovery team'.

At about 10.30 on Friday morning a hush descended on the village. From across the valley a crowd of solemn onlookers gasped as a lone USAR firefighter gingerly made his way to the heart of the disaster site. Tethered to his colleagues, Geoff Courtney inched his way across the debris to an Audi sedan. It still had its parking lights on, as they had been since the landslide occurred. The car was precariously balanced on a precipice at the base of the slide; if it fell its petrol tank could burst into flames, igniting lodges immediately below the site. Courtney secured a chain to the car so a crane could later lift it out.

Some hours later a crane removed the Audi sedan and another severely damaged car. A one-tonne truck had been dragged clear earlier. This was viewed as a significant achievement and boosted the spirits of the rescuers.

The arrival of New South Wales Premier Bob Carr and Police Commissioner Peter Ryan also helped morale. After surveying the scene from a helicopter, several thousand feet above, the pair was taken on site. For the Premier, meeting with the families of those missing had an enormous effect: 'What sticks with me is the eyes of the family members who have got people under that rubble and who live in hope that there might be life there. I am sure all of those families have hope in their spirit and, like them, we want to live in hope'.

Commissioner Ryan recognised the rescuers' frustrations: 'It's that general feeling of emotion, frustration, of wanting to get on. As the land moves everybody has to evacuate and creep back in to progress the work, but they are working extremely hard, as best they can given the circumstances'.

State Protection Group Inspector Dan Ruming was appointed the police liaison officer to deal with the victims' relatives. Sergeant Geoff Levey and Senior Constable Lenore Turner were enlisted to help him. The magnitude of this job was like nothing they had ever encountered. It was vital that the relatives and friends were kept up to date with information and that any questions or suggestions they had were acted upon where possible.

Regular briefings were scheduled to bring them up to date. During these briefings, experts such as doctors, engineers, geologists, media officers, the rescue command, the National Parks and Wildlife Service and those involved in the overall running of the operation were made available. During one of the first meetings Ruming made his position clear: 'I'm the punching bag—be as gentle as you can'. He had never dealt with anything like this before but maintained a theory that it was always best to be open in passing on information to the relatives.

The veteran homicide investigator was also given the heart-wrenching task of informing the relatives when the bodies of their loved ones were found and identified. It was a job he had never had to carry out before even though he had investigated some of the State's most brutal murders. He became an emotional crutch to many, available around the clock for those who simply just needed someone to talk to.

There was a really sharp pain in my back. A rock had been stuck in my back since the beginning. No matter how hard I tried I couldn't get that rock out. Every half hour I tried to shift a little because the pain was so excruciating from that damned rock. The pain ran the whole way along my back. That rock caused me such intense pain but actually, in a lot of ways, helped me survive—because of the pain it caused I couldn't go to sleep and run the risk of losing consciousness. I'd dig down, dig around with my hand underneath my back, I could feel it. I couldn't move it and I was thinking, 'Bloody hell, why the hell can't I move this rock?' I would dig around it with my fingernail. Sometimes I thought I'd moved it but no, it was still there.

Eventually I reached out and felt something flat above my chest. Maybe it was a picture or something, it was relatively large, flat and smooth. With a bit of effort I was able to dislodge it and manoeuvre it under me so I wasn't lying in mud. It finally put an end to that infuriating rock that had hurt so much. It was such a relief. It also felt good to not be lying in mud ... but that didn't last long. As soon as the water started flowing again I was covered with mud.

Although I was exhausted I managed to find enough strength to start wiggling my toes again. My urine only provided very temporary relief. It warmed them for a split second and that was the end of that. Every time I needed to go to the toilet I just went. The urine was pretty good actually—it was sterile and nice and warm. Because of the cold I was urinating a lot, considering I hadn't drunk anything. I was losing a lot of fluid.

Briefing the media on the task ahead, Chief Superintendent Bruce Johnston could no longer hide his own disappointment: 'The reason for the frustration that everyone has felt is that this damn slip ... we could not get in, people could not get in with any safety, or any degree of safety, for either their own lives or perhaps people who were still alive within the rubble'.

The rescuers had become worried about a number of cylinders of cooking gas and two 3,000-litre diesel storage tanks, which they feared could explode.

And movement of another large boulder, held in place by only a gum tree, once again brought work to a halt. Two backhoes, six thermal imaging cameras, two seismic listening devices, diamond-tipped chainsaws and flexi search cameras all became idle until the boulder could be secured.

I was still completely focused on survival and on the physical side of getting out. I was out to combat the world. I was fighting to survive against everything that was being thrown at me. I had a blind faith in my fellow human beings, which I probably got from being brought up a Diver, having blind faith in Mum, Dad and Euan. Never questioning anything that they did or said. And then that faith grew to include Sal, her mum and her sister, Anna. Now that faith rested on the shoulders of the rescuers.

At noon the bells of the small village chapel began to toll, summoning those who wished to offer a prayer. More than 100 people crowded into the Mary MacKillop Chapel on the banks of the Thredbo River. Father Wally Stefanski had been in the parish for the past eight years and he knew most of those trapped. He prayed for divine intervention.

'Last year when this chapel was officially opened, on the June long weekend, we were having joyful celebrations. Somehow I thought the chapel would only be used for weddings—I never thought of sad happenings, tragic happenings.

'We need something to save these people, so Lord Jesus, please tell us what to do.'

Of course I had no idea that Mum and Dad had come to Thredbo. But it was the thought of my family, Sal's family and our friends that kept me going. I still had no idea of the magnitude of what had happened but I knew there was a hell of a lot happening to try to get us out. That was another reason for surviving—these people were putting in such a hard effort, it would be pretty selfish of me to die on them.

A number of the relatives of those missing wanted to know why a 'heavy lift' helicopter, such as an American Sikorski Skycrane, hadn't been brought in to move the larger slabs of concrete, particularly one measuring 15 metres by 15 metres, that were obstructing the rescue operation. They took up their concerns with New South Wales Police Commissioner Peter Ryan, who passed the request on to Charlie Sanderson. But Sanderson had already canvassed the option with the Sea King aircrew, police aircrew, engineers and senior rescuers after the smaller police helicopter had made its reconnaissance the day before. They'd reached a consensus that it would be extremely dangerous to bring in anything more powerful. The down draught probably would have blown the roofs off neighbouring buildings and the vibrations could have triggered another landslide.

It was decided the best approach would be to drill holes in the slabs, anchor them, then cut and chisel them using water-cooled diamond-tipped circular saws and crowbars. Cranes and excavators could then remove the larger chunks.

The Divers were confident the rescuers were doing everything humanly, and safely, possible to find survivors and were worried and upset about criticism to the contrary.

Later in the afternoon some of the families of the missing were taken onto the site to view it for themselves. A police chaplain and Charlie Sanderson accompanied them. 'They were quite emotional about it,' Sanderson told reporters. 'This is a very hard thing for those people ... and I just feel so much for them.'

The Divers had declined the invitation to go; they felt that they just wanted to be on their own, as a family.

But Andrew Donald, whose background is in engineering, wanted to assess the site. 'I had one important task in my life at this stage and that was to save my daughter and Stuart,' he said. Sitting on the stairs of Leatherbarrel Lodge, alongside the slide, Andrew saw cavities in the debris and felt there was a chance Sally and Stuart had survived in one of them.

A formal investigation into the cause of the landslide had begun. Under Detective Inspector Bob Cocksedge, 12 detectives were assigned to look at every aspect of the slide to prepare a report for the coroner. Cocksedge was well known. The senior investigator had headed the inquiry into a 1988 mudslide at Coledale on the New South Wales south coast, which killed a mother and her child when their house was swept away when a drain gave way during heavy rainfall.

New South Wales coroner Derrick Hand warned that identification of the bodies from the Thredbo disaster might be a difficult and long process.

'This disaster is an open disaster, and at this stage we have no way of knowing who has actually died. I stress that it is not my function to interfere with the rescue of victims. That must be left to others. I can only say that it was obvious to me, on visiting the scene, that those charged with the rescue of victims at Thredbo are having to cope with an inordinately difficult and dangerous disaster site.'

Because the identification of victims could prove difficult, their families were asked to provide information that could help in the process. For Steve, Annette and Euan it was an agonising task. Filling in the lengthy Victims' Identification

Form was a horrible, harrowing experience. They had to recall everything about Stuart, everything they could remember down to the smallest details like moles, scars or birthmarks. But Annette was more concerned with Sally's mother, Margy, and how she would cope with filling out the details—Euan lent a hand.

The Divers spent much of their time with Margy. Occasionally they would take a walk and look back on their lives, and their children's lives. Counsellors were made available to all the victims' families—that helped share some of the burden. Both sets of parents were preparing for the worst. No matter the end result, they were proud of their children. They had utterly enjoyed rearing their children and believed both had turned out to be responsible and caring adults. Sally and Stuart had lived their lives to the full and that made the possibility that both had died that little bit easier to take. If they were gone, then so be it, they would learn to cope.

Across the valley from the site a large media contingent had grown to a small army. Footage of the rescue efforts was being beamed live around the world from trucks carrying satellite equipment. News broadcasts and current affairs shows were being presented live from Thredbo. Many locals felt their privacy was being invaded. A number of reporters and photographers tried to sneak through the police cordons, only to be turned back. There were reports some had even disguised themselves in SES uniforms. The Divers and the Donalds made a conscious decision to avoid watching the media. They had enough to deal with without adding to the stress by watching how the media was handling it.

As the daunting task of clearing the rubble continued, the danger of further slippage increased. But the emergency workers doggedly carried on pulling debris from what had been two lodges—battered books, photo albums depicting the smiling faces of the victims, clothes, some still on their hangers, and bedding were just some of the items being recovered.

Each piece was tenderly passed up the human chain to be carefully put aside for future identification. Slowly a mountain of personal belongings piled up at the sports hall in the Thredbo Altitude Training Centre. Touching the lives of the victims made the rescuers' jobs all the harder. It just added to the emotional drain. Pulling people's happy snaps off walls, or finding someone's wallet.

For those still in the village—residents and visitors—the hardship was escalating. Due to interruptions in the water supply there was a high probability of contamination. As a precaution, health officers advised everyone to boil their drinking water.

Almost two days had passed when the Alpine Way was finally reopened to traffic from Jindabyne. It was decided Thredbo had to reopen; it couldn't close out the world and hide in its own misery.

The sun set, heralding another freezing night in Thredbo. It was Friday night, normally a night of partying after a hard week's skiing. There was no partying that night; there was no cheer as once again the temperature plunged below zero.

A 24-hour kitchen had been set up and staffed by people from all walks of life in the village. Truckloads of supplies were donated by the people of the region. There was no shortage of volunteers to cook up the thousands of meals that were needed each day. One delivery of mince meat from a local butcher inspired the great 'cook off' as five locals prepared their own prized bolognese sauces. No one won—it all tasted good to the weary rescuers.

Now working longer shifts with longer breaks the rescuers, though weary, despondent and emotionally drained, ploughed on, centimetre by centimetre, into the heart of the slide. Always there to offer invaluable support were the tireless saints from the Salvation Army. No matter the hour, no matter the conditions, the Salvos were there, offering a comforting smile and a cup of tea.

But for many the grim search was becoming all too much, finding body after body with no sign of life. Psychologists and counsellors were on hand for those who needed them. Firefighter Steve Hirst was feeling the strain and rang home to get in touch with his normal life. He broke down as he heard the voice of his little girl come down the line. Trauma management consultant Bruce Parry had seen this type of emotion before: 'Being involved in something as immense as this creates emotional reactions in people that they have probably never experienced before. They really need to know what is likely to happen to them and how it might affect them and that it's absolutely normal to experience these [feelings] and that they will go away'.

What made this trauma all the more unusual was that instead of being a single sudden incident this was going on for days. Most were coping reasonably well, running on adrenaline to overcome the negativity of the situation they were in. What worried counsellors was that when the adrenaline wore off they would come crashing down to earth.

Despite there being no sign of life there was still hope. The lower side of the site was an absolute mess and most of the rescuers by now felt there was no way anyone could survive down there. But up at the top of the site they would occasionally come across voids in the rubble, voids that could sustain life. It provided fresh hope.

With darkness came the now familiar arc floodlights casting their long and haunting shadows over the rubble.

I had no idea if it was day or night. The pitch blackness was overwhelming. I was so hungry, so thirsty. I began feeling that this wasn't happening. It was some horrible nightmare. When would I wake up? Surely this couldn't go on much longer.

But I was wide awake. Although I craved sleep, something in my mind held me back from the brink. Even though I was awake I sometimes felt my mind was resting, preparing itself for the next hurdle that would present itself.

Paramedic Paul Featherstone of the Special Casualty Access Team was finding it harder to cope as time passed and body after body was pulled from the debris. He asked himself, 'Is there really hope?' The answer was always 'Yes'. In his mind there had to be hope right until the very end otherwise they might as well have brought in a bulldozer and cleared the site.

'You can't afford to think like that. History repeats itself and in the past there have been amazing endurance and saves.'

I guess I had been there for about 40 hours.

My subconscious had taken control: 'I'm going to keep the vital organs going. I'm going to keep you alive and keep the body ticking over because we don't want to spend any more energy'.

It felt like my mind had moved to another level. Moved away so it could observe me from a distance. The cold was sapping my energy so much there was no way I could see myself going on. That was when my subconscious took over and basically shut down my body into a sort of hibernation. I was no longer wiggling my feet, I was no longer moving, I was just lying there waiting—or maybe I was simply starting to die.

My mind started to produce hallucinations and really wild dreams to keep me going. I'd lapse into them temporarily then bounce back to reality. What scared me most was that some of these hallucinations and dreams were about attempting to take my life. What was going on? One minute I was running the show, determined to survive, the next I wanted to die. I was so confused—'Do I want to live? Do I want to die?' I swung from one end of the spectrum to the other, there was no control.

But I couldn't do it. Physically it would have been almost impossible to take my life. It was an option I'd had at the beginning—I could have drowned myself then easily. So many hours later there weren't many options left.

I had no other means to kill myself than to try to hyperventilate to death. I knew that hyperventilation can cause unconsciousness, and I thought that if I lapsed into unconsciousness the cold would take me and that would be the end. At least I would be out of this tomb, at least I would be with Sal.

I tried ten or 12 times, sucking in gasps of putrid air, but I didn't even get dizzy, never even passed out. All it did was charge my body with oxygen, and therefore intensify the pain and actually make the whole bloody situation worse. I was so committed to ending it there and then. The pain was by now unbearably agonising; it was all over my body but especially in my groin. It was like my testicles had been placed in a metal vice screwed up as tight as possible. Do that for three seconds and feel the agony ... try doing it for 30 hours ... that's the depths. It made me sick to my stomach.

I was unable to cope with the pain anymore. I may as well have been dead. I was lying dead still. I had no more strength. I couldn't wiggle my toes. I couldn't hold my arms over my torso. If the water had come again I know I would have just let it take me, there would have been nothing I could have done, I just didn't have any more strength to fight.

The stress was not only starting to show on the rescuers. The residents of Thredbo were angry. Angry that they had lost friends and loved ones, angry that the rescue operation was taking so long, angry that their mountain paradise had been invaded by not only terror but the glare of the media's—and the world's—attention.

Counsellors were made available to all. Leaflets were circulated warning residents of the symptoms of post-traumatic stress.

My imagination was going wild. Switching from reality to a bizarre world of dreams. I first dreamt that I was buried under the snow. I could hear people above me getting set up for a ski race. Planting the racing gates, measuring the turns. I could hear the snowcats. There was a huge team up there getting ready for the race. I couldn't work out how I ended up being beneath the snow and why I couldn't dig myself out. I was yelling and yelling but still they couldn't hear me. I was so cold, buried in the ice and snow. I woke and realised that what I was hearing was not snow cats, but excavators; not race organisers, but rescuers. I was becoming delirious.

On the surface rescuers too were becoming delirious—deliriously frustrated by the instability of the site. They just wanted to get in there, rip the debris apart and rescue people, but they knew they couldn't.

The rescuers were having some success cutting through the massive concrete slabs with diamond-tipped circular saws. But even that did little to ease the frustration of the rescue operation's coordinator, Police Rescue Squad chief Garry Smith. He sadly admitted: 'Unfortunately, the slab that we are going to uncover will only uncover another slab'.

Then I dreamt that I was in a warm, summery place and that there were fishermen up above me. There were lots of fishing huts everywhere and the fishermen were going out to these fishing huts. I was underneath one of the huts but no one ever came into it. Why the hell wasn't anyone coming into my hut? They went to all the others.

In the same dream there was an image of a silver pistol—because now they were hunting huts—there was a silver pistol in the hut directly above me. But because I was buried underneath, I couldn't get to the silver pistol to shoot myself, to put myself out of this misery.

It was Steve and Annette Diver's second night in Thredbo. Conversation was sparse as they sat down to dinner with Euan and Susie at the Thredbo Alpine Hotel apartment where they would spend the night. They went to bed early but sleep didn't come easily. 'You never knew when you were going to get a phone call or a knock on the door ... we were just waiting,' Steve said.

Margy and Colin were staying in the same apartment but couldn't sleep; having arrived that afternoon and seen the devastation of the slide, it was an image they couldn't get out of their minds. For Andrew and Carol sleep was also impossible. They'd been allocated a bed at the Riverside Cabins but soon after turning in Carol started crying: 'I can't be in here if Sally's out there in pain'. They went back out and spent the night at a roadblock just near the police command post.

In my few lucid moments I had recollections of Mum rubbing my feet to make them warm when I was a little kid at the bottom of one of the ski lifts in Thredbo. Why wasn't she here now—she'd make my feet feel better. I was concerned about losing my feet. My whole body was racked with pain; it seemed to emanate from my feet, creep up my legs, attack my groin and spread through my torso to my brain.

To block it out I concentrated on people. It was comforting thinking of Euan, Mum and Dad. Everything I'd ever done before came together in my subconscious. No single incident stood out, it was more like a montage of memories—Sally, bushwalking, skiing, rock climbing, travelling. I imagined myself in a cabin, warm, with Sal next to me, enjoying each other's company.

There was no clear-cut transition from one dream to the next. They blended in, they were all intertwined.

I would come out of these dreams when my head belted the roof. I was still in the same spot, nothing had changed. I was cold again. I would look around and see only darkness, hear the water still trickling and hear the rescuers and the saws. Nothing had changed and then off I would go again into another dream.

Every piece of equipment had now been deployed in the rescue effort. All had failed ... there was no sign of life.

But just about every rescuer maintained hope that if there was life under the rubble it would be found—somehow. The trapped person locator was being used regularly. When this piece of equipment was employed the site became deathly still; everyone silent as the operator strained his ears to pick up something, anything.

When I wasn't dreaming I was still calling out. I tried, I really tried. I had that metal pipe and with the little strength I had left I tapped on the metal bars of the bedhead and tried to make noise. Everything was blurry. What was reality? Was I yelling in my dreams or was I yelling in the real world? I couldn't tell.

I knew it was dangerous to be so close to deep sleep, but there was nothing I could do about it. I couldn't stop myself going off into dreamland. It was as though my mind was producing these dreams as a kind of stimulus, to keep itself alert and awake in case something happened that I physically had to be there for.

Several times a night utter silence would descend on the village as the rescuers put down their tools, lay down and pressed their ears to the cold concrete, praying they would hear a murmur, the rustle of clothing, a groan ... anything. For a spectator it appeared eerily strange—it looked like they were taking a rest.

When it went quiet I too stopped making a racket, thinking they had once again left the site. Maybe if I had just kept tapping during those quiet times ...

I started to have dreams of a desert scene and real

warmth. I started doing stupid things like trying to take my clothes off. I dreamed I was an actor on a movie set somewhere in the desert. I had to keep changing costumes. They'd take me down to a little bazaar—it could have been anywhere in the world—and I would go in and buy new, dry suits and clothes. I would come onto the set, put the dry suit on and then I would wet my pants. The director was screaming at me 'Hey, what are you doing. Stop wetting your pants. We've got to get this scene done'. I would go back to the bazaar and put another suit on; this repeated itself several times until finally we did the shoot and it was a wrap.

Then we'd fly off to lunch somewhere. We were flying all over the world for lunch. The big movie star. And then I would smack my head on the concrete slab above me and come back to reality.

I would find I had moved a little bit. I would have changed position and would be undoing my polar fleece jacket. I'd stay in the real world for a split second before going back and starting to abuse the guys for not changing the set. 'What are you doing? This is the same scene. We've done this scene, let's get out of it.' I had the dream over and over and over again. It was during this dream that I finally heard a voice.

It was a voice and it was really close. My mind had kept me just aware enough to respond and I did with every ounce of strength I had left.

eleven

A Voice from the Rubble

It had been a long, fruitless night. It was now some 50 hours since the landslide. The stars shone in the southern sky as the temperature once again plummeted to minus nine degrees Celsius. The cold had hampered the recovery work; water used to cool the motors of the chainsaws froze, making them inoperable without the use of anti-freeze.

The confirmed death toll so far stood at six. Three bodies had been recovered; rescuers knew the whereabouts of three others but hadn't been able to free them. To the rescuers it had brought a bizarre mixture of joy and sorrow. If they didn't recover a body during a shift they would become despondent, feeling as though they weren't doing their jobs properly. Alternatively, if they discovered bodies they finished their shifts feeling as though they had accomplished something.

Urban Search and Rescue instructor Warwick Kidd could see the effect the mounting body count was having—rescuers excited that they were finding bodies began wondering whether there was something wrong with them because of their feelings of accomplishment.

'I had to talk to these guys and explain to them that their feelings were a natural progression of what they were doing. Each and every one of the rescuers were high achievers, achieving what they had been sent down there to do,' said Kidd.

Firefighters Courtney and Hirst had been on site since 11.00pm, Friday. The pair had spent their shift dangling like puppets, secured by harnesses and safety lines from up above on the Alpine Way. They were busy cutting through the larger concrete slabs so that a crane perched on Bobuck Lane could lift the pieces out. Still no one was allowed on the centre of the slide—all they could do was attack it from the sides.

It was now Saturday, 5.37am and the pair was in the south-eastern corner edging towards the heart of the slide, just above an area that was to become known as the 'A frame' because of the shape of the fallen concrete slabs. They were clearing rubble on the edge of one slab, beneath was an abyss.

The noise was almost deafening on the site—chainsaws working in one area, diamond-tipped saws in another, excavators digging, cranes lifting and people shouting instructions. Hirst yelled to Courtney.

'I've heard something!'

'What the fuck are you talking about?' Courtney screamed back.

'Just something unusual,' came Hirst's reply.

'Go with it.'

Hirst didn't know what he'd heard; didn't know if it was a voice, but it was something.

He screamed to a bloke nearby: 'Turn off the chainsaw'. Sensing the urgency in his voice just about every rescuer on the mountain turned to where Hirst and Courtney had been working. Carefully lowering himself further down Hirst lay on the edge of the slab and looked over into the abyss. 'I'm going to look a Class A fool here if I'm wrong,' he thought.

Like just about everyone else on the site Courtney at first thought this was yet another frustrating false alarm. But he screamed for silence on the site and listened as Hirst called out again ...

I was on the movie set, wetting my pants and heading off to get changed again. I was in the middle of the dream when I snapped out of it. A voice! A voice! I don't know if that voice had pierced my dream or I was already in the real world, but from the moment I heard it I was back for good ... no more dreams.

I had been here for what seemed an eternity. Though nothing had changed and I was still in the same situation as

I'd been in all along at last I'd had voice contact with another human being.

Hirst still wasn't sure what he'd heard. The rubble was a network of conduits and there were people all over the site so he shouted again: 'Quiet on the site'. This time it brought dead silence. The adrenaline was racing through his blood at that moment. He shouted: 'Rescue party working overhead, can ... you ... hear ... me?'

A faint 'can ... you ... hear' came from somewhere beneath him. The clarity of the voice amazed the young firefighter. Although he could tell it was some distance away in the tangled mess of twisted concrete and debris, it was strong, unquavering.

I thought I heard 'Rescue party above. Can you hear me?' I screamed, 'Yes. Can you hear me?' Then he repeated exactly the same thing again: 'Rescue party above. Can you hear me?' I yelled, 'Yes, I'm down here'. Maybe he thought my first response was his voice echoing.

When I first heard the voice I heard him call out for a local quiet but this time, when I shouted 'I'm down here' he called for a site quiet. I knew he had heard me. At last, after a lifetime in this concrete tomb, I had human contact. I really believe that I was almost at the end. I couldn't feel my feet or legs. I just don't know how much longer I could have lasted. But this man's voice gave me another go at life and from somewhere I mustered more energy. I don't know where I got it from but it was there.

Obviously the euphoria of the moment—the first human voice contact after being on my own for so long—was unbelievable, just an unbelievable feeling.

Hirst was on top of the world. Tears welled in his eyes. After so long—after so much death—here was a live victim.

Sergeant Warren Williamson rushed up to the police command post and breathlessly told his superiors someone had been found—someone had been found alive.

'What's your name?' Hirst shouted down.

'Stuart Diver.'

'What's your condition?'

'I'm OK.'

The elation was short lived ... though one life had been saved he knew another might be lost.

'Is there anyone with you?'

'My wife, Sally, but she's dead.'

'Hang tight, Stuart, we're not going to get you out in two minutes but hang tight ... we're coming to get you.'

News of a voice from the rubble spread like wildfire through the village. The media was in a flap. The mood of the rescue services was buoyant.

Kidd hadn't been able to sleep and got up about 5.30am. His team's shift wasn't due to begin till 7.00am so he decided to check on a dangerous side effect of the slide: heating oil from the lodges had flowed down to the Thredbo River, near the base of the slide, and the fire brigade had set up booms and pumps across the river. All of a sudden Kidd's two-way radio crackled to life: 'We've found someone alive, someone's found, we've got someone, we've got someone'.

He ran back up to the top of the site and stood on the road, where there was already a fair bit of commotion. He could see Courtney, Hirst and a few of the others digging down into the rubble and frantically trying to organise a human chain to hand rubble back. Kidd's team was about to begin their shift; they would soon have to take over the rescue operation.

For police chief Charlie Sanderson it was news he wanted to break. 'A miracle has occurred and signs of life have been detected,' he told a packed media conference. As journalists shouted questions at the beaming policeman he told them: 'He is conscious and we are extremely hopeful of getting him out alive as soon as possible'.

Salvation Army captain and fire brigade chaplain Bob Garven's prayers had been answered. They had one miracle— they wanted 20, but at least they'd had one.

Andrew and Carol Donald were still waiting at the roadblock when word filtered back from the site that a voice had been heard. There was a rumour that it was Stuart's, that he was just below the surface. A policeman came up and told them to come down to the command centre—there was some good news. Andrew told the police where to reach the Divers.

At about 5.00am Margy and Colin had given up trying to get some sleep and had gone with Euan's girlfriend, Susie, to the Thredbo Alpine Hotel where counsellors were working around the clock.

The ringing of the telephone woke Euan from a half sleep. It was one of his mates from the fire station: 'You'd better come on down, the chaplain wants to see you'. He knew something had happened ... just what, was the mystery. At that stage he was 75 per cent hope, 25 per cent despair. He crept out of the flat, not wanting to wake his mum and dad.

As he raced into the station, breathing hard from the near sprint from the flat, he spotted a friend coming out of the operations van. He had a grin from ear to ear: 'I'm supposed to wait until Bob Garven comes down, but they've found your brother. They've found him alive'.

In a jubilant daze he made his way up to the command centre in Christiana Lodge to wait for news. He was about to ring his mum and dad when they walked in. They had no idea Euan had gone until they heard a knock on the door at about 6.30am. It was local senior constable Paul Hoyer, the first policeman on the scene some 50 hours earlier.

'Mrs Diver, can you and your husband come up to the command centre?' Hoyer asked.

Annette turned to her husband.

'They're going to tell us that they have found Stuart and he's dead.' They looked at each other and sighed. At least the waiting was over.

As they entered the command centre Euan walked over to them with a smile that told them everything they wanted to know.

'They've found Stu, he's alive and he's OK.' They fell into each other's arms and hugged away the past two days of sorrow.

Sanderson took the three of them to another, more private, area and repeated Euan's news. They'd found Stuart but it could take three hours, maybe three-and-a-half hours, to cut through the slab to get to him.

There was still a question mark over what had happened to Sally. Police found Margy and Colin in the Alpine Hotel with

Susie, waiting for counselling. The officers said they'd found somebody. Something told them it was Stuart. If Stuart was alive, maybe Sally was OK too. Margy knew that if Stuart had survived he would have done everything in his power to get Sally through. They too rushed up to the command centre.

I couldn't believe he couldn't hear me very well. I could hear him so clearly. And he could only just barely hear me.

My world was a mixture of reality and dreamland. This guy had heard me with his human ear and I probably wasn't yelling that loud—I didn't have the strength to. In my confused state I wondered if I'd even been yelling. Maybe I had just been whispering.

How did I hear his voice in my dreamland state? By that stage I was phasing in and out. I was on my last legs, I was going and I just happened to hear him and in that split second I yelled at the top of my voice. I knew I was yelling and he could barely hear me. I could hear him as if he was right there with me, talking to me. Crystal, crystal clear. 'This is bizarre. Why can't you fucking hear me? I'm right here.'

If he had not responded when I yelled back the second time it probably would have been the end. It was my one chance, I doubt I would have had a second. My mind would have just given up, just shut off and said 'See you later. We're out of this'.

Hirst's joy was contagious. They had found one; they could find another, and another and another. It was human spirit at its most optimistic. No one would give up until the very last known victim was located.

Warren Williamson would oversee this very delicate extrication. He would stay until Stuart Diver was brought out— dead or alive.

Courtney and Hirst unclipped from the harnesses, jumped down into the crevasse with Williamson and began dragging out rubble and debris. The rest of the team soon joined them. Together they dug down and cleared a trench. Within minutes two human chains of about 60 people had been formed. One to take full buckets of debris away, the other to bring them back empty.

Although the voice was clear they couldn't determine exactly where Stuart was. So they just kept tunnelling down. With each piece of rubble removed they got closer and closer, the voice so much clearer.

At one stage they heard Stuart mumbling. Fearing he was losing it they worked even more feverishly until they could quite clearly hear him humming to himself.

Courtney yelled: 'Stu, are you OK?'

'Oh yeah, yeah, I'm fine.'

'OK, just checking.'

Courtney figured Stuart was now confident of being saved and was just passing the time any way he could.

Paramedic Paul Featherstone knew that now someone had been found alive the problem would be keeping him alive. Rescuers on the mountain were being drawn to the area where the voice had been heard. Everyone wanted to lend a hand. But that created a terribly dangerous situation. With the site still unstable, if a mass of people got on top, it could collapse. Featherstone set up a perimeter of SCAT officers to help control things. They were to monitor the safety of those working in the vicinity of where Stuart's voice had been heard.

After briefing the Diver family, who were now waiting in an apartment next to the site, Charlie Sanderson went straight back to the coalface. There was a lot to be done. Paramount was ensuring that everything humanly possible was done to keep this survivor alive. It would be disastrous, after all this time, to get so close and then lose the fight.

The media was baying at his door; he had little to tell them. 'At this point in time they are still a considerable distance from where that sound was coming from with a large amount of rubble in between. We are very hopeful that it won't be a long time, but we're also working carefully because the whole point of this operation has been some degree of caution, or a considerable degree of caution. If what we do under there, for example, causes the slab to drop our efforts are in vain.'

It was unknown just how far below the surface Stuart was trapped. The rescuers suspected he was several metres down but it was impossible to determine how long the rescue could take. Early estimates suggested Stuart would be free by 8.00am, but that quickly blew out.

As Stuart's and Sally's families waited anxiously they were once again tended by the kind souls from the Salvation Army. They consumed countless cups of tea and coffee as seconds dragged to minutes, minutes to hours. And while their jubilation was hard to quell, questions about Sally's fate filled their minds. They tried desperately to maintain a positive front, if only for Margy and Andrew's sake. But as time wore on it became harder and harder. While Stuart had relayed Sally's fate the police withheld the information on the minute chance that she had indeed made it.

Margy Donald was trying hard to be positive, hopeful. Every time the police came in with an update about Stuart she would bombard them with questions: 'What about Sal? Is there any word of Sal yet?' The officers would simply reply 'No there's no word yet, we haven't found her yet'.

I knew I had been almost at the end, both of this ordeal and my life. It is very hard to put an exact time on it but I probably had a few hours left in me. I know I would have lost my feet past that time. I wasn't even sure if I still had them because I had lost all feeling below my waist.

While I had been given another chance the memories of Sal dying came flooding back. Like the water that had taken her life the memories were drowning me. Sal's screams: 'Stuart, Stuart, Stuart'. Was surviving really that wonderful? I just wished I had Sal there next to me … alive. So we could be pulled out of this hell together.

We'd gone from being asleep in our bed—which should be the most comfortable and safe place to be in—to this. Now my sole aim was to stay alive for at least a little longer so I could get out and tell Margy, Mum, Dad and Euan what had happened to tear our lives apart. I wanted them to know the truth; I didn't want them living with theory and supposition.

twelve

Touch and Go

With the initial euphoria of that first contact subsiding, now came the difficult task of extricating this miracle man. It wasn't going to be easy. It was going to take time. In the first place no one was really sure of his condition. The possibilities were endless—hypothermia, crush injuries, spinal injuries, broken bones, internal injuries—anything was possible.

Featherstone was realistic. He knew the odds, and they weren't good. His training told him Stuart was obviously going to be hypothermic, that is, he would have a low body temperature. The danger was that if Stuart began to move around, got excited, or was handled roughly by the rescuers he could suffer a heart attack and die—just as other hypothermic patients have been known to die shortly after rescue. During hypothermia the body's metabolism slows as the kidneys and liver fail to function properly. As a result the amount of lactic acid and potassium in the blood can rise to toxic levels. While Stuart's body remained still he was relatively safe, but if he moved suddenly these toxins could flood through his system, possibly resulting in death. Sudden or rough movement also had the potential to dangerously affect the rhythm of Stuart's heart.

From the moment I heard that voice I was back. I was alert ... alert as I have ever been. I suspected my feet were gone, I had basically given up on them. I was so happy to be rescued, and I was more than sure they were going to get me out in a couple of hours.

The euphoria was short lived ... my mind again turned

to Sal. How I wished she was there alive next to me. How I wished she could share this moment. How I just wished she could hear those voices too.

Though the rescue workers still had no real idea of Stuart's location they did know that he was in some sort of a cavity and oxygen wasn't a problem. They weren't sure how long it was going to take to get him out but the Westpac rescue helicopter was put on standby for immediate evacuation to the nearby Canberra Hospital.

There was a renewed hope in the eyes of the rescuers as news of Stuart Diver's survival spread—smiles appeared instantly on everyone's faces. The medical experts were amazed by the discovery and put Stuart's survival down to his fitness and perhaps to hypothermia, which may have taken his body into a sort of suspended animation.

The medical team at Canberra Hospital was ready. Doctors, including general surgeons, spinal specialists and orthopaedic and renal specialists, were on standby. But it would be many more hours before their talents were needed.

The rescuers were convinced they were only a few metres from the trapped ski instructor. At first they thought the operation would be over quickly—they'd clear away the rubble and have him out ... how wrong they were.

Melbourne fire brigade officers Mark O'Connor and Mark Treverton, federal police rescue squad officer Senior Constable Steve Neuhaus, and ACT Fire Brigade officers Steve Gibbs and Ron Hourigan had joined Sydney firefighters Courtney and Hirst. They could all hear Stuart's voice but were confused as to exactly where it was coming from because it was being filtered through layers of rubble. Slowly they dug through the mud, rubble and debris towards his voice, creating a tunnel between the concrete slab they believed Stuart was lying on, and the slab above it.

O'Connor and Treverton were using what was known as the 'search-cam'—an extendible arm with a flexible head with a camera, light and microphone on the end. Using a television monitor and headphones they adopted a system where O'Connor and Treverton would talk to Stuart for a short time and then the others would dig a little further. The probe meant Stuart didn't have to shout; the rescuers felt his yelling would drain what little energy he had left.

Featherstone was listening to the exchanges between Stuart and the rescuers. He could hear the excitement in their voices and knew that for Stuart this could be dangerous—it could so easily lead to cardiac arrest. Mentally, it was also dangerous for him to get too excited. The SCAT officer knew he would soon begin communicating with Stuart to assess his medical condition. He knew that once that contact was established it was vital to maintain the rapport and build up trust. Featherstone would remain on site until the job of rescuing Stuart was finished.

Warwick Kidd and team leaders Rob Killham, Terry Munsey and Tim Fox were watching from the sidelines. They would take over the rescue operation soon, as the others were nearing the end of their shift.

Up above they were in full-on rescue mode. I just lay there. They said they were going to try to get a camera and a little microphone down to me so they could hear me better. I could hear them fine, not a problem. From their voices I could tell this wasn't going to take long. I'd be out of my cold, muddy tomb at last.

As the rescuers dug deeper, the space between the slab they were lying on and the one above their heads got smaller and smaller, it was down to about 30 centimetres. At about 9.00am—some three-and-a-half hours after Stuart's calls for help had been heard—the rescuers realised that he wasn't lying on the same slab as them at all. His voice was being filtered and was vibrating through the debris and being carried from somewhere beneath them, through a crack in the concrete. It momentarily deflated their excitement—this was going to be a whole lot more difficult than any of them had realised.

The Divers were waiting patiently for news. Charlie Sanderson broke the latest development to them.

'We've hit a hurdle. Stuart's not on the slab we've been working on; he's under another. It's going to take a bit longer,' he told them.

They kept on saying, 'Can you see any light? Can you see any light?'. No, I couldn't see any light. Through the cracks I could hear them frantically working. Again: 'Can you see the light, can you see the light?'. I still couldn't. More digging. Then there it was—just out of the corner of my eye I saw a light up, behind me.

In case I was injured they told me not to move. They said 'Don't move towards the light, we'll get the light to you. Can you see the light?' 'Yeah, yeah I can see the light,' I shouted as I slowly slid towards it. I moved about a metre-and-a-half and found myself in a slightly bigger cavity. I had about 30 centimetres above me instead of the three I was used to.

I stopped when the light was shining right in the middle of my forehead. They asked me 'Where's the light now?' I said, 'It is shining right in the middle of my forehead'. 'You didn't move did you?' I lied, 'Only a little bit'.

When that light hit my forehead it seemed to beam a renewed hope into me. Seeing that light and hearing the rescuers' voices reinforced everything that I had ever believed in. My faith in the rescuers had been proven correct.

It was just a matter of whether I could live long enough for them to get me out. I thought it would take maybe 20 minutes, half an hour at the most and I'd be out and away we'd go. That belief, I suppose, had kept me going the whole way along. The voice and the light made reality sink in a little bit more. Sure, I knew I was going to get out, but Sal wasn't. I felt tremendous euphoria at being rescued—but at what cost?

It was Courtney who heard Stuart shout 'I can see the light'. Courtney glanced around the cavity the rescuers had made and wondered what he had just moved to allow Stuart to see the little light that filled the void they had dug. It was then that he realised they were lying on the concrete slab directly above the entombed survivor; they were actually lying on his roof—the light was shining in through a crack in the slab.

'I can see the light,' Stuart yelled again. 'I'm going to reach up for it.'

Courtney was wearing mud-covered gloves but flung them off as he saw Stuart's fingers, blue from the cold, appear through the crack. He wanted to have Stuart feel human flesh. He grabbed Stuart's fingertips—they were icy cold ... trembling. They seemed to draw the warmth from his own body.

I didn't want to let go. He said he couldn't believe how cold my fingers were. Apart from dead people he had never, ever felt hands that cold. And I thought I was feeling great. I held onto his nice warm hand and just wouldn't let go. I probably hung on for about a minute, until he said they had to make the hole bigger so they could get a camera and microphone down to me. I had to let go of his hand.

That was frightening because somewhere in my mind I felt it may be the last human contact I would ever have.

Courtney called up to the other rescuers to pass a torch down to him—it was Warwick Kidd's. Courtney passed it through the crack so Stuart could get a look at his own environment. He immediately heard a change in Stuart's voice. Stuart had finally regained some control of his life. He could see—his tomb was illuminated. It gave Stuart a mental warmth. But in some ways it also made his situation worse by enabling him to see how much strife he was in.

Now I had the torch I looked around to see if I could see Sal. I couldn't see her, and that put a few doubts in my mind. Was she really there? Had she got up and wandered off somewhere else while I was in dreamland? Had I moved around when I was dreaming? There were so many possibilities of where I could have gone and what I could have done.

At one end of the spectrum I felt extremely positive, euphoric, but at the other I felt overwhelmingly negative. Yet I hung on to the promise I made Sal—the promise that I was going to get out and tell Margy, Mum, Dad and Euan what had happened.

I really don't know what would have happened if I'd been able to see Sal at that point ... it's not something I want to think about.

It was a thought that crossed the minds of the rescuers as well, but the benefits of having Stuart take a look at his tomb far outweighed the negatives; it could mean the difference of getting him out alive or not.

Courtney realised the rescue was going to take much longer than first anticipated. Backing out of the tunnel he explained the situation to his workmates, careful not to speak too loudly in case Stuart heard them. It would not be news this tired, cold man wanted to hear.

It was vital for the rescuers to get a more accurate idea of Stuart's environment. The surface team had set up a miniature closed-circuit television with a flexible cable attached to it. They gave it to Courtney and he scrambled back down the hole and passed it through the crack. Although it provided no audio Courtney was close enough to be able to speak to, and hear, Stuart clearly through the crack, and he could watch him on the monitor. He asked Stuart to move it around as best he could. Stuart immediately put the camera on his own face.

'G'day, I'm Stuart Diver. How're you going?'

It brought a smile to Courtney's face. Here was a man who had been through so much terror, suffering and pain asking how *he* was feeling! Courtney was lying on his back with the monitor on his chest, watching Stuart. He was amazed Stuart still had a sense of humour and in their brief exchange of words he determined a tone in Stuart's voice that showed an inner strength, a mental strength, to survive.

I pointed it at my face, pointed it around, and tried to give them a rough idea of where I was and what was going on. I had the torch so I shone that around with the camera. I could hear one of them saying 'Don't move, whatever you do, don't move'. It was easy for them to say that. For the first time I could see my cavity, for the first time I could see that all along there'd been areas where I could've moved to!

Featherstone wasn't too keen on Stuart being given the torch. It could be a breaking point for him, mentally. With the torch he may have realised just how much trouble he was in. But, on the other hand, the torch could be vital in determining if there was an easier way to extricate him.

As it turned out it didn't break Stuart's mental resolve.

Yet Featherstone could tell the survivor was getting excited. The veteran paramedic knew he had to start talking this patient through it. Watching the drama unfold from the surface Featherstone took over communication. Backed up by SCAT officers Chris Wilkinson, George Smith and Peter Cribbs he would monitor Stuart, medically and mentally. As the police officers and the firefighters concentrated on getting him out, it was the paramedics who would have to keep him alive.

'G'day Stuart, my name's Paul Featherstone. I'm a paramedic. How're you feeling?'

'OK,' Stuart called back.

'Mate, everyone's out here. This is going to happen but it is not going to happen quick.' Featherstone figured Stuart was on a high after hearing people so close to him and was probably expecting to be rescued quickly. He realised that until this point Stuart would have been frustrated by being able to hear the rescuers above but unable to make himself heard. He needed to assess his patient both physically and mentally. Reassurance was the key.

'We're definitely getting you out of here but it is going to take time. It is not going to happen straight away. But I'm just telling you, stick with me.

'I'm going to be your pacer ... you're obviously a very fit athlete, you know about hypothermia, you know what you should and shouldn't do. What I am going to do is sit up here and I'm going to pace you. I am going to be your trainer. All you've got to do is listen to me and you'll get out.'

The paramedics and the rescuers set up a system—five minutes on, 20 minutes off. For five minutes Featherstone could speak with Stuart, while at the same time assessing his medical condition. For the next 20 minutes the others would dig ... and dig ... and dig. Cribbs and Smith advised and provided vital communications for Featherstone. Because he didn't want Stuart to hear, he would whisper his reports to them and they would radio them back to base.

Sometimes the rescuers could hear Stuart babbling nonsense. But it didn't matter—their aim was just to keep him talking but not concentrate too hard on what he was saying because it would use up energy.

They thought I couldn't hear them, but I could. They were talking to each other discussing what they were going to do and then I heard one of them say: 'We're really going to have a hell of a lot of trouble getting this guy out'. My heart sank— after all this I wasn't going to make it!

At first I didn't say anything but finally I called out to Feathers: 'Tell them I can fucking hear them'. That put an end to that.

It slowed the whole thing down because every time they were concerned about something or had to shore something up they had to all go out of the tunnel, away from where I was.

With the ground rules now set Stuart began guiding his rescuers to him. Courtney needed to have a better idea of his exact position. It was almost impossible for Stuart to distinguish north from south in his cavity so Courtney reached through the crack holding a pen. He asked Stuart what it was pointing at, how far away it was and how deep the cavity was. For instance when Courtney pointed the pen in a certain direction Stuart was able to describe how much space was in that direction and what he could see there, such as cavities or rubble.

From this information Courtney was able to calculate fairly accurately where Stuart was in relation to the crack, which direction he was lying and where he was in relation to the access tunnel that had been dug.

I was directing them to where I was. They were tapping, asking if they were getting closer or further away. They were getting closer. Good, good, good. 'What side do you think we're on?' 'You're on my right-hand side.' 'No, no, no. We're on your left-hand side' over and over again. 'You're on my right-hand side, you're coming down towards the right-hand side of my head.' They couldn't believe that they were coming on the right side, they thought they were on the left-hand side of me. I was telling them: 'I'm on my back. I'm facing up to you guys, you're coming in on the right-hand side'.

The rescuers faced obstacle after obstacle. The room they were digging through was clearly a bedroom; there were cupboards, drawers, a bed, chairs, a television. Each and every item had to be cut or broken through.

Pre-tensioned steel cables running through the concrete slabs were not only difficult, but also dangerous, to cut through. Once severed they could spring back through the concrete with enough speed to cut off a limb.

One of the team was lying on the slab above Stuart and was using a hacksaw to cut through some concrete reinforcing when the blade broke. 'Fuck!' he cursed. Featherstone bent down from his perch at the mouth of the void that had been dug out and made eye contact with the rescuer: 'From now on no negativity. Everything must be positive,' he whispered. Featherstone was trying to put himself in Stuart's position. He knew he wouldn't want to hear anything negative.

The site was still as unpredictable as it ever had been. Two-and-a-half hours after the first contact was made with Stuart there was another significant landslip at the top of the site, forcing yet another evacuation.

The alarms went off and one of the rescuers grabbed Featherstone by the back of his overalls. 'We're out,' he shouted. The search cam headphones popped off his head and he was dragged up, back out of the tunnel. He was ropeable; there was no way he was going to desert the survivor now that a lifeline had been established. He could imagine Stuart lying there just waiting for the water to come and rush over him again or the cave to come crashing in.

He ran up to the site commander, Police Sergeant Bill Pearce, from the police rescue squad: 'This guy will die unless I'm down there. I'm going back. I'm going down. I'm prepared to take the risk if you give me a skeleton team'.

Featherstone knew this was breaking all the rules, breaking the discipline that had governed the rescue operation so far, but he was a paramedic with some 20 years' experience. He knew the risks; he had assessed the dangers.

Up until now dozens of rescuers had been directly involved in the operation to get Stuart out, but Pearce agreed to the skeleton team. They formulated a plan to have two spotters to act as safety monitors who would watch for any signs of movement while Featherstone was in the tunnel talking to Stuart.

They scrambled back down the site and Featherstone returned to the tunnel. Putting the headphones back on he called down to Stuart.

'Howya going, mate. I just had a bit of battery trouble up here.'

Stuart knew the procedure as well as everyone else—he knew what the sirens meant.

'Don't bullshit me.'

'All right mate, we had a slide but there's not much in it. Everyone is out here working their arses off.' Featherstone had a shovel and began belting it on rocks, giving the impression that there was still a large team up there trying to get Stuart out.

I heard the whistles go and it went quiet. All of a sudden Feathers was back and told me he'd had some battery trouble and that the boys were still working up there. I could tell he was banging his own shovel on some rocks. I knew there were no other workers there at all.

Stuart said 'Mate, quit stuffing around, I know there's no one there working. I know they've been called off. Don't worry about it. We'll just sit here and wait'.

'OK. Yeah. Not a problem,' Featherstone replied.

Feathers had been found out. But it didn't matter. He didn't apologise or anything like that. Just went straight on to the next thing. It probably set the ground rules for the whole day for how we dealt with each other—there was to be no bullshit between us.

I was thinking half-hour to half-hour and then when it went on longer, hour to hour. The doubts were creeping back. Big doubts. 'What the hell is taking them this long?' Maybe that rescuer was right, maybe I didn't have a hope in hell of getting out.

The rescuers were throwing everything into the operation. Furiously cutting and moving out pieces of rubble and debris using hand tools, hydraulic shears, bolt cutters, circular saws and angle grinders—trying to provide themselves enough room to work in.

The noise and the dust were terrifying. Everything was shaking and vibrating. It was probably one of the most terrifying parts of the whole ordeal. I still had the blind faith in them—they were going to get me out because they were professionals and that is what they were there to do, but I did start to wonder what the hell was going on.

Physically I felt like I was ready just to jog out and head down to the bistro for a beer. I was asking for food. I wanted a hamburger, I wanted a Coke. That was how good I felt. I felt a million bucks. I kept telling them that there was nothing wrong with me.

But mentally I wasn't jumping up and down, cheering. I never, ever felt ecstatic or felt any real happiness about being rescued. It was certainly a great relief to be rescued, but because there was so much loss there I didn't have a feeling of jubilation. There were plenty of tears at this stage ... but they weren't tears of joy.

Although confident about the rescue operation, for Steve Diver the longer it went on the harder it became. So far he had refrained from looking into the finer details of the rescue operation but the time had come for him to see for himself exactly what was being done to rescue his son. He didn't want to be spotted by the ever-present media so he borrowed a firefighter's jacket and helmet and ventured out onto the unit's balcony to take a look. As he stood there the sirens went off yet again ... his heart sank.

Courtney, Hirst and the rest of their team had worked way past their shift; their discipline told them they must leave, despite their desire to see the rescue through. They had found Stuart Diver; they wanted to get him out. Hirst was still on a high, likening his elation to the day his first child was born.

Reluctantly, they emerged from the tunnel. Back on the surface Courtney grabbed a piece of chipboard. With a pen he drew a rough sketch of what he believed was Stuart's position, location and the suggested access points to his tomb. By earlier using the pen as a direction finder Courtney had calculated that Stuart's feet were in the vicinity of where the rescuers had made the initial opening when they first heard his voice, that is, beneath where the rest of the rescue team was standing.

The senior rescuers decided that if they made a manhole in the concrete where they were standing they would be approximately 60 centimetres from Stuart's feet. Once the hole had been cut in the concrete they could clear enough rubble away to slide Stuart down about 180 centimetres, sit him up and lift him out.

It was a blueprint that was to prove correct.

thirteen

The Emotional Roller-coaster

Warwick Kidd had been sitting at the mouth of the void that had been dug out waiting for his team to take over from Courtney, Hirst and the others. He was less than two metres from the crack from which Stuart's voice could be heard. Kidd could hear Stuart's description of what he could and couldn't see. When it was time for his team to take the lead he decided it wasn't enough; he had to see for himself. He crawled up to the crack and began chipping away at it with a small sledge-hammer and chisel. A few good whacks enlarged the hole considerably. The next thing Stuart reached up and stuck his whole hand through the crack. Kidd squeezed further up and shone his torch down.

'Put the torch on your own face,' Stuart said.

Kidd shone the beam on his own face.

'I didn't think I'd get to see another person's face,' Stuart told him.

With a chuckle Kidd apologised for it being his face.

He had the sort of face you would picture as the classic rescue firefighter's, the 'I'm going to save the world' man—he had that type of rugged face. He was 100 per cent sure he was going to get me out. He said, 'Mate, it's going to take us a bit of time. You're not in the best situation. We are going to take time. But you've got the best. We'll have you out of here, no worries. Just hang tight. We'll take care of you and you'll be away'.

I looked at him and thought, 'Yeah, no worries, they are going to get me out'.

During one of the quiet times Kidd listened as Stuart told his rescuers about a dream that he'd had where he was in Thailand or Burma and was sitting in a rocking chair on a verandah. Kidd sensed that Stuart wasn't really recalling the details but was actually having the dream. Kidd felt it was his mind removing him from where he was, deliberately trying to get him away.

Featherstone had earlier inserted a tube carrying warm air—called a 'bearhugger'—into the crack. It was the first bit of real warmth Stuart had experienced since the slide. Featherstone saw the paradox in that too. Every time he made one part of Stuart feel better it could make him realise how bad everything else was. It was a rebound effect that could have killed him.

I put it down the front of my jacket. Nice, hot air—like a reverse vacuum cleaner. Then they gave me oxygen and goggles so that all the dust and stuff wouldn't get in my eyes. They told me they were digging two tunnels to get in and it sounded like it too! Everything was shaking, vibrating—I was worried so much activity could bring everything down on top of me.

Paul Featherstone knew the mere fact that there was now hope could spell disaster for his patient. As Stuart breathed Featherstone could hear the bag of the oxygen mask crack; this enabled him to count Stuart's respirations. He'd also managed to get a probe onto one of Stuart's fingers with which he could read his pulse rate. Twice in those early stages he thought he had lost Stuart; his heart rate leapt and his breathing became more rapid and heavy. A few times he heard his patient moan and start to cry.

About six hours into the rescue operation Stuart called out to Featherstone.

'Mate I've got some stuff I want to talk about, but I don't know whether you're up to talking about them. They're pretty nasty.'

Featherstone knew what was coming: 'Mate, whatever, fire away'.

'I've got to tell you about Sally. She's dead. I've got to

tell you how she died. I just can't lie here and hold onto this stuff any more—it's tearing me apart.'

I started blurting out things about Sally, that she was dead and how she died. I opened my heart to this man I didn't even know. It was the first chance I'd had to speak about it to another person—it really started to drive home to me what had happened. It got really, really emotional. I had to talk to somebody. What else was I to do? I had just gone on for so long. I had to talk.

It was good to get it all off my chest. From that early stage onwards. Even though I was probably still in shock and in full-on survival mode I was already verbalising what had happened, mentally trying to cope with it all.

Despite his extensive experience nothing had prepared Featherstone for the emotion-charged conversation; he dropped his head as Stuart's voice filled the headphones, explaining his battle to save his wife's life. Featherstone made a promise to his patient that the conversation would always stay just between them—and it has.

It was the moment a bond was formed; a bond on which a life depended.

With warm air and oxygen already being pumped in, the next hurdle for rescuers was to get some nourishment to Stuart. But without knowing the extent of his injuries it could prove fatal. Specialist trauma doctor, Dr Richard Morris, from the Sydney Medical Retrieval Service, was part of Featherstone's SCAT unit. He concocted Stuart's first meal in days—a balanced electrolyte and nutrient solution. Featherstone inserted the tube through the crack, reached down and felt Stuart's mouth with his fingers and fed the tube in. Up above another SCAT paramedic, Chris Wilkinson, manually pumped the solution down through the tube.

Because I'd complained so much about wanting something to eat and drink, they gave me that jungle juice, two half-mouthfuls every 20 minutes. It tasted awful but it gave me a mental boost—if they were giving me food I must be OK.

Feathers was monitoring my pulse and respiration so he

could tell that whenever the rescuers started working, my pulse and respiration doubled. When the rescuers took a break they returned to normal. When it was quiet time I was fine, but when they were working I panicked. He kept on saying 'Try and stay calm' and 'Keep quiet'. Feathers had the ability to keep me on an even keel just with the tone of his voice.

Featherstone was amazed by his patient's positive attitude, even after a failed attempt to get an intravenous drip into his arm. It failed simply because he was so cold they couldn't find a vein.

Featherstone had become so much a part of what was happening in the hole that he could now interpret any movement, any change in breathing, and read its meaning. It was a critical time; it had been several hours since first contact had been made and Featherstone was worried frustration could set in. He thought to himself: 'You're a better man than me— I'd be spitting the dummy long before this'. With the emotion and frustration would come some form of physical response, and that was beyond the paramedic's control. He couldn't fully access his patient so he basically had to trust that Stuart's mental robustness would pull him through. All Featherstone could do was ensure Stuart didn't realise the seriousness of the situation he was in and the very real possibility he still might not come out of that hole alive.

Feathers and I solved most of the problems of the world. We had quite a few intellectual discussions on things. Just to fill in the time. He was basically doing whatever he could to keep my mind off the predicament I was in. Even though he was the consummate professional I could still tell he was keeping some things about the rescue back from me.

I have a kind of blind faith in people, and in humanity as a whole, and here it was again—I trusted that these people were going to get me out. Somehow I knew that Feathers was going to take care of me . . . he was going to ensure my survival.

So if he had to go and do something for two or three minutes, well, that was the way it was and I could cope. As long as he was telling me the truth, which he did all the time except for that initial occasion, everything would be OK. I knew why he lied during that early evacuation—if I had been in his boots I would have done the same.

Now confident of Stuart's exact location the Urban Search and Rescue team tunnelled downwards, removing debris covering the area where they planned to drill an inspection hole. They would then use a diamond-tipped saw to cut through the single concrete slab above Stuart's feet,

     Meanwhile, a second rescue team, the Mines Rescue squad, dug from the eastern side of the site. In front of them were about 16 metres of rubble. They planned to dig their tunnel on the same level as Stuart, but they would have to tunnel through three or four walls to reach him. It was the back-up plan; if for some reason the top-down approach failed then perhaps this would work.

The scariest times were the 20-minute periods when the guys were working, when I didn't get to talk to Feathers. I'm lying there and these guys are going hell for leather, everything's shaking, everything's moving. The biggest, loudest noise I'd ever heard. I was breathing like a madman. I went through a lot of oxygen bottles. It was a lot more terrifying than the breaks prompted by the sirens.

Warwick Kidd was part of the overhead team. As a USAR instructor he'd taught confined-space rescue and knew what it felt like to be trapped. Yet he couldn't imagine the terror Stuart was experiencing—trapped in a tomb, which had been filling up with water. It was beyond his, or anyone else's, comprehension. As a team leader he watched the rescuers emerge from their burrow and saw the emotion on their faces. These were men and women who attended car accidents every day, who recovered the bodies of children from burning homes—these were heroes—yet even for them the emotion of trying to save one man's life amid so much death and devastation was almost overwhelming.

The thing that sticks in my mind is the emotional roller-coaster I went through. From the feelings of, 'Great. I'm going to get out' down to the feelings of 'This is crap because I've lost Sal'.

Then up again: 'I can't wait to see Margy and tell her what happened to Sal'. Down to: 'This is crap because I don't really want to tell her what happened because it is going to be too nasty'. Up to: 'Great, Mum, Dad and Euan are out there'. Up and down the whole day. It really tested my whole belief system.

After their initial doubts the rescuers had become so positive about the rescue that it was contagious. But I did wonder how sincere they were. What really were my chances?

With the search cam the rescuers were able to determine that while two slabs covered the upper part of Stuart's body there was only one above his feet. As the USAR firefighters made inroads from above, the vibrations of their equipment caused pieces of debris to fall into the Mines Rescue tunnel below. Once it was clear the top-down approach was the most promising, a meeting was hastily convened on the hillside. Kidd, fellow USAR firefighters Tim Fox and Clayton Abel, and police rescue chief Garry Smith decided to opt for one rescue mission and one alone. At about noon, six-and-a-half hours after Stuart's voice was first heard, the Mines Rescue tunnel was abandoned—it was a risk but a calculated risk and one that had to be taken.

They continued digging from the top. The plan entailed making a 'pumpkin cut' through the single slab covering Stuart's feet. It was critical to make the cut just to Stuart's right otherwise they could seriously injure him.

First they had to drill a borehole to allow the diamond-tipped circular saw access. Then they could cut out a plug of concrete in much the same way you cut the top from a pumpkin, by cutting a bevelled hole that's wider at the top and narrower at the bottom.

Inserting a second search cam through the borehole revealed what appeared to be loose rubble down near Stuart's feet. They planned to make the pumpkin cut, clear out the rubble, gently slide him down to where the rubble had been, sit him upright and pull him headfirst out of the hole.

But like everything else in this rescue mission it didn't go smoothly. A mattress partially covered the area the team was trying to dig through so they could begin making the pumpkin cut. It posed an interesting predicament—how do you cut through a steel spring mattress? First the material and padding had to be cut away and then using small bolt cutters each piece of spring had to be individually cut. Because all the springs were connected it took over an hour to get through it.

They were getting closer and Featherstone could hear the crackling of the oxygen bag speed up. He knew Stuart was becoming more and more anxious the closer they got—his breathing quickened, his pulse rate sped up. Featherstone clambered back down into the hole and ordered a shutdown of digging. He felt it important to constantly update his charge on what stage they were at, constantly urge him to relax, assure him everything was safe. During these conversations Featherstone kept upping the ante.

'We've got a thousand blokes up here, mate.'

The next time: 'We've got fifteen hundred this time'.

Featherstone became Stuart's eyes above ground, painting word pictures of the mountains. It was such a contrast—here he was surrounded by death and disaster but if he stuck his head up and looked across the valley it was a clear blue day with snow covering the top of the range, sun shining, it was so picturesque.

At first it concerned Featherstone that by describing the beauty of the mountains he might frustrate Stuart more, but the mountains were clearly something he loved and it gave him something to look forward to.

'We're going to win and we're going to get you out of here,' Featherstone promised.

Once they had completed the pumpkin cut and removed the plug of concrete the rescuers faced yet another hurdle. Directly beneath the hole they'd made was the back of Stuart's lounge; it too was a difficult proposition as it was hard to cut through. They peeled away the lounge's material cover and using hammers, chisels and an air-powered hacksaw they managed to cut it out of the way—another hour had passed.

Despite his promise Featherstone harboured secret fears. This was all taking too long. Would Stuart be able to survive much longer? Again he placed himself in Stuart's position, imagined himself lying there, uncomfortable, cold and wet, surrounded by all this tragedy—'enough is enough'. Stuart's positive nature and faith in Featherstone had their drawbacks as well as their benefits. Featherstone had seen it before— people trapped for lengthy periods of time who were fine up until the moment of rescue and then suddenly deteriorated and died. There was a very real possibility it could happen here.

Garry Smith climbed down to where Featherstone was perched; they discussed Stuart's chances and what to do if his condition suddenly worsened. There were a couple of ace cards. Featherstone had a mobile phone. If he felt Stuart slipping away he would use it so Stuart could speak to his family . . . but only when the time was right. To do it prematurely could have a detrimental effect. Once that conversation took place Stuart could let himself go. Yet from his parents' point of view, if he died and they hadn't had a chance to speak to him it would be disastrous.

At one stage Featherstone feared they'd lost the fight; Stuart's heart was racing and his breathing was short— Featherstone called for the phone. But it turned out to be one of those moments when Stuart was overcome by sadness and frustration. His sobbing told Featherstone that the problem was more emotional than physical. He was ready for the highs and lows; when Stuart was down he tried to pep him up a little, lighten the mood by talking about Stuart's plans to travel and see the world—anything to make him feel just a little bit better.

Featherstone believed that deep down Stuart knew how much danger he was in—he was no fool.

At one stage Kidd was down in the hole the rescuers had cut. Reaching out to clear some rubble away his hand brushed something soft and frigid—he didn't realise he had laid his hand on Stuart's foot, it was just so icy.

Kidd clambered out allowing Featherstone to get in. Seeing Stuart's feet confirmed his fears. They were frostbitten. There was evidence of severe hypothermia and it was impossible to know just how much other damage had been done.

The partially cleared cavity gave Featherstone enough room to squirm up alongside Stuart's freezing body. One of the fire rescuers had given Featherstone a piece of webbing, similar to a car seat belt, which he wrapped around Stuart's waist.

With Featherstrone gently dragging on the waist strap, Stuart began to wiggle his way down, centimetre by centimetre, until his feet were visible in the manhole. Featherstone stopped him there. This was not going to be rushed.

Like every rescuer on the mountain, all of Australia began to wonder if this was really going to work. The nation's television networks had changed their programming to accommodate live coverage from Thredbo. Crowds had even gathered outside electronics stores watching the drama unfold. Motorists everywhere tuned to the radio to pick up the latest developments. On the hillside opposite the site a large crowd had joined the contingent of media. Eyes glued to every movement made by the rescuers. Thredbo had become the focus of the nation ... their dreams and hopes centred on one man.

It was nearing the end of Kidd's shift and he was about to brief the next team, the same team that had actually found Stuart. Charlie Sanderson spotted him on the roadway and rushed over.

'How are we going?'

'OK,' Kidd replied, 'We should have him out soon'.

For the first time in days a smile slowly spread across Sanderson's face. He'd shouldered the brunt of media criticism and doubts raised by the families of the victims. It had been a turbulent couple of days ... now his face was beaming.

Stuart was within minutes of being extricated but Kidd knew the regimen: his team's shift had finished so they must pull out. But he faced rebellion. None of them wanted to leave—they had come this far, they would finish the job.

'I'm going so you are too,' he told them. Slowly, one by one, they downed tools ... all but one who flatly refused. Kidd had to make a decision. The man had become quite distressed and to push the issue could have worsened the situation. Kidd reluctantly relented but left with a warning to the next team leader.

'This bloke is not to lift a shovel, he's not allowed to do anything—once Stuart's out he has to leave the site.'

Rested and eager to take over after their break, Courtney, Hirst and their team returned to the front line. Courtney slid down into the pumpkin cut and lay down to make sure enough rubble had been removed so that when they slid Stuart down he would be in such a position that they could lift him up and take him straight out—it was a dress rehearsal.

We got to the 11-hour mark and they had finally managed to make a hole down near my feet. Feathers told me the doctor wanted to come down to put an IV drip into my foot—he assured me he was the best doctor in Australia. He tried to find a vein but I was just too cold, he didn't have a hope, so eventually he had to make a cut near my foot to put the IV in. It took about 20 minutes.

The rescuers reached in through the manhole and placed warm towels on one of Stuart's feet in an effort to draw up a vein. After several attempts to locate one the trauma doctor had to make an incision, hook a vein and insert the IV into it. Courtney was lying next to Dr Morris as he made the incision. There was no blood. Courtney shook his head, 'there's no blood; there's just nothing,' he thought.

For the next half-hour they fed their patient more warm fluid through the IV drip, re-hydrating his body in readiness for what lay ahead.

Stuart's remarkable calmness during the procedure surprised everyone. 'This is one incredible young fella,' Featherstone thought as he again squirmed his way alongside his patient to attach ECG leads to Stuart's chest so he could be monitored by the other paramedics on the surface. Featherstone glanced up toward Stuart's head. He could see a tiny gap between his chest and the slab above him. It had a picture frame on it—he wondered what the picture showed.

'Mate we're going to do this two inches at a time,' Featherstone whispered.

'Come on you bastards, just get me out of here,' came the desperate reply.

'We're nearly there. Nearly there. Just relax, everything is going fine.'

Now they had established the escape hatch Featherstone was finally starting to feel more positive. The only thing worrying him was the clinical side. He knew this was the most dangerous part of the whole operation—when Stuart's body position changed from lying down to sitting up.

Feathers came down. 'No worries, mate.' He was adamant that I wasn't to move because he was sure the toxins in my blood would spread. He came down, scrambled all the way up the confined space and told me they were going to drag me down inch by inch to the hole, place a harness on me and lift me up. Out of the hole. Down flat onto a rescue board. Thanks for coming—I'm out of here.

With Featherstone in the cavity Hirst and Courtney positioned themselves so they could reach down, through the hole up to where Stuart was lying. Slowly, carefully, Stuart began to wiggle his way down towards the manhole, the rescuers helping him as much as they could. On the surface the rescue board was put in place.

Centimetre by centimetre he was manoeuvred into the cleared area beneath the manhole. It was as though everyone on the site and around the nation collectively held their breath. Those on the surface gradually saw Stuart Diver ... first his feet, then his ankles, legs, waist, chest, neck and finally, his face.

'Thank God you got me out in daylight because I thought I would never see daylight again.'

No one could forget the look on his face as the daylight hit it. For Stuart the temptation was too great, he lifted his head, trying to get himself out. Featherstone reacted quickly, placing his hand on his forehead.

'No mate. Remember this is all about pace.' Featherstone was now more concerned than ever about Stuart's physical condition—this could be it.

It was a moment of euphoria—to see that sky. Feathers had promised it all day long. He said the sky was blue ... he was right ... it was fantastic. The only thing that disappointed me was I didn't see anything else because they had to keep me flat.
I struggled to lift my head so I could get a better look.

The joy on Stuart's face was indescribable—Featherstone could only liken it to someone 'showing him the world'.

'Mate, stop,' Featherstone warned.

By now Featherstone's voice had become crucial to Stuart's comfort zone. Yet again Featherstone was able to talk his patient down.

'Right oh mate, now concentrate on slowing yourself right down. I just want you to go into dreamtime now, relax, think about something really nice, but just stay there. Just calm yourself right down.'

Immediately his heart rate dropped, his breathing slowed. Featherstone was amazed Stuart had such control over his body, that he could calm himself so quickly—he'd not seen many patients like it.

Steve Hirst could now put a face to the voice he had heard what seemed a lifetime ago. The lump returned to his throat. He couldn't believe Stuart looked so well—it was as though the miracle man had brushed his hair for the cameras. He appeared so calm, so in control. Hirst couldn't believe his ears as Stuart declared: 'What a bunch of ugly bastards'.

It blew everyone away. Each and every rescuer there was trained to handle grief—none of them expected Stuart Diver, trapped for some 65 hours—to come out with his spirits soaring.

Dr Richard Morris had done what he could to stabilise his patient; he hoped Stuart's fitness would do the rest. But the fitness was only part of the equation—Stuart's willpower was the other vital element and he'd seen enough to know Stuart had incredible strength of spirit.

Now was the critical moment. Within minutes Stuart could have a heart attack and the battle would be lost. Now it was time for the mobile phone. A line to the Divers was quickly established. There was barely a murmur from the rescue team—they all knew just how crucial the next few seconds would be.

A chaplain passed Steve Diver the mobile. The family was still waiting in an apartment next door to the site. They felt it was better to stay out of the rescuers' way and wait for news; they had been constantly updated by Charlie Sanderson.

There was total silence on the hillside as Featherstone placed the phone next to Stuart's ear.

'How are you going tiger?' Steve asked.

'Yeah, bloody good, just happy to be out of here.'
'Hang in there son, we'll see you very soon.'
'Yeah, I'll be with you Dad.'

I was crying and I suspect Dad had tears in his eyes as well. I wanted to talk to Mum and to Euan but either the telephone signal dropped out or the battery died. That was the end of that. Dad said, 'How are you?' 'Good.' 'I'll see you when you get out.' 'Yep, great'—peeeeeeep—that was the end of that. Silence.

Featherstone was surprised the conversation was over so quickly. He thought that perhaps neither Stuart nor his father wanted to dwell ... they just wanted all this to be over. He grabbed the phone.

'OK Stu, here we go. What I need you to do is not to struggle, don't push, don't pull, don't do anything, just let us lift you out. Just let us do all the physical, let us do the grunt and you just relax. When I get you out and on this board I want you to do exactly what we've been doing all day—bloody relax.'

This was it.

Carefully Featherstone wrapped another piece of webbing tape around Stuart's chest. It, and the waist strap, would be used as a makeshift harness, which the rescuers would grab to help lift him out of the hole.

They were ready. Hands went under his arms, others grabbed the tape, and the rescuers began to gently lift Stuart's upper body. As they sat him up the rescue board was put into position behind him; with his back resting against it they gave one final heave and hoisted his entire body onto it. Now lying flat, but almost vertical, they whisked him out of the manhole and placed the rescue board onto a stretcher.

At 5.17pm, Saturday—more than 64 hours after the landslide—Stuart Diver emerged from his concrete cocoon. It had taken almost 12 hours.

As they passed him out of the hole Featherstone tracked Stuart's vital signs on the monitor—everything was stable. Everything was going to be fine. A human chain formed to carry Stuart to a waiting ambulance; loud applause and cheers echoed from across the valley.

'Mate, hear that, that's the whole bloody world cheering you,' said Featherstone.

Hand to hand they passed Stuart's stretcher up the hillside. When they reached the ambulance Featherstone cleared away the crowd, bent over Stuart and whispered: 'Lift your head up and look over there, I told you you'd see them again'. Stuart looked over Featherstone's shoulder ... there, in all their majestic beauty, were the mountains he loved so much.

As they passed me up that human chain I saw the faces of so many of the rescuers ... they were all smiling. It was just unbelievable. I will never, ever forget that moment. At that moment I forgot about absolutely everything else that had happened except the fact that I had survived. I'd made it out alive.

fourteen Painful Warmth

*W*as this yet another dream? No, life couldn't be that cruel. Or could it?

As they passed me up the line, hand-to-hand, all I heard was 'Good on you'; 'Well done, buddy'. But what had I done? I'd just survived.

Mum, Dad and Euan were at the top. I couldn't say anything to them, the words wouldn't come. I couldn't tell them what had happened. They came up to the back of the ambulance as I was being pushed in and one of them, I think it was Mum, asked me how I was. 'Bloody great,' I replied and away I went. Physically, I really did feel great—mentally, though, it was an entirely different proposition.

Unlike most of the country Steve, Annette and Euan Diver had refused to watch any television coverage of the event. The first they knew that Stuart was out was the roar of the spectators. Within seconds a policeman rushed into the apartment, where they had spent the day waiting for just this piece of news.

'They're putting him into an ambulance, you better come on up,' he said.

The three of them almost ran up the steep hillside, reaching the top just as the paramedics were wheeling Stuart into the back of the ambulance.

Euan called out to his brother: 'Good on you, buddy, we'll see you shortly'.

Steve Diver leaned across the stretcher, removed the oxygen mask covering his son's face and gave him a kiss. He couldn't believe his eyes, Stuart looked so good. He looked so physically well. 'See you soon son,' he said. After trying so hard to remain positive throughout the entire rescue mission Steve Diver felt a tremendous sense of relief. His dread had grown as each body was removed from the site. He had been told of their condition and he had always feared that Stuart, despite being alive, could have suffered horrendous injuries.

Annette was at Steve's side; she watched father kissing son. 'Thank God,' she thought. Despite the obvious relief of Stuart making it out alive and being relatively OK, as Annette glanced at Margy, who had joined them at the back of the ambulance, that relief was quickly tempered by thoughts of Sal's death.

The look on Margy's face portrayed her conflicting emotions. While elated at seeing Stuart alive and well she was also dealing with the realisation that Sal had not survived. All she wanted was official confirmation—for someone to tell her that her daughter had died.

It had been such a hell, a living hell. I had a feeling of, 'I'm out of here, I've finally made it and got out of here'. It was a euphoric feeling.

I was on my way down to the bistro for that beer as far as I was concerned. As soon as they pulled me up through the hole I was back.

But in the back of the ambulance I started to fade—I had come to the end. There was nothing left. The tank was empty. I was totally out of energy. I lost my sense of reality a little as I began to get warm. Having been awake for 65 hours my body felt it was about time I went to sleep.

On the mountain the euphoria was short lived; there was still a job to do. Courtney, Hirst and their team gave each other a pat on the back, and then it was back to work. Clambering back down into the crevasse from which they had freed Stuart, they felt an obligation to find Sally. But Sally was dead—Stuart had already told them that. While there was still a chance—even a slim chance—of finding other survivors that had to remain their focus. So they headed off in another direction, digging towards the area where voices had been reported immediately after the slide.

I was lying there, sleep was gnawing at me and my mind turned to Margy. What she must have been going through. The only reason I had come out was to speak to her and it crossed my mind that I hadn't. I hadn't been able to tell her Sal was dead. I wanted to speak with her so much, tell her Sal's death had been quick. That had been my mission.

I had lost Sal so I couldn't care for her anymore. Now I had to concentrate on the people closest to me and Sal. If it had only ever been Sal and me, without the people closest to us, it would have been very, very hard for me to survive.

I was disappointed that I hadn't seen Margy but I really didn't have that much time to dwell on it. Before I knew it they were wheeling me out of the ambulance into the Thredbo Medical Centre. There were doctors and nurses rushing about, they'd been awaiting my arrival.

For Sally's mother and father it was a stressful time. Confined to the apartment to wait for confirmation about Sally the stress was reopening old conflicts. Margy and Andrew were snapping at each other—the tension, at one stage, became overpowering. There with them, though, were Fire Brigade chaplains Bob Garven and his wife Genness. It was a difficult situation for them as they had been told that the rescuers suspected Sally was dead. During one heated moment Genness suggested they pray together. It seemed to calm the whole room down.

After Stuart had been extricated, rescuers scrambled back down into his tomb. It wasn't long before they found a woman's body partially buried in the mud just near where Stuart had been lying. Paramedics checked for any sign of life—there was none. The news filtered back to the rescue operations centre. Inspector Garry Smith swallowed hard— this was the task he had been dreading. He went down to the apartment where Sally's parents were waiting and broke the news. While a positive identification could not yet be made, he told them, they had found a woman in what appeared to be Stuart and Sally's flat—she was dead.

The parents had been preparing themselves for this but the realisation numbed Margy from head to foot. She sat silent for a while ... disbelieving ... wanting beyond all want for Sally to come walking through the door. All day long Andrew and Margy had refused to admit to themselves their worst fears—at least now the waiting was finally over.

Andrew's greatest fear since his arrival in Thredbo had been that if Stuart had died and Sally had survived, entombed in the rubble, would she have been able to cope or would she have been driven out of her mind? At least now he knew she was at peace.

The focus now had to be on Stuart—he had made it—he would need their support to get through his ordeal and his loss. 'I can't imagine what he sees when he shuts his eyes,' Margy thought.

I was pretty much out of it but I soon came back to life when the medical team started getting to work, causing me intense pain. All I could think about was the pain. Why are these guys causing me all this pain when I feel so good? I hadn't had a painkiller. I hadn't had anything. They inserted a catheter in my penis and tubes in my nose, and it seemed like I underwent every test known to man. There were about eight doctors rushing around.

They told me they were just prepping me for the helicopter ride to Canberra. 'Doc Steve' was there—he's the local doctor, Steve Breathour. He asked me about my feet and I said, 'My feet are fine. It's the rest that's hurting'. I had needle after needle. Things in the heart, the head, the leg. It was unbelievable. I still had urine all over me. I desperately needed a wash. Eventually a nurse came over and gave me a wipe down; I started to feel a little bit human again.

Doc Steve was near my head at this stage. He asked me what I wanted and I said, 'Just give me some fucking painkillers'. All the doctors turned around and looked at me.

Steve, Annette and Euan were only minutes behind the ambulance. They still couldn't believe how fit Stuart appeared when they saw him briefly at the top of the site. They anxiously waited for the doctors to let them in.

I could sense my family was nearby ... all I wanted was to be with them. It seemed like ages before they were allowed in to see me. What was I going to say to them? I just wanted to wake up and discover this had all been a nightmare.

Annette and Steve walked into the emergency room first. Annette walked up to her son and gave him a kiss.

'Sally's dead,' Stuart told them, 'she drowned.'

'We know,' Steve said. They only had a couple of minutes, so much else was going on around them. Before they knew it they were being ushered out: 'See you in Canberra'.

Euan was then given a few minutes with Stuart. Choking back a tear Stuart told his brother, 'You realise that Sal's dead'.

'Yeah mate, but you're here.' It was very brief. Neither brother knew what else to say ... there was nothing *to* say. As Euan walked out the door he whispered to himself: 'tough bastard'.

'Where's Feathers?' Stuart asked. 'Why isn't he here?'

Featherstone had watched the ambulance drive off towards the medical centre. He felt a need to still be with Stuart and followed on foot. But by the time he got there the emergency room was so hectic he didn't want to interfere and waited outside.

I thought he would have stayed on the site. 'Job done' sort of thing. He'd finished his job with me and had delivered me to the doctors—that's where we just shake hands and say good-bye—that's the end of it. But I wanted him to be there. He had been such a crucial part of my life and my living.

Once the team in the Thredbo Medical Centre had done what they could to stabilise Stuart's condition it was back into an ambulance bound for the Village Green just near the chapel. In the ambulance Stuart could hear the church bells ringing.

The rotors were winding up as the ambulance came to a stop and they bundled Stuart's stretcher into the rescue chopper. The whine of the engine all but drowned every other sound; still the church bells rang, seemingly farewelling a miracle. On take off the air traffic controllers radioed their best wishes as the nose of the chopper tilted down and it headed off up the valley.

, Featherstone watched the chopper take off and despite needing to rest, something drew him back to the site ... he knew Sally was dead and was still buried under the rubble but he needed to see for himself. Stuart Diver had bared his soul to this man all day ... somehow he too felt emotionally attached to Sally.

When I got in the air ambulance I tried to sleep, but it was too noisy. By that time it was dark. I couldn't see anything. I was in a neck brace and feeling pretty uncomfortable, with these things up my nose, down my throat, in my penis.

Premier Bob Carr echoed a nation's thanks for the miracle: 'The moment when Stuart Diver was brought to the surface will be remembered forever by anyone who watched the rescue. I speak for the people of New South Wales, when I say, we send all our hope and prayers to Stuart for a full recovery and to his family. But our thoughts remain with those still trapped and their families and friends'.

fifteen

Echoing Cheers

The cheers that greeted Stuart Diver's rescue were but an echo down the valley as darkness descended on Thredbo village that Saturday evening. Feelings of jubilation were short-lived as rescuers returned to the task at hand.

During Stuart's miraculous rescue the body bags had continued to be carted to the temporary morgue at the top of the hillside. Police confirmed a total of six bodies had been located in the rubble, there were still a dozen people believed entombed. Charlie Sanderson once again faced reporters: 'I guess we can hope and pray that miracles will keep happening and we might find somebody else'.

While the job on the mountain was hard, so too was the little down time the rescuers were allowed. Being in a small community they couldn't help but rub shoulders with the relatives and friends of those missing. Steve Hirst, Geoff Courtney and the other team members who pulled Stuart out of the rubble finished their shift at 11 o'clock that night. Still buoyed by the rescue they headed off for a beer before turning in. A woman approached them. She told them they were doing a tremendous job and said she was waiting for her friend to also be rescued. She was crying in anticipation that they would be able to give her some good news.

They told her they were doing their best. Then she said her friend's name.

The rescuers exchanged glances—they had located her friend's body just half an hour earlier.

Messages of sympathy and encouragement flooded in from around the world. A wall at the bistro was covered with facsimiles of hope. Tragically one was addressed to Wendy O'Donohue—one of those still missing. Many were from the nation's young. Students from Nelson Park School penned this note.

> 'To the emergency workers and volunteers. We have been watching the Thredbo disaster on TV and would like to express our admiration for the courage, bravery and determination that you have shown us. We are very proud of your efforts and send our deepest sympathy to the victims and their families.'

The Thredbo Family Relief Fund had been set up to help the relatives of those killed. Village managing director David Osborn pledged 10 per cent of the mountain revenue for the remainder of the season.

The Thredbo village community addressed an open letter of thanks to the nation:

> 'We would . . . like to thank the thousands of people throughout the country who have contacted us with expressions of support, sympathy and kind offers of assistance.
>
> 'It has been a great comfort for us to know there are so many people who care for Thredbo and the Thredbo community as much as we do.'

That Saturday night the temperature crashed again to minus nine degrees Celsius. For the first night since the effort began the floodlights were gone. Instead, giant floating lights normally used in the film industry illuminated the mountainside scar. It was the first time the 'Air Stars' had been used in such a mission. Enormous helium-filled balloons with halogen bulbs inside, they were anchored to the ground by cables and gave the site a mystical appearance.

Expensive diamond-tipped circular saws, which had arrived the night before, were to be used to cut through some of the larger slabs. They were provided by the firm Concut. One of the firm's owners, David Rees, had been a member of the team involved in cutting through the concrete bridge that collapsed on a train at Granville in Sydney in 1977, killing 83 people.

In the early hours of Sunday morning the sirens once again brought work to a stop. A number of boulders and slabs were dangerously close to tumbling down and had to be shored up before work could commence again. It was a situation that was to be repeated a number of times over the following hours as the rescue efforts became more frenetic.

At the morning media briefing Sanderson told reporters what no one wanted to hear: the debris on the site had moved almost half a metre in the past 36 hours. Sixteen metres of tunnels had been constructed; more bodies had been located but not removed. He admitted the chances of finding anyone else alive were very small. The death toll stood at nine.

The waiting was torment for the families of the victims. For the relatives of 32-year-old front office manager at the Thredbo Alpine Hotel, Steven Urosevic, grief was mixed with anger. 'It's too slow. Why?' his father, Milan Urosevic was quoted in the newspapers. 'I can't understand why. They're not looking to do anything; they're just looking around.'

But Steven's sister told reporters she knew the rescuers were doing what they could: 'They're trying their very best. They're doing their very best. It's just taking so long'.

Sunday night was a night of significant breakthroughs for the rescue team. For the first time they were able to safely manoeuvre a 'trackscavator', an excavator on wheels, onto part of the slip site just below Bobuck Lane. The trackscavator was able to remove large amounts of sodden earth and rubble, speeding up the operation.

At the same time a team of carpenters braved the sub-zero temperatures to construct a 30-metre chute which rescuers could use to transport debris instead of passing it hand-to-hand along a human chain. This freed up the rescuers who had up until now made up the human chain.

With many of the volunteer rescuers nearing exhaustion, relief came in the form of a task force of 150 fresh State Emergency Service workers from around the state.

But there was a new hurdle on the horizon: weather forecasters predicted snow and rain. State Emergency Service personnel made preparations to cover the top part of the slide with Monaflex, a semi-rigid plastic and wire mesh.

Now, five days after the disaster, investigators revealed some much-needed good news. Susan Green, the woman who was initially believed to have been swept away in the slide, had been found safe and well. Mrs Green and her husband, Mark, from Forbes in rural New South Wales, had been on holiday in Thredbo and were walking along Bobuck Lane when the slide swept past them. They had become separated in the chaos that followed. Mark Green notified police that he couldn't find his wife. However they later reunited and left Thredbo to return home to Forbes—it had just been a mix-up. Police eventually tracked down the couple and established that both were safe and well.

Despite the good news nothing could staunch the tears flowing at a memorial service for the dead and missing at the local chapel. Ideological differences were forgotten as senior politicians united, joining several hundred people at the Thredbo village chapel. Led by Catholic Archbishop Francis Carroll and Anglican Bishop George Bowning, it was also attended by New South Wales Governor Gordon Samuels and Governor-General Sir William Deane.

With pain etched on his face Sir William told the tearful congregation: 'We are sure that the Snowy and its people, who hold such a special place in our nation, its achievements and its folklore, will come through these tragic days with their legendary determination and courage'.

Bishop Bowning told the rescuers that they had 'united Australians in a way that could hardly be imagined'.

Candles for each of the dead and missing burned at the altar as Snowy Mountains Christian Centre Pastor Clare Singleton prayed:

> 'Hearts have been broken but the great mysteries of love, compassion and the capacity for tireless self-giving have been revealed.
> '. . . The scars on the mountain we will carry always. May these scars help us remember that true love and life never end.'

Father Wally Stefanski invited the relatives of the dead and missing to come forward to receive one of the commemorative candles from a clearly emotional Sir William Deane. Two distressed women collapsed, requiring treatment by paramedics on standby.

On the site itself the rescue mission had once again been stalled as tree stumps believed to be binding soil on the landslip were removed. Some rescuers made their way to the chapel to listen to the words of hope. They joined the congregation in the hymn 'How Great Thou Art'.

The tears were barely dry when the siren once again signalled that work could resume in the search for survivors.

A new weapon in the battle to break up the concrete slabs had arrived—100 kilograms of a chemical called Bristar. Holes were drilled in the slabs and the Bristar inserted; once inside the slab the chemical expanded, breaking up the concrete. A concrete x-ray machine from Sydney had also arrived. One of only two in the country it was hoped the 'Ferro Scan' would help in the search for survivors.

In darkness the tenth victim was located, a woman. Six men and four women were now confirmed dead.

As rescuers removed the concrete and rubble on the lower part of the slide SES workers frantically assembled the Monaflex cover that was to, hopefully, stop any further slides in the event of rain. Fire brigade officers scrambled to build a drainage system for the rainwater.

Efforts were once again stalled when geological experts warned it was too dangerous to continue excavating under the concrete slabs. A mines rescue team was sent in to shore up the danger areas.

Out of all the devastation and despair grew something quite beautiful yet haunting. As the rescue operation continued, Jodie Young, a former Thredbo resident, composed and recorded the song 'Winter Grows Colder', to help raise money for the Thredbo Family Relief Fund.

I see it so clearly our last conversation
it really was nothing but I hear every word
and somewhere within the hello and goodbye
I love you was spoken in between the lines

I say it out loud now that I can't hold you
and winter grows longer and winter grows colder.

I can't be lost without you when this is my home
and I know it as well as I ever will
but it's different here now, somehow it seems older
and winter grows harder and winter grows colder.

Now there's only missing you so I do it well
and if I never told you, now I can tell
like a Polaroid I see your face in my mind
in the last place you smiled and the first place I cried.
I say it out loud now that I can't hold you
and winter grows longer and winter grows colder.

It's amazing to me that when I close my eyes
the look you give me takes the chill off the air
and I'll always love winter though I wish she were kinder
she brought you to me and now she keeps you here.

I see it so clearly our last conversation
it really was nothing but I hear every word
and somewhere within the hello and goodbye
I love you was spoken in between the lines.
I say it out loud, now that I can't hold you
and winter grows warmer and winter is over.

In the early hours of Tuesday morning the whistles once again heralded another stop in the work. More movement had been reported. Overnight overseer of police rescue, Sergeant Mark Powderly, checked with the surveyors across the valley—they hadn't sighted any significant shifts.

Powderly could see the rescuers were becoming understandably complacent as the rescue operation dragged on and they neared exhaustion point—one was almost crushed by the swinging crane. From a perch on Bobuck lane he gave the men and women what was later to become known as his 'sermon from the mount'.

'We are becoming sloppy. Our attitudes are getting out of line. We are still committed to a task and we are starting to risk ourselves,' he said and stalked off back to the command post as the 150 personnel got back to work—this time with a fresh enthusiasm.

The bad weather was due within the next 24 hours and there were still eight people unaccounted for. The weather bureau issued a warning to rescue coordinators. Driving rain and gale-force winds of between 55 and 75 kilometres per hour were predicted. Snow would likely follow.

By 10.00am Wednesday the death toll had climbed to 13 with another three bodies located through the night. Light rain had begun falling ... heavy snow clouds were approaching. As SES workers secured the Monaflex sheeting more than 3,000 sandbags were laid at the top of the landslide in a bid to keep water off. Rescuers were equipped with warmer snow gear to ward off the change in conditions. So far the weather had been an ally ... it could soon become the enemy.

Up until now the rescuers had been working in two- or three-hour shifts. Now, because of the weather, the shifts would be reduced to one hour to lessen the danger of exposure.

After lunch the toll climbed to 15—nine men and six women—leaving just three people unaccounted for.

At 11.30 that night the skies broke and rain began pelting the site. Fierce winds lashed the area, making the operation all but unbearable. Doggedly the rescuers continued and one by one more bodies were located and extricated until only one known victim was still missing. Sergeant Powderly was in the middle of briefing the other agency commanders inside the command post when a cold, wet and breathless rescuer rushed in, caught Powderly's eye and held up his finger—the last victim had been located. It brought a lump to Powderly's throat. 'We did it. We did it. It's all over,' he thought.

Just after 2.00am, Thursday, August 7th, the last known victim was carried up the face of the mountain; by now the rain was drenching the site.

Powderly called the 200 rescuers together. 'It's been a long hard haul,' he told them. 'We've achieved a result to the point where we think we've recovered all the bodies that we are aware of. I can't thank you enough. Let's go get some sleep.'

The rescuers were stood down en masse. The site was

left to the rain. Police Region Commander Eric Gollan thanked God the weather had held off so long: 'I don't know whether you believe in it or not but there is such a thing as divine intervention. Perhaps the grieving process can now commence'.

For Charlie Sanderson it was an emotional end to a traumatic exercise. For the first time his troops downed tools and relaxed. Throughout the village locals and rescuers mingled, hugged, patted each other on the back. Charlie Sanderson was heartened by the community support. He had wished to save more lives, to finish the job more quickly, but above all else he was confident the rescue team had gone about the operation the right way—the only way—methodically and carefully.

While arrangements had been made for Andrew Donald to formally identify his daughter's body in Sydney the police now told him there was no need because dental records had been used. At first he didn't really feel the need to see her, wanting to remember her the way she was, but when he was given the opportunity he decided he wanted to. 'Sal was just lying there and she had a tiny mark on her cheekbone, and a little bruise on her forehead,' he said. 'She was just lying there exactly as if she was asleep, exactly as I had seen her thousands of times. A peaceful face—the spirit was still there—she still had a glow to her.'

That night snow blanketed the pretty alpine village. It was time for the hundreds of rescuers to let off a little steam; they had a mammoth snow fight with locals and the media. The next morning Thredbo had been transformed. The ugly site which had been a brutal reminder of the carnage of the past week was now covered in white, virgin snow … it was almost as if Mother Nature was saying sorry.

sixteen

The Only One

As we touched down in Canberra I could hear the sound of car horns heralding our arrival. The doctor told me a crowd and a large media contingent were waiting. With an oxygen mask, a neck brace and nearing exhaustion I was in no state to face the media throng.

'Mate, I'm just going to pretend I'm asleep and you just take me straight through them.'

As the cameras flashed and the questions flew the medicoes wheeled me on a trolley for about 20 metres, straight into the back of a waiting ambulance for the drive to the emergency ward of Canberra Hospital. I could hear people clapping as the paramedics closed the ambulance door ... I wondered why they were clapping.

I remember lots of whiteness and bright lights. I always expected hospital emergency wards to be full of people, with doctors and nurses running everywhere, but there was no one there. This very lonely feeling swept over me. I wasn't with anyone from Thredbo. New paramedics, new doctors, new nurses. It was unbelievably frightening. I had been feeling so good when I came out of the rubble and now I was in so much pain. Maybe there *was* something seriously wrong with me.

My feet were finally starting to warm up and this took me to new levels of pain. It was excruciating, the throbbing ache racked my whole body. I'd already had so many needles and then they whacked in some more IVs. I still hadn't been properly washed. Even though they'd cut my clothes off, I smelled pretty ordinary.

By this stage I had been awake for 67 hours; all I wanted

to do was curl up and go to sleep. I was in an environment that was all white and bright—feeling pain, feeling absolute total loneliness—so sleep seemed like an impossibility.

A doctor came up and told me they were worried because my temperature was fluctuating and that they needed to put a thermometer in my oesophagus. I already had a tube going down my oesophagus and into my stomach to stop me from throwing up. Now they wanted to put in another tube with a thermometer.

'If you come anywhere near me, put anything else in my nose, another tube anywhere near me, I'm going to kill you,' I said.

The doctor reeled backwards.

'I'm serious. I'll get up and I'll kill you.'

Finally the doctor agreed to wait half an hour. Sure enough, within that time my temperature stabilised ... he didn't have to put any more tubes in and I didn't have to kill him.

Mum, Dad and Euan came in soon after I arrived. They basically just had time to say hello because the doctors wanted to do more tests on me.

The Diver family had arrived courtesy of a police escort travelling at breakneck speeds from Thredbo to Canberra. The trip had given Euan time for a little reflection. Although not surprised Stuart had made it out, it made Euan wonder how he would've faced such adversity. But above all else Euan felt an overwhelming pride in his younger brother. He kept shaking his head, thinking 'tough bastard'.

Salvation Army colonel Don Woodland had spent much of the day with Stuart's family. He spoke to reporters outside the hospital: 'At the end of the day, when their emotions have been stretched and are still being stretched, they just want to say thank you very much to every person that's been involved. The support that they've got has been absolutely marvellous. They've just asked me to say thank you for your love and your care and your prayers ...'

The tests took about another three hours and I had to stay awake the whole time. I had to have every part of my body x-rayed, and then all the blood tests they'd done at Thredbo had to be redone in hospital again.

I'd felt so fit when I came out of the rubble, maybe because there were so many endorphins flowing through my body at the time or maybe because I had just come out of 65 hours in hell—I felt great. But from the moment they'd got me into the medical centre I'd felt nothing but pain—mental and physical. After losing Sal, the 65-hour ordeal and then what the medical team had to do to me, I was getting fed up with everything—I just wanted to get the hell out of there.

I began hassling them to take the tube out of my nose and the catheter out of my penis—they were just so bloody uncomfortable. It was explained to me that the catheter was needed to monitor my urine output and to measure my electrolyte balance. This way the doctors could get a good idea if any internal organs, such as my kidneys, had been damaged. I had more x-rays and what seemed like 50 million other tests before I finally got into the intensive care unit. I was in a real daze. I'd had a few painkillers by then. I could just press a button and give myself as much intravenous painkiller as I wanted.

The doctor came in and said they were very concerned about the frostbite on my feet. He hinted at the fact that I might lose all the toes on my left foot; he held out pretty good hope for the right foot and thought I might just lose a bit of flesh off a couple of toes. Neither foot looked too crash hot. When I came out of the hole my left leg from halfway down my calf to the foot was completely black. My right foot from just above the ankle joint down was also completely black. They said if the skin had been really shiny I would've been in bad strife—mine was dull so they held out some hope.

They decided to put my feet into hot water in an effort to bring them back to life ... and I thought I had already been through some intense pain. Frozen feet into what felt like boiling water. I was screaming for them to stop. Instantly my feet blew up to the size of footballs. Apart from my toes my feet went from black to pink in two seconds. The blood just came straight back. As soon as that happened, even though my toes were still black, the doctor came in and said they should be OK. They placed my feet in the hot water for

20 minutes, took them out for 20 minutes and back in again for 20 minutes, for the next two hours. The painkillers definitely helped but no painkiller in the world could completely take away the agony of placing my feet in that water. I'm sure that if I hadn't had painkillers it would have been comparable to what I had suffered when I was trapped under the building in the cold.

I just kept pushing the button on the IV painkiller. Even though it limited the amount I could have each hour it was still a good feeling to press that button. In a way it was the first time I had some control over what was happening to me.

Since the landslide I'd hungered for real warmth, the kind of warmth you have when you're snuggling up to someone in a nice, warm bed. The first real warmth I experienced was in the intensive care unit. The nurse brought in this big container of warm water and cleaned me up properly. She had also given me the self-administering painkiller, so I thought she was wonderful.

I thought that everyone else, except Sal, had survived. It was only Sal who had died. Thinking that others had survived helped because that meant that everyone else was going through what I was now going through, I shouldn't complain too much.

I was still starving and thirsty. They were giving me nutrients through the IV but I couldn't stop thinking about my empty stomach. I hadn't had any fluid down my throat except for the tiny little bit they gave me when I was under the rubble. They had to wait for the results of my tests to make sure my kidneys were all right.

By now I'd been awake for 72 hours—there was nothing left in me. My mind was so rattled. It was about two o'clock in the morning by the time I finally got some sleep. It was more a drug-induced haze than real sleep. The pain was so intense. I woke up about three hours later.

That morning a nurse came and took me for my first shower. Beautiful. I thought it was the best. Because my feet were like balloons there was no way I could walk so she took me in a wheelchair. That shower felt just sensational. Finally I could wash the 65 hours of caked-on mud out of my hair. It was in the shower when reality took a momentary hold: 'Sal's gone'. But I was so drugged up everything seemed slightly unreal.

Finally they removed the catheter. It hurt even more taking it out than putting it in. The nurse who pulled it out could see the agony I was in and said that the catheter *was* rather large. Somehow that knowledge didn't take the pain away.

I had cuts everywhere and they were worried about infection, so they made sure they were all thoroughly cleaned. The pain of the cuts was nothing compared to my feet. The pain now was like a big, rusty nail being driven into my foot every 10 seconds, over and over again. I was worrying about it too much to think about anything else.

I was dealing only with what I *had* to deal with. When will I get to eat something? What's going on? The reality of what had happened and my emotions really didn't enter my mind that much. It's very hard to be emotional when you are in so much physical pain. Except for being emotional towards the physical pain. I got angry with my feet. I was abusing my feet. I wasn't too happy with them.

There was now no need to keep me in intensive care so they transferred me up to the burns ward. My own room. It gave me a chance to think about what had happened, what had happened to Sal.

Mum, Dad and Euan came in to see me. I think they were still in a state of shock that I had actually managed to survive at all. We kissed each other. Before this we had never felt the need to express our affection—before this we had so much love and affection for each other that it went without saying. But here were Euan, Dad and I actually kissing each other on the lips—not too many Australian males do that.

I know I never would have gotten through this ordeal without my family. While we were never a cuddly family we always had a lot of mutual respect for each other. Since the disaster we've become a lot closer, a lot more physical. Euan, Dad and I kiss each other now—kiss, hug, touch. We never used to because we never felt the need.

I owe a lot to my parents for my survival. I have no doubt that my upbringing is what got me here today. As a kid I learned what was right and wrong—that's such a crucial and basic ingredient in life. I don't have any regrets. I would if I had done nothing with my life, but my parents gave me so many great opportunities as a child and teenager, which I firmly believe helped to build the mental and physical strength I needed to survive.

I told them all that had happened, from beginning to end. I amazed myself because I was able to hold myself together as I told them how Sal had died in my hands. I was still doped to the eyeballs so that probably overcame the emotion that raged through my body. I'd be halfway through a sentence and I would suddenly fall silent. Mum later told me my eyes just seemed to haze over as if I was reliving it all again. Then, 30 seconds later I would pick up where I had left off. After a while they left—said something about a press conference and were gone.

With Don Woodland there for support Steve, Annette and Euan answered a barrage of media questions. From Steve Diver came a heartfelt thanks: 'This comes from Stuart as well. To the people who did perform the rescue, all the people on the site, and there were 1,500 or so up there working, thank you, thank you very much for performing a miracle'.

'I always thought he was fantastic ... he's now even more fantastic,' Annette told the reporters.

It was about this time I met Marina Boogaerts. She was one of the senior nurses in the trauma ward. All the nurses were great—they'd come in with their fantastic smiles—but she just stood out. She was the one who told me to just take it really easy and that it *was* going to hurt. She explained to me that it *was* really OK if I wanted to cry. She helped take a little bit of the pressure off—I didn't have to maintain this macho image that I was invincible.

Marina was always there if I wanted to talk.

For Marina it was a traumatic experience. Silently she listened to Stuart's account of the disaster. An hour-and-a-half later she walked out of his room and headed home ... she cried the whole way.

'He put on such a brave face, especially to his family. I

think he was being strong for them, protecting them. He didn't seem to be able to just let go,' said Marina.

'There would be times at night, when he was alone, and I would go into his room and he had such a sad look on his face. I remember he would sometimes ask about his wedding photos, if they had made it out of the landslide, he didn't seem to care about any of his other possessions.'

I began to look forward to Marina's shift. I became attached emotionally to her. She had all the qualities that I needed at the time—compassion and a smiling face. Maybe she reminded me of Sal in some ways. In the space of four days I had gone from happily married and having a special relationship to having nothing. There was a huge void in my life and Marina helped fill that with her caring and compassionate attitude.

The doctors told me the tests had come up clean. Apart from my feet, I was 100 per cent, no broken bones, nothing. It wasn't a surprise to me at all. I could have told them that at the beginning—I knew all along I was OK. I had been in that freezing mud for 65 hours, I'd have known if I'd broken anything. I knew that the only concern was going to be my feet. So I said, 'Oh great. Thanks for that. Can I now have something to eat?'

They brought me eggnog and porridge. Dairy, high carbohydrate food. It was pretty usual hospital fare but it was good. They only gave me a small meal. I took a couple of mouthfuls and tried to swallow but it was as if my throat had contracted. I managed to get some down but immediately began to feel sick so I didn't finish it. After being so hungry the whole time I was buried suddenly food didn't interest me that much.

The police wanted to speak with me; I did an hour-long interview with them, which was unbelievably hard. Mum and Dad had left the room and I was alone with these two policemen. I still didn't know what was going on—no idea—and they were asking me all these questions. I honestly thought, by the way they were talking, that I had knocked the building down. They asked me how many people there were in the building; did I speak to any of them; did I notice any cracks in the building? I was still under heavy sedation and painkillers, so I was a bit paranoid. I was scared. I had never been interviewed by police in my life. They weren't rude but they seemed very officious. Honestly, I thought they were going to go away and investigate *me*. There was that hole I drilled in the wall for the hook to hang a picture. Maybe that had weakened the whole building and it had fallen down. As soon as I was better they'd cart me off to jail.

I figured that they had interviewed all the other survivors as well and I was just adding this piece to the picture. I did think it was odd when they showed me a map of the building and asked me to mark where everyone had been living. I thought that was a funny question, but I answered it anyway.

They also asked me about Sal so I told them what I could remember. It was amazing, all of a sudden everything that had happened to Sal and me became so clear—my mind had switched from a blurry haze to crystal clarity. What I told them became the basis for my official police statement. It was one of the toughest things I've ever had to do—reliving the night our lives were torn apart.

'On Wednesday the 30th July 1997 Sally and I went to Jindabyne and did a bit of shopping. We returned to Thredbo at 7.00pm. We both had dinner and went to bed at 8.30pm. We didn't speak to anybody else in the Bimbadeen Lodge before we went to bed. I went to sleep shortly after that. The next thing I was awoken by a massive, roaring, exploding sound. Sally and I were asleep in a short four poster bed, which was situated on the centre wall of the apartment.

'When I heard the noise I lifted my head up to see what the noise was. This was done in a split second. I lifted my head up and then instinctively put my head straight back down on the pillow. There was a huge amount of choking dust, and it was pitch black. Sally and I were both screaming. I attempted to get off the bed to find a way out. Unable to do so I returned to try and assist Sally. Sally said that her legs were trapped and I felt up to where I thought her head would be, found her head and realised that she was pinned to the bed. I attempted to lift the bedhead off her upper torso to free her as there was now water cascading down on top of us.

'Being unable to free Sally I attempted to find an air pocket for myself so I wouldn't drown. Sally's scream stopped so I realised that she was dead. This whole process from the collapse until now, took approximately thirty seconds.'

Talking to the police was a bit of a reality check. I began thinking about who else had been in the building such as my friends Wendy O'Donohue, Mike and Mim, and Col Warren. I thought, 'There were a fair few people in that building. I hope they're all OK'. The police didn't say anything. I must admit I didn't ask them; subconsciously I probably didn't really want to know. I hadn't even seen the devastation. When they pulled me out of the hole I was looking at the sky so I didn't see anything else—I had no idea.

That afternoon I met Don Woodland from the Salvation Army. This man seemed to exude an inner strength, which radiated to me. It was clear he would always be there to offer support.

Dad was unbelievably protective about who came into the room. The pain was so excruciating that I couldn't sleep but Dad tried to give me times when I could at least rest. He'd kick everyone out. He'd come in and say, 'Everyone out. He's having an hour's rest. See you later'.

Don and Dad began to sort out what to do with the media. The hospital had put a blanket on all information and just released hourly reports: I was 'still alive, stable and doing well' but Dad had 150 messages on his answering machine and 50 more on his mobile phone. And because Susie was Thredbo's media manager she was plagued as well. It was out of control. I just couldn't understand why there was so much interest in me.

Dad had no idea how to handle the media. Don Woodland recommended we get an agent and one suggestion was the Media Management company run by Harry M. Miller. Miller had worked with the Salvation Army previously. We hadn't heard of Harry before so Susie made a few phone calls to some of her contacts to check him out. They advised her that Harry was the right man for the job.

Mum and Dad thought Harry would help gain some control of the media coverage, some control over what they did with the information. They felt that a lot of incorrect information had already been published and broadcast and they were adamant about putting up a barrier between the media and me.

Dad told me the pressure from the media was mounting. We decided that we had to do *something* so we agreed to let one television crew come into the hospital; they would then share the footage with the other stations. I wanted to say thanks to the people who had got me out. The producer came in with a script but I asked him, 'Do I have to read that?' He said, 'Oh, no, no, we just wrote that in case'. So I put the script aside, looked straight down the camera and said what I wanted to say. I said a few words about the Thredbo Family Relief Fund as well as this thankyou message:

> 'I'd just like to thank everyone who was involved in my rescue, the fire brigade, and all the rescue services along with the medical teams at Thredbo and here in Canberra and all the people who prayed for me and gave me so much support over the last couple of days.
>
> 'It's been overwhelming and I don't think I'd have made it through without the involvement of all those people.
>
> 'It's been fantastic, and thanks very much.'

I didn't get a lot of time to myself that afternoon because Mum and Dad wanted to stay around me. No one really knew what was going on in my head. They thought it was a little bit strange that I hadn't cried and I seemed to be smiling and laughing with the nurses. So they kept a fairly close eye on me. I still probably wasn't 'with it' all the time. Yet I couldn't have done a police interview, talked to the media or made decisions of the magnitude that I had to make without having a fair grasp of reality. Again I was swinging between opposite ends of the spectrum—between both the unreal and the real world.

I think my positive outlook was my mind's way of protecting itself so I didn't go crazy. Blocking out what had happened and trying to live in the present. From that early stage I knew that I had to live—I was alive—therefore I had to live. I had been positive my whole life so why should I change now? I didn't want to sit there bawling my eyes out in front of people. Sal was one of the only people who had ever seen that side of me. I was alive and I felt relatively good. Life had to go on. I knew from day one that life had to go on. Showing the world a positive face was my way of starting to put the roots in place from which life would one day sprout again. That was exactly what Sal would have wanted me to do.

On Sunday I was finally left alone. I turned on the television. Every channel was still on Thredbo. It was then that I realised the devastation of the site. I thought I was the last one out and that the site would have been cleared by now. I called out to Dad and he rushed in. I asked if they got everyone out. He told me that they hadn't, they were still trying to get other people out. It didn't occur to me to ask him if there was anyone else alive—deep down I don't think I wanted to know.

It was to be another fitful night. I could sleep for about two hours, then I'd wake for half an hour, and go back to sleep for another two hours; this went on throughout the night. The self-administering painkiller became a problem because I would wake up to give myself the next injection. They started giving me an extra little booster at night to try and knock me out. Every time I woke up there was a nurse there. It was good because I never woke up in complete darkness.

The next morning Dad came in and started going through the pile of mail that had arrived. Mum decided to go shopping because I had nothing. She went out and bought me some toiletries, undies and clothes. That made me realise I had nothing left, I couldn't go and grab my favourite shirt or jeans. At 27 years of age here I was, my mother buying my clothes.

That morning Dad came in and said that he'd organised Harry M. Miller to handle the media for us. Soon after I met

Harry for the first time. Harry said he would be dealing with Dad on everything and that he already had a couple of ideas about what to do. He emphasised that his utmost concern was me, Mum, Dad, Sal and Sal's family. He said I was his number one concern at the time and that's all *I* wanted to hear. I looked at him and thought: 'Yeah, good, that sounds very good to me, mate. Great'.

I was beginning to wonder more about why all the media attention was focused on me. Mum told me friends were coming from everywhere to see me. Iain Groves was even travelling back from Tanzania. I again asked Dad if they had got Sal's body out yet. I wanted to see Margy. I began to wonder about everyone else.

'Dad, did I do something special? Am I the last one out and that's why they're focusing on me, waiting for the next one to come out? Where's everybody else? Are they here in Canberra Hospital? Can I go and see them?'

Dad looked me in the eyes and almost whispered, 'There is no one else'.

'What do you mean there is no one else?'

'They haven't found anybody else alive.'

It hit me like a sledgehammer—I had never felt so alone in my life. No ... one ... else. We were both silent as the reality sank in. What could I say? I looked down and just sat there. It was like someone put something through my heart.

With no one else to share this with how could I cope with Sal's death? I had thought I could go and talk to Mike or Mim Sodergren or Wendy O'Donohue—anybody—at least they would be able to relate to what had happened. I was alone again, just like when I was buried under the rubble. I sat there by myself thinking 'This just can't be right'.

It added to the monumental emotional nightmare I was trying to deal with. It put an extra nail in the coffin of my mental stability.

Somehow I still managed to present a positive attitude. On reflection that positive attitude was my way of building a barrier against the trauma. That's the only way I survived. If I hadn't done that, I don't think I'd be here today—I'd be in some padded room somewhere. I put up barriers—I had to— to survive.

I held onto the hope that if they hadn't got everybody out yet then there was still a chance there'd be more survivors. Maybe some of my friends were still in there, alive. There was a chance they'll still come out. Dad agreed there was still a chance. We turned the sadness around and got some hope back again. I had made it out so there was no reason why anyone else couldn't do the same thing. Maybe it was just my mind blocking out the reality because I had too much else to deal with. I was trying to deal with Sal's death—that was my main focus.

I still hadn't seen the person I really wanted to. Margy had been in Thredbo waiting for news about Sal. Finally on the Tuesday morning Dad came in and said: 'Margy's here to say hello'.

'Fantastic, bring her on in.'

Margy walked through the door. Despite everything that had happened it was the same old Margy—her usual smiling, happy face. It was the first contact I'd had with a blood relative of Sal's and it brought it all home. It was the first time I really started to realise how much my life had been torn apart. We hugged ... we cried. I was still in a lot of pain and had the intravenous drips coming out of my arms. So it wasn't really a big hug, but it was great. Here I was hugging someone who had been so close to Sal—that hug gave me strength. We held each other for a while.

The tears rolled down my cheeks as I told her, 'I wanted to survive for you, because I knew you would be so upset'.

I couldn't bring myself to tell her the details of what had happened, which was really strange because that had been one of the strongest incentives for getting out. The words wouldn't come. There was nothing I could say. She knew that Sal was dead and I knew she was dead. What could I say? What could anyone say? What do you say to a mother who has just lost her daughter? What do you say to a man who has just lost his wife? The best thing to do was to say nothing. The hug said it all. We didn't have to talk and that's the way it's always been, that's the beauty of our relationship. I suppose it's because Margy is one of my last remaining connections to Sal.

seventeen

Where's Home?

My hospital room was beginning to look like a florist shop. Flowers were coming from everywhere, so many flowers that we were able to distribute them to all ten floors of the hospital. Flowers and chocolates, everybody got them. The kids' ward was full of cuddly toys and balloons. There were cards by the bagful. I just couldn't believe the support I was getting.

Apart from a few people from Thredbo and an old schoolmate, the only people I'd seen were doctors, nurses, hospital media liaison people and close family. On the Wednesday Iain Groves showed up, which was a huge boost. He'd travelled all the way from Tanzania.

Obviously he was devastated about what had happened to Sally and me but we went straight into the same old routine— he came in and cracked a joke and I gave him one back. Even though he'd been in Tanzania for three months it was like he'd never been away. The fact that he had come all this way to see me was a reality check because it proved how serious the situation was but then to see him being as positive as I was, was fantastic. I couldn't believe he was there. He had just got off a 51-hour flight and had come straight from the airport. It was a moving moment when he walked through the door.

Grovesy had been working in Mwanza, a remote Tanzanian city, when he got a call from our friend Greg Beanland— at the time of the call there wasn't much hope of finding Sal or me alive. But the next morning Grovesy got a fax from another friend, Steve Prothero. It read:

Stuart Diver found ALIVE at 5.30am.

55 hours after landslide.
Trapped between two slabs of concrete—minor injuries and
hypothermia. Conscious and in good spirits.
All efforts are being made to rescue him. It's a long slow job
due to the unstable ground. Expect to take 2–3 more hours.
No news of Sally. Three other bodies recovered—no names
released.
Take care mate.
Steve P.

Grovesy was a bloke who could always put a smile on my face
and he didn't let me down this time. He told me a funny story
about his nightmare trip from Tanzania and made me smile
for the first time in days. It began at the airport in Dar es
Salaam. Grovesy is about six foot one and his black Tanzanian
travel agent was about four foot two. Grovesy had paid someone
US$2000 to get a ticket on the next flight out—there wasn't
another one for two days. But the plane was full. Five minutes
before it was due to take off he was still standing at the service
desk pleading and arguing with the airline staff. There was
just no way they were going to let him on so his travel agent
yelled at the airport staff 'You have to help this man!' When
they asked him why he said, 'Because he is my son'. The whole
place erupted in hysterical laughter. But can you believe it?
They let him on!

Grovesy only realised the enormity of the situation when
he got to Bangkok where he had an eight-hour stopover and
spotted a huge picture of me on the front page of a newspaper.

I just couldn't tell him everything that had happened—
there was no time. That was the problem. If I had been able
to sit down with him for eight hours that day I would have
told him everything.

During that week in hospital I never had time to say
anything really personal to anyone . . . or maybe I didn't because
I was trying to block it out myself. People would ask, 'How are
you going?' and I'd say 'I'm feeling pretty good actually. My
feet are hurting, but other than that I am feeling OK'. That
was about the limit of my conversations.

Even now there are a lot of things I still haven't told
people that one day I would like to tell them. Either they're

not ready to hear these things or I'm not ready to tell them. There are obviously a lot of things I will never tell anyone because they're mine ... Sal's and mine.

It was while I was in hospital that Harry M. Miller organised an agreement with Network Seven and *The Australian Women's Weekly* magazine. The contract was signed in hospital. It was all organised in three days. Dad told me Harry and the lawyers were working around the clock trying to sort things out. Right at the end, when Harry was just about to walk in to collect the final contract for me to sign he came up with another proposal, something that he thought would be good for us. So the lawyers had to go back for another few hours and rewrite the contract.

I left the decision-making to Mum and Dad—I had absolute faith they would do what was best for me. They told me the Network Seven agreement included going to the 1998 Winter Olympics, which sounded like a great opportunity, but the reality of the contract and its details were so far removed from what I was going through that none of it made any real difference to me. I knew it meant that I would only be dealing with Channel Seven—we hoped that this would ease the media pressure. We hoped that once we were aligned with one network and one magazine the others would leave us alone.

Day after day I got more mail. Of all those cards and letters, and I figure there would have been about 5,000, only one was negative—one out of 5,000. Mum accidentally let me read it. It was some guy extolling the virtues of me joining the media 'scum'. Now that I'd joined the media I was no longer to be respected. Basically I should go and cut my wrists and end it all. That letter infuriated me. It was signed with a return address; I came so close to writing back to him but then I thought, 'no, he's not worth it'.

But the positive letters were fantastic. I couldn't believe that what had happened to me had had such an effect on people. Some were from kids, just four years old or younger, writing classic lines such as, 'I'm sorry the mountain fell on you'.

There was one in particular: 'I watched all day and I prayed and prayed that I would get a Labrador for Christmas'. That brought a smile back to my face; letters like that were superb. There were a lot of primary school teachers who gave their students assignments to 'write to Stuart Diver' so I got piles of letters. There would be 40 letters in each envelope, and paintings.

A lot of the letters I received had religious overtones—a lot of people believed that the Lord had saved me. Some were a little dubious, like the cults who sent me proposals to become their leader—I can just imagine myself a sect leader! Other people shared their stories of grief and told me 'You'll get through it in the end'. I must admit, at the time, they were a little depressing but I realised they were trying to show me that you can overcome adversity, that you can go on after a tragedy.

But the letters from children were classics: 'I'm sorry the mountain fell on you' or 'We're sorry for what happened and it was really bad but let's look to the future'. Children can get their message across in ten words where it takes an adult five pages—the kids' simple attitude captured everything that needed to be said.

A lot of the letters started with 'I have never, ever written to anyone in this situation before' and most ended with something like 'You've been such an inspiration and you've made me really look at my life and consider what I am doing and hopefully change something'. Those letters helped my recovery; to have that amount of goodwill coming from so many people was just so uplifting.

Two kids sent me their teddy bears. I think they were three and four years old and here they were sending me their own teddy bears! It was just so special when you consider how important a teddy bear is to a child. The letter that came with them was from their grandfather. He said that he tried to talk them out of it, explained the loss of their teddy bears, but they insisted, they wanted to send me their teddy bears—I've still got them.

People knitted things for me, made me big quilts and sent me lots of slippers 'for your cold feet'. It made me realise just how caring and compassionate people are. That's what's kept me going. I think I've now got about 20 teddy bears and each and every one of them is very special.

To sit there every day reading letters from all these

people who had gotten inspiration out of what had happened to me and then promised to change their lives for the better—at the time it was exactly what I needed. I thought of each person sitting in their house writing one little letter, not realising that there were 5,000 people doing the same thing. It reinforced my faith in humankind and helped take away a lot of the anger that I had because I had lost Sal. It made me realise that it was possible to get something positive out of something so negative.

On the Thursday the Fire Brigade and Salvation Army chaplain Captain Bob Garven and his wife Genness, who was also a captain in the Salvos, came in to present Warwick Kidd's torch to me. This small yellow torch, covered in mud, was so significant because it was the one that was passed to me when I was buried in the rubble. It had given me some semblance of control over what was happening around me. I've still got that torch and it still has some of the mud on it.

That afternoon I took my first steps. The doctors had encouraged me to get up and walk even though my feet were still the size of balloons and had massive compressive bandages on them. They taped a little bit of rubber on the bottom and I began stumbling around with a walking frame. I had been lying down since I went to bed on the night of the disaster and here I was trying to walk again—it was a weird sensation. I got half a lap around the ward and thought, 'bugger the walking frame' and tossed it. I had a nurse on one side and Grovesy on the other and I was rocking along like a drunk. I managed to get back to my bed, with the other nurses asking, 'What are you doing without the walking frame? You've got to have the walking frame'. No, I was over the walking frame. The pain became even more excruciating because as I put my feet down on the ground the blood flowed straight to them.

By Friday I was really improving and the doctors said I would be allowed to go home soon. That afternoon the firefighters Geoff Courtney, Steve Hirst and the rest of the team paid a visit. They stayed for about 20 minutes. We chatted but we didn't talk about Sal, we just mostly talked feet.

Steve Hirst will never forget the moment: 'We were all pretty filthy and we all went up in this elevator. I was taking deep breaths trying to get the emotions back in check before we walked into his room. I was worried that I was going to lose the plot, break down or wouldn't know what to say.

'But when we walked in he said, "G'day, fellas, how are you? Come in. Have a chat". He welcomed us and seemed as bright as a button. His attitude boosted my spirits. This is one tough bastard—not in a physical sense but mentally—he's got his head together. After going through what he had and losing his wife I thought this man is handling it real well.

'But it didn't hit me until days later—he never asked us what had actually happened to make the building collapse.'

Geoff Courtney: 'It was quite funny because he looked far better than we did. We looked like shit. I'd look at Stuart and then I'd look at the other guys and I thought "If I look as bad as they do, they look shocking". And here's Stuart sitting up in hospital, his feet are all bandaged and everything like that. I thought, "He looks pretty good".'

As they were going, just as they were about to leave I said, 'Thanks a lot guys, for everything you did'. That was it, they were gone. It was pretty simple really. They knew they'd done an unbelievable job. What could I say to guys who had put their lives on the line for eight days saving my life and trying to save 18 others? What do you say? I still have that trouble now.

By this stage I was itching to get out of hospital. All the IVs were finally out. I ended up with about 20 puncture marks in my arms. I felt like a pincushion.

I was now taking oral painkillers. That was good because I could slowly wean myself off them. The problem with painkillers is that they begin to rule you. You wake up every four hours to take them. My aim from early on in hospital was to get off the painkillers as quickly as I could. Even though I was in agony it was better to get off them because then at least at night, once the mind had shut out the pain, I could sleep for eight hours.

When they signed my release papers I was faced with the problem of where to go. I didn't really want to go to Mum and Dad's because we figured the media would have staked out their house. Harry offered me his farm so we could get away from people up there, but I didn't want to go there because that was foreign to me. I suppose I just wanted to go back to Thredbo and head down to the bistro—that was what I really wanted to do. My home was gone. I had no home. I had nothing.

Mum, Dad and I decided on Melbourne. Harry had an idea to take me to Canberra airport and fly me there but the media had us under siege. There were concerns that we would meet a media horde at the other end—it would have been hard to cover up, especially going by plane. I didn't really want to fly anyway because I still had to be horizontal with my feet elevated the whole time. So Dad came up with a solution. He had a van so he suggested throwing a mattress and some pillows in the back.

On the Sunday morning, seven days after I had been pulled from the rubble, they backed the van up to a rear door at the hospital and we left through the children's ward. Even though the hospital had released a statement saying that I had already left 'bound for an unknown, warm location' to put the media off the scent they were still out the front. There would have been 40 or 50 people waiting for me to come out.

There we were at the children's entrance taking photos to mark the occasion, meanwhile about 100 metres away and just around the corner, there was a mass of media waiting for me to come out, their cameras at the ready.

I got into the back of the van and we took off. It was almost like taking a step back in time to when I was a boy. Like being back in the Kombi. Even though I wasn't in the happiest frame of mind, it was the same. We'd pull into a rest area on the highway and Mum would come around, stand me up and drag me out so I could go to the toilet. It was like being a little kid again. Mum feeding me sandwiches, a cup of warm tea from the thermos. I had gone a full circle and come back. That was comforting in a way. It was awkward because of my feet but I've always loved sleeping in the back of vans—a nice, big mattress and more pillows than I knew what to do with.

It was an eight-hour trip from Canberra to Melbourne. By the time we hit the outskirts of the city it was late at night. The sights and sounds of Melbourne took me back to the early days with Sal. But now she wasn't here. Sure, it was going to be good catching up with other people but, in reality, I didn't want to see anyone else. I'd had it. I just wanted to disappear.

The media knew Mum and Dad's address and we were worried they might have surrounded the house so I went and stayed at Margy's place for the first night. That was hard. Whenever Sal and I came to Melbourne we would stay with Margy so it brought back a lot of memories. It was so hard going to bed that night ... that's when it really started to sink in that Sal was gone. In a way it was strangely comforting, because I felt that Sal was still there. Sal and I had lived in every room of that house so every room had memories. But the memories only lasted for a short time because I was still in so much pain.

I couldn't sleep alone that night so I slept next to Margy in her bed. I didn't want to be left alone—I needed to feel the warmth of another human.

The next day I went back to Mum and Dad's house. The media who'd been staking out the house seemed to have got tired of waiting and had left. It was hard going back to Mum and Dad's. I had been married for two years, in a relationship for five years and hadn't lived at their place since I was 19. The last thing I'd planned on, as a 27-year-old, was to go back to my parents' place.

There were photos of Sal and me on the walls and Mum asked me if I wanted them taken down or left up. I said, 'Leave them up. Why would I want them taken down?' Since the slide I hadn't seen a photo of Sal except for a glimpse once on television, and an image of her in one of the newspapers. It was our wedding photo that I picked up. I sat there and bawled my eyes out. It brought back so many memories. I sat there staring at the photo and Mum came over and started crying as well.

On the Tuesday of that week the media interviews began in earnest. The arrangement was that I would spend the next few days being interviewed by various Channel Seven programs and a team from the *Australian Women's Weekly*. The interviews controlled my life for the rest of the week.

It was good in a way because I had to sit there for hours

on end and talk. The journalists were all very understanding and didn't push points that they saw were affecting me—for that I was grateful. Dad was always in control of the situation and he set a timetable where every hour I would get a break for 30 minutes, a breather. The media couldn't come into my room, so I could get away from them whenever I wanted.

At the end of each day I would spend an hour or two in the shower bawling my eyes out. It was the first time I had really started to cry. This was just way, way beyond the strength that I had. I just couldn't deal with it. I was finally starting to realise the enormity of what had happened, how my life had irrevocably been changed.

I was missing Sal. Every single day, every single night, every single hour, every single minute. All I wanted was for Sal to be sitting next to me doing those interviews so that we could bounce things off each other as we always had done. We could talk to the media—together. I was feeling the pressure. Sure it might have looked OK when I was talking on TV. I said the things I wanted to say and didn't get angry with the world or bawl my eyes out but the bottom line was I didn't want to be there doing it by myself. A very real feeling of loneliness swept over me.

During a lot of those interviews they kept asking, 'Why aren't you crying? You shouldn't be able to sit here and rationally talk'. They just couldn't understand it. I replied, 'When I get up in the morning I know you guys are coming so I focus on it'. I wouldn't have got through what I have got through if I couldn't focus.

I would've been happier without the media attention but it was probably very beneficial because it got me talking about what had happened. From the beginning I had spoken about the landslide with the police, Mum and Dad, Euan, Margy, Harry and Grovesy. Then to the media, five times in four days. Talking was probably my best tonic.

During that week I got to see Feathers for the first time since the rescue. Channel Seven's 'Today Tonight' flew him down for a reunion story.

I was sitting in a chair and the cameras were rolling. I had no idea that he was even coming. All of a sudden he came into the room. With the cameras there it wasn't really personal.

It was such a surprise to see him I didn't know what to say. It ended up: 'Paul, how are you going?' 'Great.' 'Good.' 'How are the feet?' 'Good, mate.' It was all a little staged.

'Today Tonight' host, Peter Luck, was doing the interview. He was trying to get the emotional angle on our reunion but Feathers and I were just happy to see each other. We just sat down and started chatting as if we had known each other all our lives—it was straight back to where we had left off. You've got to remember I told Feathers everything the day they found me. He knew me back to front, from that 11½ hours that day. So it was just like one of my mates coming around for a chat.

The camera crew filmed everything: Feathers walking in, us shaking hands and sitting down talking, but about 20 minutes into the interview Feathers stood up and declared we were taking a break. I think he saw that I was doing it a bit tough in front of the cameras and he wanted to know if I *really* was coping. We walked into my bedroom and I broke down.

'Are you OK?' Feathers asked. 'How is it all going? I know it must be hard doing all this.'

'Yeah, I'm OK, I'll be fine,' I assured him. 'I feel within myself that I am coping OK.'

I explained to him how I mentally prepared myself for the interviews and that afterwards I would go and bawl my eyes out. I needed my quiet time.

Then we went back out and got back into it, until Feathers thought I'd had enough again and he would just stand up and walk out with me. He probably wasn't the easiest person to deal with as far as the media was concerned. But for me he was fantastic, his compassion for me, his concern for me, was the utmost. Before he got there Dad had been running the show, but Dad had had to go out for a while so Feathers took control. All the rest of the people in the house were from Channel Seven or the *Women's Weekly*.

When we were alone Feathers admitted to me for the first time that he really thought there was a strong chance I was never going to make it out of that hole. I suppose deep down I realised that fact but had not really wanted to face it. I knew it and he knew it but to openly talk about it made it seem so much more frightening.

Our mutual understanding comes back to the amazing bond that developed between us during my rescue. Our relationship has the same things that were important to me with Sal. It's trust. It's respect. It's compassion.

The affinity and the closeness we—Sal and I—have with Feathers, will always be there. I know I will never lose touch with that man. One day Feathers and I plan to just disappear, go to a beach house or something like that. We're both so busy with our lives but one day we'll get there. I think there are things about what happened to us during those 65 hours that he still wants to tell me. And I've got things I want to talk to him about ... one day we'll get away by ourselves and just talk.

I would have liked to spend a week with everyone involved in the rescue and I still would. I've still yet to meet one-tenth of the people who did unbelievable things for me and it is likely that I will never meet all of them.

The host of Channel Seven's 'Witness' program, Paul Barry, asked a fair few pertinent questions during my time with him. One particularly sticks in my mind—he asked me how, after all that happened, I could remain so positive.

I just looked him in the eyes and replied, 'After what I've been through, how can you be so negative?'

That took him back a bit. That night he and his crew went back to their hotel and had a long discussion on that one question. They realised they were so used to seeing negativity and being negative yet here I was being so positive. Paul didn't think it was possible. What did he want me to do? Did he want me to be a blubbering mess because that's what the media and the general viewing public has come to expect?

I was confronting what had happened to Sal and me, talking about it openly and trying to find something positive. The mere fact that I was sitting there, two weeks after the disaster, was a tonic. Just living day-to-day, dealing with what life was throwing at me, was something I wanted to achieve. I didn't give up when I was buried—I was not going to give up now.

I suggested we try it from a positive perspective and see how that went. I think it worked. The end product on the

'Witness' program challenged many people because it got them thinking: 'What the hell is going on? How can he be so positive?' During the program I deliberately tried to show that you could get through something very tragic in your life and still come out and *live*. It was no front—I was sitting there openly talking about the most painful event in my life to try to show people that despite what life throws at you, you can still go on.

It forced me to think about how I survived and how I was going to continue to survive. It reinforced my belief in my inner strength. I've no doubt that strength comes from my parents. Mum always said, 'Survival is a very interesting phenomenon ... if you've got something to survive for you'll survive'. I had plenty of reasons to survive.

Some people still can't work out where that strength to control my emotions came from. But the answer is pretty simple—it's purely because you've got to have that positive attitude. Every morning I woke up and I said to myself, 'Whatever you do today, Stu, do not cry on television'. The last thing I wanted to do was to be in tears on national television because I couldn't see that that would achieve anything. I'd made a decision not to cry and I didn't—publicly. Sure, I was an emotional mess for hours afterwards. But that didn't matter. That was me. My personal time. It was not something I wanted to share with 2.2 million viewers.

Don't be mistaken—every minute I was being interviewed I was upset. I controlled it purely because it would be more beneficial for the viewer (and for me) if I could coherently get my message across. I couldn't believe the feedback I received afterwards—such a large number of people were inspired by my survival, but more importantly, many were *more* inspired by the way I was coping.

Some months later the American ABC's 'Prime Time' came to Thredbo to interview me.

They focused more on my emotional recovery whereas the Australian media tended to focus more on the factual side. They decided to interview me on the site of the landslide. I had visited the site a number of times beforehand so going back there wasn't as emotional as they had hoped. I overcame any emotion I experienced by concentrating on what I had to do. Sure, to stand there where it had all happened was difficult but I'd made up my mind that it was not going to get to me.

At the end of a three-hour interview the journalist, Elizabeth Vargas, asked me, 'How can you talk about losing your wife and about all this obviously hugely emotional information and not be breaking down, crying?' I told her a little bit about focus. I said 'I get up in the morning and I come out here and I know that I have got to do a three-hour interview with you. So I focus on that'. I have always been able to focus on the job at hand.

I said, 'I come here, I focus, I do the job. But once it's finished I go home and hit huge emotional lows. It's not as if I'm not dealing with it, that I don't realise what's going on'. At the end of the interview she and the producer—both pretty hardened journalists—were near to tears. The camera operator was as well. The show went to air in the United States to 22 million viewers—it was hugely positive to think so many people might have gained *something* from my experience.

eighteen

Bye, Sal Pal

T he one thing that I still had to face was Sal's funeral. I was still very much focused on the future and what was going to happen to me mentally and physically—what the future held in store. I was dodging the other media, which was a lot of pressure, and I was still in intense agony most of the time. Those nails being driven into my feet kept my mind off my loneliness—in a bizarre way the pain did me a favour by blocking out the emotional pain for the first few weeks. It also helped strengthen my resolve—I would survive through this pain. When I was in the shower I would sit on my little stool with the warm water running over me and the pain would ease ... then the tears came ... and came. After the media left I didn't stop crying.

In the shower I felt warmth. I suppose it felt a little like someone cuddling me. Physical contact was what I needed. For the first few nights out of hospital I couldn't sleep alone. I slept in the same bed as Margy, Mum or Dad. I didn't want to be on my own, that was the last thing that I wanted. During the days I had people coming in all the time so I had human contact, lots of hugging and kissing. It wasn't joyous but it was so good—it gave me the strength to realise I wasn't facing this alone. I started to see more of my friends. All of Sal's friends, our university friends, Sal's family.

It was about this time that I met a Melbourne psychiatrist, Paul Valents. Doctors at Canberra Hospital had referred me to him. At first he just gave me a few pointers on what was probably going to happen to me, emotionally, in the short term. He told me how my mind would take me into survival mode, how it would help me get through by blocking out a lot of the emotional and physical pain. He broadly told me where I was at, mentally, and warned me it was going to get harder. I thought, no, it couldn't get any harder than this. I'd had it.

I began seeing Paul more regularly to help me through. He really helped me out.

We talked about the different feelings that I was having. One session, I told him I had a pain in my chest. We talked it through and found that the pain came from an explosive anger that I was being deprived of organising Sal's funeral. Paul asked me what I meant. I told him I thought the funeral was being stolen from me, that there was too much publicity and it would be a very public affair. We worked out that it infringed on the sense of intimacy I needed to have with Sal to say goodbye to her properly.

We continued to talk it through and it became clear that I basically felt helpless and powerless—the whole process had been taken away from me. Paul asked me if I had checked out if I was as powerless as I felt. Once we had brought this feeling out into the open I was overtly angry, but the pain in my chest had gone.

Paul said, 'Well, if you need to have your own funeral maybe you can'.

That was the impetus I needed. It had been a long delay— Sal had been pulled out of the rubble about two weeks earlier. So her funeral became my focus. There was the question of who to invite ... who do you invite? We invited friends and relatives Sal would want there. It was to be a cremation out at Fawkner Crematorium and Memorial Park. I didn't want the media to know about it so we didn't list it in the newspapers and asked the funeral home for the utmost confidentiality.

The day before the ceremony I went to say goodbye to Sal—that was hard. I went with Dad. Mum didn't want to see Sal because her last memory was the beautiful, smiling Sal, doing the ironing in our flat in Bimbadeen. Mum didn't want to destroy that image.

At the funeral parlour a man came out talking in quiet, hushed tones, asking me what I wanted done on the day. I had no real idea so I basically let him take over the organising. Then he took us to see Sal. She was lying in a little chapel. I walked up to where she lay and saw her for the first time since we had gone to bed on the night of the disaster. She looked different—time had obviously taken effect, her skin was deteriorating and she looked a lot thinner—but she was still my Sal.

They had made her up beautifully and she was wearing one of her favourite dresses, which had been in a cupboard at Margy's. She looked at peace. But she wasn't the Sal that I remembered, the Sal I wanted in my arms, smiling Sal's smile. I felt a need to reach out, to touch her, so I kissed her. I said 'See you later Sal pal' and that was it.

The man from the funeral parlour came and asked me if I needed more time—I didn't. I'd said goodbye. What else could I do? Dad waited for me down the back. When I had finished he went up to say goodbye to her. When he'd finished we held hands and walked out together.

It's something I'm so glad I did because my final memory of Sal, even though I couldn't see her face, was of a terrified young woman screaming bloodcurdling screams. I had to see her at peace otherwise all I would ever remember was a mirror of terror.

She still looked beautiful. I'm so glad I went to see her. Bye, Sal pal.

Even though the funeral was an emotionally hard day, it was a day that I enjoyed because all of Sal's friends were there. It was good to see them all paying tribute to my wife. For me it was the real closure of Sal going—the cremation, the little jar of ashes at the end of it. I had actually looked forward to the day because I knew what sort of day it was going to be. A day to celebrate Sal's life.

Somehow the media found out what day it was on and staked out our home. But Euan and Susie managed to sneak me out the back door. There was no media at the chapel.

I read the eulogy:

'As we all know Sal was a unique, loving, caring and sharing person. She gave her love not only to myself but to her family, friends and everyone she came in contact with.

'The last few days I spent with Sal were living

hell. What gave me the strength to survive was the immense love I had for Sal, but more importantly the immense love Sal had for me. Without her spiritual support over that period I would not have survived.

'I found a short poem which I feel sums up that time.'

I chose two poems by Michael Leunig:

'Love is born
With a dark and troubled face
When hope is dead
And in the most unlikely place
Love is born
Love is always born

'We all now have a journey to take. Sal's path is set but ours is a much more difficult road to follow, I ask us all not to dwell on the tragedy and loss but to build on all the positives of Sal's life and use this as a base to grow even stronger.

'Let it go, let it out
Let it all unravel
Let it free and it can be
A path on which to travel.'

I was shattered by the time I'd finished. Sitting back down in the front row I just stared at the candle, the flowers and the photos of Sal and me that adorned the front of the chapel. It kept going through my mind that this wasn't something I expected to have to face at the age of 27.

Anna read an open letter to her sister which, in part, read:

'Dear Sal,
We had such fun you and I. All those times keep flooding back ... and I smile ...

'Sal, none of us knew that you would go so soon and none of us were ready. But I just want to thank you for the precious and beautiful memories I have. I promise I will keep the 'Donald girls' spirit going. Thanks for helping me and being my friend as well as my sister. I love you Sal Pal.

Love Anna.'

As well as the private funeral we decided to have a memorial service on August 29th. Hundreds of people crowded the small community hall in Eltham, where Sal had grown up. I think just about the whole of Eltham was there.

It was basically the same service as at the chapel but this time family and friends got up to say goodbye.

Sal's cousin Sarah Jarvis was one of those who spoke.

'Life can be so cruel
but not as harsh as death
Life is loud and busy
and death a silent rest
At least I know she's resting
yet I suffer from such pain
The darkness stole her smile
and my tears fall down like rain
All my memories are happy ones
but all I do is cry
I'll remember her forever
and in my mind she'll never die.'

Sal's dad, Andrew, wrote a note, which appeared on the back of the service booklet.

'To our lovely daughter Sal,
Thanks for stopping by and sharing this past 27 years. We loved that special brand of beauty that only you could find.

What a joy it's been to watch you grow from that beautiful little golden girl into the beautiful young woman who unselfishly shared her warmth, compassion and love with all who came to know the sunshine of her smile.

Your courage and determination to make life into an adventure has, at times, left us in awe. You achieved so many goals in the art of living and giving.

We miss your quiet dignity.

We should have known that the time would pass too fast and that all too soon you would have to fly away ... just say goodbye ...'

'There were about 600 people crammed into that hall,' Andrew said afterwards. 'Friends from her primary school days through to her adult life were given the opportunity to speak about Sally. It was the little bits and pieces you learn about your child that are the greatest thing to have. Sally and Stuart had a life together that everyone would envy.'

'We had a daughter who lived for 27 years who did more things in 27 years than most people do in 50 years. While she was here she gave great joy, and she received enjoyment, but mostly she gave great joy and that's the thing she should be remembered for.'

If there is one thing losing Sal has taught me it's that you've got to enjoy today because it is quite possible that there is not going to be a tomorrow. Sal and I enjoyed every minute of our time together so, in a way, I feel that her life, no matter how short, was full.

I began reading newspapers and started to realise the magnitude of what had happened. It was nearly a month after the landslide and it was still big news. It wasn't until Princess Diana died in the Paris car crash that Thredbo—and I—were finally off the front page.

After Sal's memorial service I returned to Thredbo and moved into Cootapatamba apartments with Euan and Susie. It's on the same side of the valley as Bimbadeen. A lot of people couldn't understand why, or how, I could face coming back: 'What are you doing moving back to that side of the hill, to an apartment so close to the landslide?' Why wouldn't I? It was my home ... where I felt closest to Sal.

In the first few months I slept between 12 and 16 hours a day. It was about four months after the disaster that the dreams began. The first was about Sal—Sal and me together at home on the couch. It was so real I woke up thinking she was actually there. I've had that dream a lot—it's a nice ending for her, she's not mangled or hurt, just Sal the way I want to remember her. The dream ends with us going to bed. It's a really comforting dream. It's like she's right there. Still with me.

I guess the dream reflects what happened the night before the landslide. We always sat on the lounge before we went to bed. We'd talk to each other for a while and then we'd go to bed. A very happy, very intimate scene.

I wake up from this dream feeling Sal's presence. I wake up expecting her to be there, the dream is so real. My eyes open. I reach out and she's not there—that brings me back to reality.

You see, my whole life, every single second of the day in Thredbo, is a reminder of Sal. Even sitting in a house that Sal was never in, I feel she is still here with me, she's part of everything I do. Every day I walk past where she worked. Everything I look at in Thredbo has a connection to her— where we had done this or done that. Even my car—I've still got the same car, and every time I get into it I expect Sal to be in the other seat.

I have had to face what happened—I haven't tried to escape it. I have this fantastic dream as if Sal was here and wake up in the morning and she's not. I just roll over and think, 'Oh, that's right, here we go again. Another day in hell,' and get up.

Going back to Thredbo was good for me because it made me confront my loss—what was the point in hiding from it? I loved, and love, Thredbo: its people, its lifestyle, its beauty.

Sometimes people come up and stare at me, as if I'm somehow different or strange. Some people can't understand why I haven't gone around the twist. They're amazed that I haven't hit this big wall and crumbled. Instead I'm still smiling and still seem to be coping fairly well. I can see their minds ticking over: 'How can this person be like that?'

Since the disaster there are two Stuart Divers. One is the public Stuart Diver that I allow people to see; the other is very private and rarely do the two meet. I try to present the positive side of myself in public, whether on television or out at a restaurant. That's the image I want to portray to people. I feel that showing that life goes on even after a tragedy is most beneficial to them and, in the long term, most beneficial to me. But there's this other person who very few people get to know because it's mine; it's not for sharing.

nineteen

Life, the Universe and Nothing

I used to think I was invincible. I now know I'm not. When you go through something like I did you look back and you analyse every little thing about your life.

I met my psychologist Daren Wilson when he was engaged to assist the staff of Kosciusko Thredbo Pty Ltd. I knew I needed to speak to someone so when the opportunity arose to see him I grabbed it. I saw him on a fortnightly basis. With these sorts of relationships, it takes trust, and normally it takes time to build up trust but I got on with Daren from the word go. He was really easy to chat with and helped me with day-to-day issues—how to survive in the present with the loneliness and the immediate physical and mental pain. At that stage, I wasn't emotionally ready to delve into the real trauma of the disaster.

I felt a need to get away overseas for a month to visit friends and relatives. I thought it would be good therapy but in the end it became excruciatingly hard because they all, understandably, wanted to ask me 'What happened?' No matter where I went I still couldn't escape what had happened. Even in a tiny pub in Limerick, Ireland, a woman who happened to be in Sydney at the time of the landslide recognised me.

I came back pretty emotionally drained and was ready to just disappear. I went back to Thredbo and tried to hide but it was impossible. I had previously agreed to do work for numerous charities and probably overcommitted myself—I basically ended up with no time to myself whatsoever.

I hadn't seen Daren for about six weeks and that, in psychological terms, was dangerous for me. I saw him several times when I returned and with his help soon began to deal with things reasonably well. It was almost Christmas.

By New Year's the build-up had begun for the Winter Olympics in Nagano, Japan. I had agreed to be part of the team covering the games for Network Seven. It was a daunting prospect.

I had to go to Japan for a week to shoot some stories in preparation for the Winter Olympics. I had a brief session with Daren before I left but we only skimmed the surface. He suggested we shouldn't open up the can of worms at that stage because I had to get through the Winter Olympics. I'm sure he could see that I was about to hit the psychological brick wall he had been expecting me to hit.

The day before I left I was thinking: 'What the hell am I doing? I have so much to deal with in my life without doing this'.

When I first met the producer, Stuart Goodman, he gave me some priceless advice: 'Whatever you do, always be nice to the camera operator. If you aren't nice to the camera operator he or she will make you look shocking. Secondly, be nice to the sound operators as well because they can make you sound awful. Lastly, and most importantly, be nice to the producer—if you aren't nice to the producer you'll end up in a lot of trouble'.

The hardest part of that whole trip was when we visited the Zen Kogi Temple, one of Japan's biggest Buddhist temples, to film a couple of 'stand-ups'—short pieces where I address the camera. Stuart, the producer, said, 'Isn't this fantastic?' I replied: 'Mate, this is unbelievable. What a great experience. But it actually means nothing to me because I can't share it with Sal'. I was enjoying scenery that I know Sal would've loved, and that's when despair hit me in the face again.

When I came back I told Daren I was ready to go deeper—to handle whatever my mind was ready to throw at me. He was concerned as I had to go back to Japan for the Winter Olympics coverage within the week but agreed to do four four-hour sessions. Normally the sessions would be shorter and spaced out over a longer period but because I was living in Thredbo and travelling to Sydney to see him we decided to do it all in a seven-day period. It was really hard. He dragged me emotionally lower than I had ever been before. We broke down the whole tragedy into minute episodes and examined each one in detail. It was an overwhelmingly sad and painful process.

The second trip to Japan was a bit easier because I now had a better idea of what was going on. Yet I felt that I had been thrown in the deep end when I was asked to do a live interview in the studio. I was sitting there thinking, 'This is getting even more bizarre'. I had make-up on, nicely brushed hair and there I was sitting under the bright lights of the studio—prime time in Australia—talking about skiing conditions.

My confidence grew and by the end of the games I was going out with my own camera crew and a driver. I had a great time. It was so much fun, and it was good therapy because I met a lot of people who genuinely liked what I was producing. For the first time I was dealing with people who treated me as Stuart Diver the person, not Stuart Diver 'the survivor'. With next to no television experience the whole thing could've gone terribly wrong but it turned out to be a hugely rewarding experience.

After the Olympics I headed for the States and Canada, to where Sal and I had spent a winter working. It was strange sitting in the restaurant where Sal had worked as a waitress—sitting there alone I felt like I was drowning in the memories. At Beaver Creek I met up with some close friends of Mary Phillips, a friend who hadn't survived the slide. It was an emotional time for me and for them as they hadn't spoken to anyone so directly involved with the disaster and I was able to give them an insight into what had actually happened. There were tears as well as laughter as we shared our memories of Mary. They took me to where they had scattered her ashes on a secluded ski trail in a snow-covered pine forest.

Before I knew it I was home again. Home again to face reality. It was the end of March 1998 and it was time for me to start re-focusing again. I hadn't seen Daren for about eight weeks so we picked up where we left off.

I really believe a person's mind is their most powerful weapon. Some use theirs better than others, so therefore some cope better than others.

I believe that the mind can be divided into thirds—33 per

cent is genetic, what you get from your parents. My parents have very strong minds and their parents did as well—so I was just lucky there. The next third comes from a person's environment, how they were brought up. My childhood was great and helped sculpt me into a decent human being with a good moral base—compassion, love, happiness, caring and sharing. I was also put through a lot of outdoor adventuring, which showed me how much I could take without falling to pieces.

The remaining 33 per cent is what you *do* with the first 66 per cent. A person could have the first 66 per cent but not use any of it and then it'd be useless, wasted.

Daren said that my mind 'was psychologically robust with a strong, flexible and dynamic ability to adapt to the traumatic horrors' I was exposed to. Many people think my survival *made* me stronger and maybe it will in the long term. But in the short to medium term it was the original robustness of my mind that made me able to deal with that amount of trauma.

When I first met Daren he warned me there would come a time when I would realise that I should really start working on the emotional side of my recovery. He had a pretty simple way of explaining what I was experiencing. Everyone has a short-term storage area and a long-term storage area in their brain to process emotional experiences. The short-term storage area acts as a filter system for long-term memory storage. The information comes in; the short-term storage area filters it, gives it a little tag and puts it into the long-term storage area for access at a later stage. In everyday life the system works fine—information comes in at a speed that your short-term storage area can cope with.

But when you experience trauma, whether it's a car crash, or something like I went through, the information surrounding the event enters your mind too rapidly for your short-term storage area to be able to sort it. According to Daren the traumatic information can't be filtered like everyday events 'because of the sheer volume, volatile nature and rapid absorption rate of information that enters the mind when a person faces the very real terror of fighting for their lives'. The problem is that it doesn't just disappear; it bypasses the short-term filter and goes into no man's land, somewhere between both the short- and long-term storage areas. It remains volatile and raw, waiting to be sorted and moved into long-term storage so it can be accessed in the future.

It's possible to control all that volatile information for a time but one day it may emerge; this can be enormously damaging, possibly leading to a mental breakdown. For me at this point, some of the volatile information was beginning to emerge and I was losing control. I was suffering a constant ache in my chest as though my heart was being crushed; I was openly crying and beginning to resent people around me for no reason. It frightened me so I decided I really needed to sit down and begin doing the hard yards. My motivation was that Daren had said that if I worked at it and sorted these emotionally volatile memories into long-term storage, they wouldn't come back to haunt me.

But to do that Daren had to get the information back out in the open. He took me to the lowest of lows so we were able to re-sort my memories, balance them with my positive beliefs and file them for long-term future reference.

We sorted the information in a way that balanced the worst and best of my memories. I confront a negative thought immediately as it enters my mind and match it with a positive thought.

Whenever I have to talk about the landslide that's all I do: *talk.* I have already processed the negative aspects of my experience and replaced them with positive memories. This allows me to talk about the landslide to any person I want, for as long as I want, and really show very little external emotion because the memories are so well placed in my mind.

I have already dealt with the emotions with Daren, when he was helping me to pull all those memories out. I could never get emotionally lower than that; I was just a sobbing mess.

We used a time line of the disaster as our structure for working through the memories. To begin with we looked at the first 30 seconds and worked on releasing all the memories of that crucial period. I was shocked by the amount of material in my head relating to those first 30 seconds. Until I started working with Daren I had a fairly simplistic view:

the building came down, Sal died, that was it. But when we began analysing that 30 seconds I realised how many important things did happen. It took us about 18 pages to write it all down.

The memories came out in no order at all and at a million miles an hour. We spent eight hours drawing out and analysing the first 30 seconds. Then we put them into some semblance of order by selecting the crucial pieces of information, such as Sal screaming or me having my hand over her mouth when the water flowed in.

When we analysed everything that happened and everything I did under the rubble some very significant points emerged. I looked for a way out—that was self-preservation. I tried to help Sal—I was trying to care for others. And then my attention returned to self-preservation. To know that I had the ability and inner strength to get through it is very comforting now. I think: 'Well who cares what happens to me now? I already know I've got that inner strength, that robustness, to get through the worst'.

We studied the whole 65-hour period, broke it down into a number of incidents and concentrated on each one. There might be several negative aspects attached to one incident— what we had to do was think of something that related to it in a positive way. Obviously I had really wanted to take care of Sal, because I tried to stop the water flowing in. I couldn't stop the water but I knew that Sal and I had always taken really good care of each other and tried to care for others, and this is a positive. It's the positive that, in the end, balances the negative aspects of my experience.

Daren and I created positive reference points in my mind. When I think of any aspects of the landslide that could be really, really negative, my mind immediately flicks to the positive thought of how Sal and I cared for each other. The idea is that over time negative aspects of the landslide will actually start to leave me with a positive feeling of Sal and me caring for each other.

If it weren't for Daren's work I wouldn't have the quality of life I have today because I'd be constantly depressed. I still hit deep depressions but now I have some control. Daren knows how to help me lift myself back up.

To many men, seeking help flies in the face of the old macho Aussie bloke image: the myth that males don't need psychologists because they're tough and don't need people like that. But communication is the key. When you need help you should go and talk to someone—anyone—an independent person. Females don't seem to have a problem talking to people about their problems but males, I think, very rarely talk about their emotional side.

None of this has been an easy learning curve. My recovery has been bloody hard and it still is. I have never really been one to like hard work but if I can see a point to doing something I'll work unbelievably hard at it. It's been tough, physically as well as mentally. I've still got all my toes but some aren't too good. The frostbite has affected the circulation in my left calf so the muscles in my foot are wasting. My foot aches constantly. I'm seeing a physiotherapist regularly who has to virtually dislocate my toes over and over again. I hear the tendons crack as my toes get pushed back—it's agony.

A lot of letters I received after the landslide referred to me as 'an inspiration'. But what did I do? I'm just an ordinary bloke. The people who wrote those letters may not realise that they were, in turn, an inspiration to me—they inspired me to take up public speaking. It's yet another alien world I've been thrown into. I would never have entertained the idea of speaking in front of hundreds of people before the landslide.

I've had no formal public speaking training. Usually I just write down about ten words and go from there. I've always believed that if you have the knowledge and a belief about a particular topic it is very easy to talk about it.

I've presented speeches where 20 per cent of the audience has ended up crying and I wasn't even touching anything *really* emotional. Their tears have made me realise that maybe I *can* have a positive effect on people—that I *do* have a message to give. That message changes depending on who I'm talking to but mostly it relates to the general theme of overcoming mental and physical pain or adversity. If I sense there's people in the audience crying or starting to get too emotional, I immediately back off because I'm not there to cause people pain. But I've always liked to test and push the boundaries. So I do. If there is something positive to be gained from me taking them down to that emotional low and then bringing them back up, then I will.

One of my opening lines is: 'If I'm getting on my preacher's box someone put up their hand and tell me because I don't want to be preaching to you. I don't want to be lecturing you about Stuart Diver's solutions to the world's problems. What I want to do is share some things with you. You can take them or leave them. You might not agree with what I say or you might agree and think it is fantastic. And that's great. That's what we are all here about, challenging our minds and challenging ourselves.'

A Salvation Army officer came up to me after one of my speeches and said, 'What you've done, Stuart, is you have made these people go away and think. Maybe the majority of what you have said here hasn't sunk in yet but tonight they'll get home, they'll be sitting around talking to their family or friends and they'll think about it'. That's great. If I talk to 300 people, then they go and talk to another three people each, before you know it, almost a thousand people have heard my message.

I can imagine Sal up there looking down at me, laughing: 'What the hell are those people listening to him for?' She would find it quite funny. But I seriously think she would be completely behind what I'm doing.

twenty

Surviving Life's Landslides

I feel I am, overall, the same person now that I was before the landslide. What happened to me simply reinforced everything I already believed in. I suppose you could say that my experiences have made me stronger because I had to use every single reserve I had—physical and mental—to get through.

I can understand some people listening to me thinking: 'Yeah, that's fine for you. You were put through that. You came out of it so you know you can survive the worst. But what about me? I haven't been through anything like that so how do I know my own inner strength? How do I know that I too would be able to survive adversity?'

I believe that it *is* possible to prepare yourself mentally for adversity. This doesn't just mean disasters such as the Thredbo landslide, it can mean any of the stressful or traumatic experiences that life might throw at you. I've done a lot of thinking since the landslide and have spent time analysing the key factors in my survival and recovery. I believe these can help all of us survive life's adversities, or recover from traumatic experiences.

Family and friends are the most important assets you have

The most significant conclusion my psychologist Daren and I arrived at, after months of analysing what happened to me, is that family and friends are the most important assets you have. During the time that I was buried the over-riding focus for me was my family, my close friends and, although at the time I didn't know them, my rescuers. By concentrating on surviving to see my family and friends again I was able to conjure up an amazing feeling of strength and power. I wasn't going to let myself die, as I had to see them again. On top of that I knew that my family, friends and rescuers would be doing all they possibly could to rescue me and, even though at times doubt crept in, that knowledge gave me the strength to survive.

As time has progressed the importance of family and friends has magnified. Without their support it would have been a lonely existence. Sometimes we take our family, friends and especially our partners for granted. It's not until we lose them or are in a position where we really need them that we realise just how vital they are.

Stability in life is crucial

Whether it is stability in a relationship, financial stability, stability at work or home or a stable group of friends, stability in life is crucial to our mental and physical wellbeing. This is because it gives reassurance, contentment and provides a great base from which to expand and grow. Stability was central in my relationship with Sal. When Sal died that stable part of my life was physically gone, but spiritually she is still here—still providing support, reassurance and giving me the mental strength and drive to go on.

Stability comes ultimately from within you. By feeling content with what you're doing in life you will feel a calmness which gives you the strength to go on to challenge, and survive, life's ups and downs.

Have respect and compassion for others

The kindness and hard work of the many people who helped me during and after the landslide reinforced the importance of having respect and compassion for others. Selfless volunteers, such as those from the Salvation Army, the SES, the Volunteer Rescue Association or the Red Cross, as well as the tireless efforts of the professional rescue organisations, amaze me—their respect and compassion for humankind seem boundless. My faith that there were people out there trying their hardest to rescue me helped give me the strength to survive on my own underground.

You never know when you are going to need volunteers like the Salvation Army, or a rescue or medical team to save your life, but there's no doubt you'll hope that they'll be there showing respect and compassion. If we are to hope that others will be there to help us when we need it, then it is only fair that we too try to develop the same respect and compassion.

Keep going, keep persevering, never give up

Overcoming adversity is not an easy task. There were many times while I was buried, after Sal died, when I hit the depths of despair and felt like quitting. I was physically and mentally pushed beyond my boundaries into areas I hadn't been, even in my worst nightmares. My survival showed that as humans our over-riding natural instinct is to keep going, to survive. Even when I tried to quit, to end it all, there was a part of my mind that wouldn't let me go. Maybe it was a blind faith in my inner strength, Sal, my family, friends or the rescuers. Even when all seems lost, keep going, keep persevering and never give up because even though it may take a long time you'll make it to your goal in the end.

Communication is the key to recovery

We all need someone to talk to, especially in times of tragedy or hardship. We need to not only talk about physical events but about the emotion attached to these events. Talking about the feelings attached to a certain event with a friend, family member or a professional such as a psychologist can release the pain and sadness and allow you to move on. It is possible to keep all this emotion within you but from my experience to do that will slow the path to full recovery, to fully getting over a problem, small or large. Communicating about my fears, hopes, dreams and despairs was the key to releasing my pain and sadness and gave me the ability to be positive and get on with life.

Community is strength

The day they dug me out of the rubble was charged with a positive energy coming from the faith of millions of people who were watching and praying. Imagine if we, as a community, could channel that energy every day. Imagine what a positive world we would live in.

If Australians could use the friendship, the mateship and what I like to call the love that come out of crises such as Thredbo—if they could harness those things all the time— then Australia would be a much more positive place. Why does it take a tragedy like the Thredbo landslide or the Port Arthur massacre for us to pull together? Look at how Australians have pulled together during war and other crises. Why can't we find that spirit all the time, not just in time of crisis or hardship?

The Thredbo rescue operation showed what we could achieve as a community, as a society. As individuals we can accomplish a lot but as a community we have the ability to achieve seemingly unachievable goals.

Live for today but plan for tomorrow

I think that if there is a philosophy that guides my life this is the one: live for today but always plan and dream about tomorrow. That's what I do. That's what keeps me going. If anything, the landslide taught me that we must live for today— we don't know what's going to happen tomorrow. Enjoy each moment to the full. At the same time make sure you have a plan for the future so when tomorrow becomes today you'll be ready for it.

twenty-one | The Jigsaw Puzzle

My life is now a jigsaw puzzle with lots of little pieces missing. It has gone from being a nice, easy two-dimensional 100-piece jigsaw puzzle with a very simple pattern to being a three-dimensional jigsaw puzzle of the Empire State Building. Someone has come along and taken out crucial pieces of the foundations so that the Empire State Building is looking a little shaky. But there is no reason why I can't find new pieces and go on with my life.

Even considering all the pain and grief in my life the opportunities now before me are unbelievable. In my wildest dreams I wouldn't have imagined half of them. My dreams get bigger and better and I find more reasons to live every day. So I get up and live. If I didn't I'm sure Sal would be extremely disappointed because I, like all of us, have so much to live for. I lost so much but I have so much to live for.

My survival, and the media attention that followed, have allowed me to touch the lives of many people so I want to make sure that I touch them in a positive way. That may be through my work with the media, charities or public speaking. I also know that in the future I may one day again share my life with someone special, which is a very exciting prospect.

Time these days doesn't seem to be my own, which has been a problem for me. There are so many external pressures, pressures that have come with being a 'survivor'. Put simply, if I'd had a choice I wouldn't be in this situation. But, seeing as I am, I want to make certain that I take full advantage of those pressures—such as the media and public speaking—and make sure I use them in a positive way.

I have made some life-changing decisions since the landslide and every one of them hasn't just involved me, my family and friends but also 18 other people and all their families. These decisions, whether it was moving back to Thredbo, working with the media, public speaking, buying a house to live in or just *living* are all monumental in their own way. Any public decision I make has to take into consideration the effect it might have on the other victims' families.

One thing I'm thankful for is that I have had the right people around me to guide my decision-making process. If I didn't have the right people around me—whether it's my family and friends, Daren Wilson, Harry, my accountant or a good solicitor—I've got no idea how I would have ended up. I couldn't have done it on my own.

I haven't retreated from having to make choices in my life because the landslide reinforced how vital the decision-making process is. Sure, people can make bad choices and continue to make them but one day, hopefully, they'll make the right choice and that will turn their life around. What's important is that people keep making choices in their lives and never give up.

I owe my life to a lot of people. The pressure for me to carry on is fairly great because I don't want those rescuers to have put their lives on the line for nothing. And I don't want those 18 people—those 18 fantastic people—to have died for nothing. I often wonder where their spirits went after they died. Their bodies were in that building but where did their spirits go? I hope that perhaps a part of each and every one of them was somehow transferred to me so that I have some of the special and good qualities that they had.

Obviously Thredbo has taken a lot away from me. I can't deny that. It took half my life away from me. But the bad memories are not what I picture when I look at Thredbo now because of all the positive things I associate with the village— the good times, the good memories. I can sit here now, gaze out my window and look straight at the landslide site, look at where Sal died, where I was lying for 65 hours, and of course I have very negative thoughts. I can't and won't hide from what happened but my mission in life is to turn what happened into a positive force. I have photographs of Sal next to my bed, but how long that will last I don't know. I may get to the stage where I want to keep her memory in my mind, without physical reminders everywhere. I'm going to set aside a little place as a memorial to her … I'll always have that.

I will never forget Sal. I simply don't want to. What I aim to do is concentrate very hard on the future while still holding on to the important memories. I've seen people who have lost loved ones who never detach themselves from the past and end up destroying their lives. I know that I have got to go on.

I'm not ashamed to admit that one day I hope to have another intimate friend. That is a part of my life, a part of my dream. One day I hope that the right person will come along and I'll be able to share my life with someone again. I know that's what Sal would want me to do. I have a list of things missing in my life. It's not very long: an intimate friend.

Sal's sister, Anna, came to visit me about two weeks after the landslide. She said that as soon as I was pulled out alive and she found out Sal didn't make it, all she hoped was that, some time in the future, I would meet someone as fantastic as Sal.

Shortly after my rescue I met Wendy O'Donohue's father Tom. What he told me had an enormous impact on me. His wife had died and he had eventually remarried, and he said, 'Stu, don't worry mate, you'll get married. You're only 27 and life will go on'. I thought that advice showed incredible strength and compassion coming from someone who was going through so much grief of his own at the time, having lost his daughter in the landslide.

I do worry that anyone I become emotionally attached to in the future will face enormous pressures. I'm carrying plenty of baggage, which hopefully I will manage to cope with. That baggage includes what happened to Sal and me, it includes the media, the attention of the public, my friends and family. Anyone I meet will probably find themselves under the public microscope and that does concern me—I don't want to hurt someone else, enough people have been hurt already.

I am never going to forget anything about my prior life but I do have to draw a line so that I can make a fresh start. I can't live in a dream world thinking that Sal is going to walk in the front door one day. There's got to be a separation somewhere along the line so life can go on.

With the tools that Daren, my psychologist, gave me to convert the negatives into positives I'm able to look at the myriad of negative reminders and achieve something beneficial, whether that might be a feeling of calmness or an overwhelming urge to help someone else.

In a way I was lucky because when Sal's life was taken almost everything we ever had together was taken too. I didn't have to go back into the bedroom and empty all of Sal's clothes out of the wardrobe. The landslide was so final. When I came out and arrived at Canberra Hospital I had nothing, absolutely nothing, left of our relationship. Now my most treasured possession is on the third finger of my right hand. There, sparkling for all to see, is Sal's engagement ring. I've got my wedding ring on that same finger—it's amazing the internal strength that I can muster just by rubbing them.

When Sal and I were separated while I was away for work or off on some adventure I would have a physical ache in my heart. I missed her and I would feel that ache. The ache hasn't been there since Sal died because there's no point aching for something you can't get. I can't get her back. Gradually the ache has been replaced by a calmness.

Being positive is my main aim in life; 99 per cent of the time I am yet there is still that one per cent when I question why I persevere. But having made it this far, I am going to keep going. Nothing will ever be as hard as what I have already been through so therefore it has got to get easier . . . one day.

I'm still living for today . . . but planning for tomorrow.

Roll of Honour

I'm certain there are people who played extremely significant roles in Thredbo during the landslide tragedy who I have not mentioned in *Survival*. Here is a list of rescuers and support staff which was compiled based on similar tributes published in *The Daily Telegraph*, *The Sydney Morning Herald* and *The Australian*. It does not, however, name every local in Thredbo even though each and every one lent a hand one way or another. They know who they are and my thanks will always be with them.

NSW Police Service

Aalders, Mick
Adams, Paul
Ahern, John
Allman, Paul
Ashton, Stephen
Baker, Craig
Baker, Terry
Ball,
Barker, William
Barry, Matt
Beacroft, Lindsay
Beasley, Kel
Begg, Michael
Bell, Stuart
Bernasconi, Geoff
Bowditch, Mick
Brodie, Dave
Burcham, Brett
Burden, Andrew
Butterworth, Bradford
Cacciola, Guiseppe
Callander
Cameron, Carl
Chaplin, Paul
Charleston, Fiona
Clarke, Chris
Clarke, John
Clarke, Mitch
Clarke, Norm

Coady, Kevin
Cocksedge, Bob
Cole, Paul
Connolly, David
Coombes, Don
Cripps, Stephen
Csorba, Derek
Cunningham, Anthony
D'Bras, Rod
Daley, Kevin
Daniels, Phillip
Davies, Alan Bradgate
Davies, Peter
Day, Stephen
De Lorenzo, Stephen
Debruin, Ron
Denham, Warren
Dobell, John
Doble, Jason
Dohnt, Steven
Downes, Phillip
Doyle, Dam
Doyon, Paul
Drake, Glenn
Duncan, Ray
Elliott
Ellis, Ike
Emery, Jeff
Emms, Brian
Evans, Craig
Fairweather, Bob

Farr, Darren
Ferguson
Fitzer, Peter
Floor, Tony
Forbes, David
Forbutt, Peter
Ford, Michael
Ford, Michelle
Frazer, Russell
Friel, Peter
Gaunt, Andrew
Gill, Andrew
Glascock, Adam
Golding, Bob
Goodchild, Andrew
Gough, Roger
Green, Garry
Green, Mick
Gregory
Grima, Rachel
Grose, Andy
Grose, Brett
Hahn, Anthony
Hale, Jason
Hancock
Hancock, David
Hardinge, Ian
Hargreaves, Mark
Harvey, Ian
Hayes
Hayman, Michael

Hayson, Mark
Henshaw, Cameron
Hill, Anthony
Hill, Barry
Hinton, Tony
Hodder, Steve
Hoyer, Paul
Hubble, David
Hughes, David
Hurst, David
Ingram, Chris
Jarvis, Kevin
Johnson, Bruce
Johnson, Mark
Johnson, Moira
Johnson, Rob
Jones, Brad
Judkins, Greg
Keene, Don
King, Stephen
Kornberger, Wally
Lackenby, Glenn
Langdon, Colin
Langridge, Bob
Lawrie, John
Levey, Geoff
Little, Rex
Maddy, Brian
Mahony, Philip
Manchester, Wendy

Marcon, Peter
Mares, John
Markham, Steve
Martin, Richard
Mayhew, Michael
Mayo, Darrin
McCallum, Mark
McCarthy, Ian
McCarty
McCloghry, John
McCloskey, Phil
McClure, Steve
McCoullough, Andrew
McCrae, Darren
McGee, Ian
McGrath, Stephen
McKay, Andrew
McLay, Peter
Mealing, Tim
Michelle, Janine
Millar, Gordon
Mitchell, Mick
Moore, John
Moroney, Ken
Moroney, Peter
Moronte
Morris, Colin
Morrison, Belinda
Morsanuto, Paul
Mouawad, John
Murphy, Mark
Neilson, George
Neilson, Wayne
Nisbet, Kevin
Nixon, David
Nunan, Nicole
Nyholm, Douglas
O'Connor, Gerard
O'Connor, Mark
Opryzsko, Mich
Parker
Parker, Ian
Parrish, Barry
Parsons, Neil
Pearce
Pearce, Philip
Pearson, John
Phillips
Porta, Michael
Powderly, Mark
Purcell
Rawnsley, Shane
Ray, Bruce
Rayner, Mervyn
Redpath, Derek
Richards
Robertson, Tracey
Robinson
Ronning, Sean
Ruming, Dan
Ryan, Michael
Ryan, Stephanie
Salmon, Greg
Sanderson, Charlie
Saunders, Philip

Schreiber, Paul
Sharp, Michael
Sladden, Max
Slingsby, Graham
Smith
Smith, Gary
Stephanjec, Peter
Stephenson
Stibbard, Ian
Stocks, Warren
Storey, Gary
Strik, Peter
Sullivan, David
Sullivan, Kevin
Sutton, Adam
Sweeney, Mark
Taseski, Peter
Taylor, Kim
Taylor, Paul
Toscan, Claude
Traunter, David
Tuck, Darryl
Turner, Lenore
Van Leeuwen, Lyle
Varley, Chris
Veltman, Irene
Verzosa, Emmanual
Vincent, Andrew
Wadwell, Rory
Wall, John
Wallace, Lindsay
Weir
Wheeler, Gerard
Whitbread, Stephen
Williams, Craig
Willis, Scott
Woods, Jason
Woodward, Stewart
Wright, Dean

Federal Police

Anderson, Rod
Braun, Roger
Carter, Rod
Davis, Peter
Fitzpatrick, Kate
Guy, Fr Peter
Kearney, Gavin
Laidlaw, Peter
Laing, Mark
Mitter, Cameron
Neuhaus, Steve
Roberts, Tim
Sargeant, Steve
Szarbo, Steve
Thomas, Gavin
Travers, Mick
Usback, Mark
Walker, Rod
Weise, Bob
Whyte, Ian
Williamson, Warren
Willis, Ben
Woodyatt, Ross

NSW Fire Brigades

Abel, Clayton
Aisbett, James
Allan, John
Allison, Clayton
Arnold, Bob
Arton, Peter
Ashforth, Bob
Askell, Michael
Atkinson, Royce
Ayers, Les
Bailey, Paul
Baldwin, Jonathon
Battaerd, Hans
Bearman, Steven
Benson, Ossie
Berg, Julie
Beudeker, Martin
Bird, Peter
Black, Mark
Bland, Jay
Boon, Darryl
Bowles, John
Boyton, Andrew
Brennan, Quinton
Bresnik, Frank
Bresnik, Mike
Brewitt, Neil
Bridges, John
Brown, Arthur
Brown, Michael
Brown, Tim
Brown, Tony
Buckley, Alan
Buckley, Peter
Butler, Michael
Camilleri, Tony
Campbell, Paul
Carroll, Michael
Clifford, Bill
Coleman, James
Cooper, Craig
Corbin, Doug
Courtney, Geoffrey
Cousins, Rick
Covey, Bruce
Cowie, Roy
Cox, David
Coyte, David
Crocker, Paul
Crocker, Sam
Crowe, Shane
Cunningham, Grahame
Curtis, Mick
David, John
Davies, Catherine
Davis, John
Day, Bob
Day, Laurie
Demkin, Robert
Denny, John
Deustchbein, David
Deveau, Pat
Dew, Chris

Diver, Euan
Dover, Guy
Dowling, Benjamin
Dryburgh, Peter
Dunbar, Darryl
Dunn, Ken
Durrant, Michael
Edmonds, Keith
Edwards, Brent
Elliott, Kevin
Erland, Ted
Evans, Richard
Ewin, Chris
Fabri, Chris
Farmer, Brian
Farmer, David
Fell, Jeffrey
Ferguson, Ross
Fitzgerald, Rob
Fletcher, Thomas
Fox, Tim
Freeman, Ross
Frust, Chris
Gallagher, David
Gallagher, Kim
Gardner, John
Garven, Bob
Garven, Genness
Geeves, Robert
Gehrig, Les
Giles, Bernie
Gillies, Les
Goldsmith, Rita
Golik, Rene
Goodwin, Dave
Gough, Mark
Graham, Steve
Gray, Leigh
Guiney, Sean
Guymer, Mick
Haddon, Craig
Halcomb, Graeme
Hall, Ricky
Hamilton, James
Hampshire Robert
Hampshire, Neil
Hands, James
Harley, Robert
Harris, James
Hastings, Matt
Hatton, Phillip
Hayes, Col
Henry, Glen
Hewitt, Colin
Hine, Ian
Hinton, Ross
Hirst, Steve
Hitchens, John
Hockey, Steven
Holland, Oliver
Houston, Gregory
Hughes, Bill
Hyland, Ross
Hyman, Steve
Irwin, George

Juniel, Norman
Kachel, Bill
Kelly, Ray
Kidd, Warwick
Killham, Robert
King, Gary
Kinlyside, Stan
Kirwin, Peter
Knight, Paul
Kop, Aart
Krimmer, Ian
Kursawe, Christopher
Lang, Bill
Langdon, Mark
Lapsley, Craig
Leone, Joseph
Lewis, David
Lidbetter, Geoffrey
Lindsay, Phillip
Lochart, Glen
Loche, Bradley
Lomas, Terry
Love, Keiran
Lynch, Paul
MacDougall, Ian
Maddox, Kris
Major, Bob
Mark, Andrew
Marr, Andrew
Marshall, Thomas
Marshall, Trevor
Mattheus, Rudolph
Matthews, James
Maynard, Dawn
McDonald, Michael
McDonald, Sidney
McDonald, Steve
McDonough, John
McGrath, Phillip
McIlrath, David
McLean, Peter
Meagher, Gary
Mechielsen, Ardie
Meers, Gary
Meeuwisse, Raymond
Meldrum, Ross
Messenger, Doug
Meunier, Serge
Milliken, David
Mills, Gavin
Mills, Michael
Mitchell, Greg
Mizon, Gary
Mockeridge, Dave
Mugridge, Garry
Munsey, Terry
Murray, Dave
Murtagh, Chris
Mylnarz, Ted
Neal, Trevor
Neale, Robert
Neely, John
Newson, Noel
Nicholls, Bede
Nicholls, Fred

Nugent, Damian
O'Brien, Chris
O'Connor, Kevin
O'Mara, Pat
O'Sullivan, Michael
Owen, Neville
Packham, Robert
Palmer, John
Parker, Charles
Patterson, Rod
Perkins, Steven
Peters, Hartmut
Pinnock, Bruce
Potter, Justin
Povey, Peter
Purdom, Mick
Rafferty, Paul
Reeks, Christopher
Reid, Robert
Richardson, Steve
Roach, Les
Roberson, Colin
Roberson, Robert
Roberts, Wayne
Roche, Jeff
Rose, Paul
Rouse, Scott
Rugg, Paul
Ryan, Stephen
Sandner, Walter
Sayer, Peter
Sefton, Andrew
Shields, Ross
Shires, Ricki
Sinclair, Kevin
Smith, Jim
Smith, Peter
Snow, Darryl
Speldwinde, Lindsay
Stacey, Peter
Staples, Wayne
Steltzer, Martin
Stevens, Wayne
Stringfellow, Mark
Sutton, Stuart
Swinney, Michael
Sykes, Christopher
Tait, Graham
Taylor, George
Thistleton, Stanley
Thompson, Terrence
Toms, Alan
Towle, James
Travers, Mark
Trueman, Roderick
Tucker, Phil
Van Der Meulen, Nathan
Warner, Tim
Warren, Garry
Warren, Mal
Watson, David
Watson, Greg
Wheeler, Andrew
Williams, Mark
Woodlands, Don

Wormleaton, Bob
Wright, Alfred
Young, Andrew
Young, Chris
Young, Wayne

ACT Fire Brigades

Barr, Conrad
Batho, Gary
Baulman, Brett
Bennett, Ian
Bennett, Jon
Blake, Pat
Bland, Ian
Bourne, Todd
Brandreth, Ian
Brideson, Mick
Brighenti, Danny
Brookhouse, Marc
Bryce, Graeme
Burns, Mick
Camilleri, Danny
Canham, Phil
Cartwright, Peter
Chavasse, Keith
Comerford Kevin
Cornock, Peter
Covington, Paul
Dance, Jim
Daniel, Ray
Edwards, Steve
Evans, Bernie
Evans, Kerry
Falconer, Des
Flanagan, Warren
Flynn, Brian
Fraser, Peter
Gallop, Stu
Gibbs, Steve
Gilbard, Dave
Goodwin, Neil
Hannon, Kel
Harrison, Norm
Hobbs, Michael
Hobbs, Peter
Hourigan, Ron
Ingram, Paul
Jones, Pat
Kaylock, Gavin
Kennedy, Ross
Kent, Greg
Lloyd, Martin
Mackin, Dave
McCleary, Ian
McGregor, Rob
McMillan, Barry
Meredith, John
Moore, Andrew
Moore, Ian
Munday, Rob
Newham, Peter
O'Brien, Peter
Prince, Dave
Prout, Nigel

Raymond-Jones, Ernie
Ross, Tony
Saunders, Neville
Scheetz, Jeff
Seery, Russ
Shaw, Wayne
Stafford, John
Streatfield, John
Streatfield, Russ
Swan, Jack
Talbot, Brian
Thompson, Andrew
Thornthwaite, Darrell
Turton, Brian
Van Der Sanden, Martin
Walford, Darrell
Walsh, Jim
Weston, Ron
Willimott, Wayne
Zeitelhoffer, Chris

Victorian Fire, Rescue

Arnold, George
Belot, Eric
Cheshire, Robert
Egan, Gary
Goland, Michael
Harris, Rod
Lucas, Neil
Nunan, Justin
O'Connor, Mark
Pearce, Tony
Pfeiffer, Bruce
Roach, Andrew
Swift, Peter
Treverton, Mark
Walker, Ken
Wilson, Barry

Queensland Fire, Rescue

Littlewood, Gary
Parker, Ross
Tinsley, Shane

West Australian Fire, Rescue

Bailey, Lloyd
Johnston, Bruce

Tasmanian Fire Service

Brown, Michael
Jones, Hugh

NSW Rural Fire Service

Aitchison, Barry
Alcock, Rowan
Allen, Andrew

215

Allen, Craig
Allison, Bob
Anderson, Ron
Andrews, Janet
Ayliffe, Mark
Bartell, Alan
Battig, Andre
Beckett, Michael
Bennett, Jan
Bennett, Keith
Bennett, Mark
Brewis, Ossie
Brown, Neil
Butters, Adrian
Clarke, Mark
Clear, Murray
Climpson, Ray
Cogan, Brian
Coman, Casey
Constance, Ashley
Cooper, Gary
Cooper, Mark
Coughtrie, David
Cullen, John
Currey, Gordon
Davis, Peter
Dicker, Ian
Dixon, Darvall
Edwards, Craig
Elliott, Geoff
Evans, Kerrie
Everett, Peter
Filmer, Jenny
Filmer, Peter
Fitzgerald, Peter
Fitzpatrick, Paul
Fletcher, Bill
Fletcher, Tim
Forbes, Steve
Furnter, Bernie
Gammell, Brad
Glasson, David
Golby, Alan
Golby, Max
Grant, John
Heany, Andrew
Helliar, John
Hinkling, Peter
Inskeep, David
Ivers, Peter
Jamieson, Peter
Jardine, David
Jennings, Rick
Jennings, Tony
Jones, Steve
Kay, Glynn
Kelly, Robbie
Kent, Mark
Kleinman, Monica
Liston, Tony
Litchfield, Gordon
Lynch, Neil
Mackay, Colin
Mackay, Steve
Mansfield, Bill

May, Stuart
McCrow, Bill
McKenzie, Kevin
McRoberts, Barry
Mugridge, Rodney
Myers, David
Myers, Terry
Nagy, John
O'Neill, Mike
Olsauskas, Daris
Olsen, Richard
Peet, Rein
Peisley, Gary
Percy, Joe
Peterie, Bill
Peters, Tom
Phillips, Winston
Porter, John
Power, Bernie
Power, Rob
Reader, Paul
Reid, Philip
Roarty, Mark
Robinson, Joe
Robinson, Pippa
Robinson-Obst, Fay
Russell, Rob
Russell, Tim
Saillard, Walter
Seymour, Alison
Seymour, Wayne
Sherlock, Ross
Sidorenko, Ray
Slater, Tony
Spratt, Peter
Suthern, Dan
Suthern, Gary
Suthern, Sue
Thompson, Lenny
Thompson, Lochy
Tidmarsh, Graham
Tidmarsh, Rodney
Van Dongen, Jack
Vermik, Pierre
Wallace, Ron
Walters, John
Walters, Ross
Ware, Alan
Ware, Michael
White, Ben
Wilkinson, Dunbar
Wolfe, Roland
Woods, Fred
Wright, Eddie
Wroe, Raymond

NSW Ambulance Service

Alden, Norman
Allen, Jim
Andronicos, Nick
Annetts, Peter
Armstrong, Grant
Arthurson, Dr. Robert

Aspinall, Gordon
Aynsley, Rev. Steve
Baker, Ron
Barlow, Ken
Barnes, Kevin
Bartley, John
Bates, Stephen
Bayliss, Dr Geoff
Beaven, Denis
Beazley, Mark
Benson, George
Birch, Rev. Gray
Black, Tony
Bradbury, Richard
Brennan, Tony
Brotherton, Phillip
Brown, Rodney
Burrows, Michael
Carey, Ron
Cherry, Peter
Childs, Greg
Choi, Rhoda
Clark, Geoff
Clarke, Barry
Clements, Peter
Coghlan, Jim
Coppin, Bill
Cotsios, David
Cribb, Leon
Cribbs, Peter
Crisante, Sergio
Croft, Peter
Croll, Neil
Cutler, Martin
Daniel, Peter
Davey, Genevieve
Dell, Peter
Dent, Allan
Dent, Gary
Devlin, Jim
Doughty, Chris
Dunlop, Wayne
Eadie, Malcolm
Edge, David
Edward, Paul
Ellems, John
Evans, Laurence
Farnell, Peter
Featherstone, Paul
Ferguson, Daniel
Ferguson, Tom
Field, Graeme
Flamank, Bruce
Fraser, Steve
Gargett, Craig
Garnham, Warren
Gately, Tony
Gatt, Harry
Gilliam, Jeff
Girr, Father Paul
Goff, Joseph
Goodridge, Steve
Goodwin, Dane
Grant, Darryl
Gray, Melissa

Gregg, Peter
Grimson, Kim
Gruer, John
Gulesken, Greg
Haddon, Jeff
Hansen, Greg
Hare, Tony
Harrold, Bob
Harrold, Stan
Hart, Don
Hennessy, Col
Herring, Ray
Higgins, David
Higgs, Larry
Higham, Peter
Honeyman, Col
Hughes, Steve
Humphries, Adrian
Hutchins, Craig
Isles, Ken
Jamieson, Chris
Jamsek, Anton
Jenkins, David
Johnson, Michael
Jones, Shirley
Kenny, Peter
Kernick, Paul
Keys, Scott
Knowles, Alan
Kruit, Rick
Lees, Chris
Leopold, Peter
Lilequist, Gus
Ling, Grant
Lumsden, Alison
Maher, Michael
Maiden, Baiden
Manson, Paul
Marks, Eric
Martin, Paul
Martz, Steve
Matheson, Steve
McCabe, Peter
McCarthy, Ian
McCormack, Judy
McDonald, Dale
McIlvanie, Howard
McKendry, Terry
McLachlan, James
McLennan, Paul
McQueeney, Chris
Meagher, Paul
Meillon, Lynn
Mewburn, Scott
Michael, Joe
Michlmayr, Frank
Miller, Rohan
Milligan, Robert
Mills, Michael
Monaghan, Michael
Mooney, Peter
Morgan, Dominic
Morris, Bob
Morris, Paul
Mower, Adam

Nelson, Terry
Newburn, Scott
Nicholls, Craig
Nicholson, Charles
Nicholson, Harvey
Noonan, Glen
O'Connor, Danny
O'Connor, Kerri
O'Donoghue, Peter
O'Toole, David
Osypenko, Rick
Parker, Laurie
Parsell, Brian
Plumb, Darren
Porter, James
Power, Wayne
Preston, Julie
Price, Rev. Phil
Pritchard, Ken
Purse, Jeff
Rebett, Mick
Reid, David
Ridge, Leyton
Rowlands, Peter
Rubino, Joe
Russell, Hugh
Ryan, Andrew
Sadowksi, Terry
Scullin, Lindsay
Shaper, Les
Sheers, Dave
Shepherd, Neil
Short, Craig
Sinclair, Gary
Smith, Ailsa
Smith, George
Smith, Keith
Smith, Sam
Sommer, Ron
Sopniewski, Peter
Sparks, Peter
Spencer, Ian
Spiller, John
Spowart, David,
Stone, Rev. Kevin
Straw, Chris
Symons, Garry
Taylor, William
Tebbatt, Stephen
Tester, James
Thompson, Kerry
Traynor, Murray
Turner, David
Turner, Garry
Vassallo, Alex
Walsh, Raymond
Wasley, John
Wasley, John
Watkins, Charles
Watmore, Peter
Watts, Graham
Webster, Graham
Webster, Susan
Wheatley, Mark
Whelan, Dr. Trish

White, Brian
Whiteley, Cheryl
Whitney, Bob
Whittington, Neil
Wilkinson, Chris
Williams, Anthony
Williams, Keith
Williams, William
Willis, Graeme
Willis, Ray
Willits, Louise
Willits, Rev. Tony
Wunsch, Andrew
Wunschl, Ralph

ACT Ambulance

Abigail, Michael
Blewitt, Michelle
Bohun, Michael
Callahan, Bob
Findlay, Ross
Hardie, Leanne
Hardie, Paul
Hastings, Matthew
Holdom, David
Hooper, Craig
Keogh, Chris
Manton, Ashley
McKenzie, Bruce
McKie, Peter
Mitchell, Steve
Nulty, Ross
Nuss, Darryl
Paulsen, Ken
Quiggin, Jon
Ribbons, Paul
Seddon, Richard
Snadden, Sally
Sutton, David
Wren, Howard

Doctors

Anderson, Brett
Belessis, Andrew
Breathour, Steve
Carroll, Vic
Corr, Craig
Edwards, Keith
Evers, Justin
Fischer, Chris
Fulde, Gordian
Harris, Roger
Hill, David
King, Michael
Kumar, Ajay
Kumar, Sashsi
Kumar, Simon
Lawrence, Hugh
Lockley, Scott
Manning, Ron
Meaney, Steve
Morris, Richard
Murray, Lindsay
Prineas, Stavros

Proctor, John
Ross, Gary
Sauvage, Alain
Talbot-Stern, Janet
Tall, Gary
Truskett, Phil
Woo, Michael

NSW State Emergency Service

Abbott, Alf
Abbott, Chris
Abel, Ron
Abernethy, David
Abrahams, Grahame
Ackerman, Conrad
Adams, John
Agustin, Greg
Alavanos, Peter
Alcott, Howard
Alcott, Roxanne
Alderson, Ross
Alderton, John
Alderton, Wilfred
Alexander, Franklin
Alexander, John
Alexander, Robyn
Allen, Craig
Allport, Damon
Allsop, Martin
Allsop, Murray
Amos, Michelle
Amos, Owen
Anderson, Duncan
Anderson, Kevin
Anderson, Malcolm
Anderson, Mathew
Anderson, Russell
Anderson, Steve
Anderson, Timothy
Andrews, Brian
Andrews, David
Andrews, David
Andrews, Mark
Andrews, William
Angel, Richard
Ansen, Coleen
Anson, Alex
Apps, Wayne
Ardern, Judith
Armanini, Sonya
Armstrong, Janet
Arnold, Terry
Arnot, Wal
Askew, Barry
Aspinall, Terry
Astill, Jeff
Astill, Jenny
Atkins, Lyn
Atkinson, Brett
Avery, Scott
Avery, Todd
Avis, Peter
Azzopardi, Paul

Bailey, Linda
Bailey, Richard
Baker, Bob
Baker, Gary
Baker, Kerry
Baldock, Tina
Banks, Norman
Barbic, David
Barnett, Hannah
Barrell, Mathew
Barrett, Ross
Barry, John
Barry, Wayne
Bartlett, Kevin
Bateman, Barbara
Bateman, Bill
Bates, Scott
Baxter, Peter
Beal, Suzanne
Beament, David
Beaver, Cherrie
Beaver, Jeffrey
Bedbrook, Arthur
Bedbrook, Jenny
Beddy, Anthony
Bekema, Claire
Bell, Andrew
Bell, Carey
Bell, Duncan
Bell, Paul
Bell, Robert
Bell, Robin
Bendeich, Trevor
Benson, Lorraine
Benson, Roger
Bere, David
Berry, David
Berzins, Michelle
Berzins, Zigic
Betty, Alexandria
Betty, Andrew
Beverstock, James
Billingsby, Malcolm
Birchall, Nathan
Birchall, Sandra
Birmingham, Paul
Bishop, David
Bismare, Graham
Black, Wallace
Blackman, Philip
Blanchard, Jeremy
Blank, Margaret
Blank, Tracey
Blewitt, Darren
Blicharz, George
Blow, Gordon
Blundell, Adam
Blundell, Peter
Blyde, John
Bobbin, Gayle
Boileau, Duncan
Bolton, Allan
Booth, Greg
Booth, Susan
Borgar, Kim

Borrowdale, Ian
Botting, Tamasine
Bourke, Pat
Boyce, Adrian
Boyd, Sue
Brand, David
Bratton, Christopher
Bray, Peter
Brennan, John
Bridge, Peter
Briggs, Peter
Bright, Patrick
Brill, Merv
Britt, Paul
Britt, William
Britton, Shannon
Brookes, Jannine
Brooks, Kimberly
Broome, Michael
Broomhall, Sue
Broomhall, Tony
Brown, Alan
Brown, Chris
Brown, Colin
Brown, Dale
Brown, David
Brown, Ray
Brown, Sean
Brown, Todd
Browne, Sarah
Bruce, Bonita
Bruce, Chris
Buckley, Paul
Bull, Andrew
Bullock, Matthew
Bully, Paul
Burgess, Terry
Burke, Michael
Burns, Andrew
Burns, Debbie
Burrell, Geraldine
Burrows, Mal
Bursill, Geoff
Bursill, Richard
Burt, Greg
Burton, Julie
Bush, Darrell
Butcher, Timothy
Butler, Allan
Butler, David
Butlin, Fiona
Butt, Joel
Byrne, Melba
Byrne, Ryan
Byrne, Stan
Byron, Brett
Byron, Garth
Caletti, Steven
Camarotto, Peter
Cameron, Beth
Cameron, Gaye
Cameron, John
Cameron, Leslie
Camm, Kenneth
Camm, Vernon

Campbell, Bronwyn
Campbell, Bruce
Campbell, David
Campbell, Keith
Campbell, Leisa
Carey, Bernard
Carey, Mick
Carlisle-Jones, Su
Carlson, Ian
Carlson, Scott
Carmichael, Drew
Carney, Ian
Carney, Michael
Carran, Bernard
Carrol, Mike
Carson, Maureen
Carson, Wayne
Cary, Warwick
Casilles, Harry
Catchpole, Douglas
Catchpoole, Margaret
Catlin, Kerrie
Catteral, David
Cave, Chantelle
Cawthorne, Noel
Chamberlant, William
Chambers, Peter
Chaplin, Ian
Chapman, Scott
Chapman, Tim
Chase, Troy
Chatwin, Peter
Chen, Richard
Cheney, Chris
Cherry, Cristian
Chifley, Angela
Chifley, Matthew
Childs, Susan
Chin, Steven
Chisholm, Grant
Christie, Trevor
Christmas, Kevin
Churches, Lee
Churchill, Amber Jane
Cinque, Peter
Clague, Patrick
Clancy, Colleen
Clark, Ben
Clark, Jeremy
Clarke, Deryck
Clarke, Steve
Clayton, Ron
Clegg, Adrian
Clements, Philip
Cliffe, Stephen
Cochburn, Craig
Cockburn, Mark
Coleman, David
Coleman, Justin
Coles, Donna
Coley, Michael
Collard, Anita
Collins, Danny
Collins, Graeme
Collins, Norm

Colquhoun, Robert
Colwell, Mark
Connolly, Les
Connolly, Ramsay
Conroy, Michael
Constable, Mark
Cook, Greg
Cook, John
Cooley, Donna
Cooper, Colin
Cooper, Liam
Cooper, Robert
Cooper, Robert
Cooper, Vicki
Cordwell, Richard
Corneliussen, Eddie
Corrie, Danielle
Corrie, Samantha
Corrigan, Brett
Cosgrove, Bob
Cotter, Natasha
Cotter, Patrick
Coulston, Warren
Couvee, Michael
Cox, Colin
Cox, Peter
Cox, Stephen
Craig, Graeme
Craig, Susan
Criddle, Anthony
Croker, Barry
Crombie, Terry
Cross, Ron
Crump, Doug
Cummins, James
Cunneen, Geoffrey
Cunneen, Peter
Cunningham, Michael
Cupitt, Reg
Curley, Anita
Curley, David
Curll, Roland
Currie, Neil
Currie, Rita
Curtin, William
Cuthbert, Mark
Cutler, Raymond
Dale, Peter
Daly, Chris
Daniel, Brett
Darling, Mark
Darman, Andrew
DaSilva, Andrew
DaSilva, Louise
Davey, Rod
Davidson, Allan
Davidson, Lyn
Davidson, Samantha
Davies, Adam
Davies, Belinda
Davies, Evan
Davies, Greg
Davies, Judy
Davies, Kylie
Davis, Scott

Davison, Kristy
Dawe, Keith
Dawson, Michael
Debrincat, Joe
Deitz, Derrick
Dekrell, Michelle
Delaney, Adrian
Demenezes, Lloyd
Denniss, Louise
Denny, Rowena
Denny, Wendy
Dent, Kevin
Dentler, Ray
DeRidder, Brian
Dernelley, Peter
Devine, Danielle
Dix, George
Dixon, Bert
Dixon, Sue
Dodd, John
Doherty, Lynne
Doherty, Peter
Dohnt, Rachael
Dollisson, Garry
Dollisson, Janelle
Dompedro, Rick
Donlan, Matthew
Douglass, Jeff
Douglass, Lois
Downs, Phil
Doyle, Dianne
Dregde, John
Drew, Carl
Drury, Rev. Paul
Duff, David
Duff, Mal
Duffey, Brian
Duffey, Kama
Duggan, Patricia
Duggan, Trudy
Duke, Aaron
Dumbrell, Maxwell
Dunkley, Karen
Dunlop, Brian
Dunning, Suzanne
Dunning, Vernon
Durkin, Anthony
Dutton, Phillip
Dwyer, Barry
Dwyer, Chris
Easterbrook, David
Edwards, Kevin
Egan, Jeffery
Elliott, Craig
Ellis, Malcolm
Ellis, Sam
Ellis, Tim
Ellison, Herbert (Jim)
Ellul, Simon
Elms, Megan
Emmet, Jim
English, Rebecca
Englund, Graham
Ensbey, Ron
Evans, Robert

Evans, Troy
Eyres, Justin
Fairhall, Christine
Fairhall, Jason
Farac, Gary
Farkas, Sue
Farnsworth, Lincoln
Favell, Keith
Fearnside, Catherine
Feilen, Alison
Fellowes, Bruce
Fellowes, Jamie
Fellowes, Neil
Fellowes, Richard
Felmingham, Kevin
Fenech, Dominic
Ferguson, Keith
Fergusson, Angus
Field, Brian
Field, Matthew
Filmer, Jenny
Filmer, Peter
Filmer, Tracey
Finiss, Anthony
Finlay, Scott
Finn, Michael
Finnie, John
Firman, Stanley
Firminger, David
Firminger, Eva
Fisher, Brenda
Fisher, Paul
Fisher, Robert
Fitton, Colin
Fitzgerald, Maurice
Fitzgibbon, Steve
Flack, Neil
Flanagan, Rhonda
Flanagan, Stephen
Fleming, Steven
Flint, Ben
Flood, Terry
Foley, Kathleen
Foley, Ron
Foley, Sandra
Forbes, Martin
Ford, Jason
Forknall, Donna
Fortheringham, Malcolm
Forty, Judith
Foster, Cas
Foster-Percy, Rodney
Fox, Bettina
Fox, Lucas
Francis, Angela
Franke, Kayleen
Franzi, Brett
Fraser, Tammie
Fredericks, Lawson
Freeman, Doug
Freeman, Kim
Freer, Robert
Freer, Stephen
Freeth, James
French, Jarrod

Fromaget, Muriel
Frost, Andrew
Frost, Chris
Fry, Gary
Fry, Pamela
Fry, Robyn
Fulton, Corey
Gambacciani, Fausto
Ganderton, Timothy
Gannon, Greg
Garancsi, Kathy
Garda, Rolf
Gatehouse, Stephen
Gates, Ross
Gatien, Paul
Gatt, Ray
Gauci, Steven
Gay, Anthony
Gaymer, Ronald
Geddes, David
Gers, Malcolm
Gescke, Dieter
Ghysen, Dave
Giannone, Dominic
Gibbons, Kathryn
Gibson, David
Giddins, Melissa
Gilbert, Andrew
Gilby, Jeanne
Giles, Belinda
Giles, Timothy
Gill, Susan
Gillies, Ron
Gillingham, Jon
Gilmore, Roy
Girvan, Mark
Girvan, Robert
Glazebrook, Robert
Godde, Jim
Godfrey, Jamie
Golden, Matthew
Goldsworthy, Trevor
Gonzales, John
Goodhew, Kenneth
Goodwin, Ian
Gordon, John
Gordon, Sean
Gorman, Chris
Gosden, John
Goshn, John
Gothard, David
Gothard, Rosanne
Gothard, Ross
Gould, Darren
Gould, Mark
Grainger, Brian
Grainger, Mark
Grange, Lorna
Grant, Anthony
Gravett, Tony
Gray, David
Gray, David
Grech, Craig
Greco, Joanne
Green, Barry

Greenway, Andrew
Gregory, Dean
Gregory, Martin
Grey, Keith
Grimm, Phil
Gunter, Trevor
Gurney, Mark
Hadden, Ian
Hahn, Michael
Haigh, Mandy
Hainsworth, Peter
Haley, Robert
Haley, Tamie
Hall, Andrew
Hamilton, James
Hammels, Paul
Hammond, Jean
Hancock, Thelma
Hanlon, Olivia
Hanna, Rebecca
Hannon, Megan
Harder, Kevan
Harding, Andrew
Hare, Rick
Hargreaves, Ken
Harker, Peter
Harlem, Monica
Harpley, Steven
Harragon, Barry
Harragon, Timothy
Harris, Lee-Anne
Harris, Richard
Harris, Ryan
Harris, Stephen
Harris, Tim
Harrison, Martin
Hart, Rachel
Hart, Richard
Hartigan, Natalie
Hartin, Denis
Harvey, Neil
Harvey, Ron
Hastie, Brian
Hatch, Anthony
Hawke, Phillip
Hawkes, Ken
Hawkins, Delma
Hayden, Lance
Hayes, David
Hearn, Craig
Hedges, John
Heldon, Stuart
Hely, Margaret
Hennell, Andrew
Hesketh, Robert
Hewat, Peter
Heyer, Nathan
Heyer, Robert
Hillman, Andrew
Hillsley, Russell
Hindi, David
Hine, Andrew
Hinton, Delwyn
Hjorth, Peter
Hoare, Michael

Hobbs, Bruce
Hockey, Steven
Hodges, Allan
Hodges, Bruce
Hodges, Mark
Hodgins, Gary
Hoffman, Damien
Holden, Linda
Holland, Arthur
Holland, Shane
Holmes, Joan
Holmes, John
Holwell, Suzanne
Holyoake, Sabrina
Hood, Kerry
Hook, Geoff
Hopper, Robert
Horner, Leonard
Horner, Monica
Horton, Alicia
Howard, Brian (Hori)
Howard, John
Howard, Peter
Hudson, Derek
Hughes, Nicole
Hughes, Peter
Hughes, Teresa
Hulkanen, Carl
Hulme, Gary
Hume, Gerard
Hume, Robin
Humphreys, Paul
Humphries, Elizabeth
Humphries, Joanne
Humphries, Louise
Hunt, Paul
Hussain, Sunny
Hyne, Matthew
Inglis, Ben
Irvin, Peter
Irving, Carla
Irwin, Bradley
Irwin, Linda
Jackson, Brett
Jackson, Ken
Jacobs, Brad
James, Greg
James, Jimmy
James, Rhonda
Jardine, Trevor
Jay, Ian
Jefferson, Tim
Jehn, Greg
Jelinek, Jerry
Jenal, Scott
Jenkins, Alan
Jenkins, Andrew
Jenkins, Michelle
Jenkins, Neil
Jennis, Anthony
Jeppesen, John
Jesshope, David
Johansson, Wolfgang
Johnson, Andrew
Johnson, Caroline

Johnson, Noel
Johnson, Pat
Johnston, Barry
Johnston, Colin
Johnston, Glenda
Johnston, Paul
Johnston, Peter
Johnston, Ray
Johnston, Richard
Johnston, Tristan
Jol, Catharina
Jonas, Peter
Jones, Alan
Jones, Athol
Jones, Christopher
Jones, Emma
Jones, Gary
Jones, Josephine
Jones, Joy
Jones, Kevin
Jones, Kevin
Jones, Mark
Jones, Merien
Jones, Michael
Jones, Tim
Jud-Brettingham, Marcel
Jumeau, Paul
Kalssen, Arnold
Kaszonyi, Rob
Kaye, Peter
Kelland, David
Kelly, Andrew
Kelly, Steve
Kelsey, David
Kelson, Robert
Kennedy, Brendan
Kenner, Daniel
Kent, Adam
Keogh, Paul
Kerr, Darren
Kerr, Libby
Kerr, Susie
Kershaw, Robert
Kidd, Marilyn
Kielbicki, John
Kielbicki, Katherine
Kiley, Brendon
Kiley, Claire
Kilsdonk, Kylie
Kinch, Andrew
King, Daryl
King, David
King, Jeff
King, Noel
Kirkwood, Elizabeth
Knapman, Amelia
Knight, Garry
Knight, Warren
Kohlhagen, Kevin
Kopko, John
Kopko, Wendy
Kristen, Wil
Kwan, Ken
La Cava, Peter
Lahey, Lynn

Lake, Peter
Lalor, Peter
Lamrock, Michael
Lane, David
Lang, Peter
Lasker, Janelle
Laszuk, George
Latham, Belinda
Latham, Christopher
Latham, Kim
Lauritzen, Matthew
Lavin, Brenden
Lawdy, Neil
Lawes, Don
Lawrey, Christine
Lawson, David
Lawson, Edith
Lawson, Mary
Lay, Edna
Lea, Brian
Leahy, Geoff
Lebreton, Sean
Lee, Joannah
Lee, John
Leech, Nathan
Lees, Brett
Lehmann, Ruth
Leigh, David
Lennon, Murray
Leov, Mark
Lester, Kim
Lewis, Earl
Lewis, Wayne
Lim, Irene
Lines, Kate
Lines, Stuart
Link, Stefan
Lintern, Ray
Liston, Malcolm
Little, Mark
Lloyd, Jack
Lock, Neil
Lofthouse, Dennis
Loneragan, Anna
Lonergan, Stephen
Long, Byron
Long, Faye
Longhurst, Mark
Lord, Cheryl
Lord, Peter
Lotze, Mitchell
Love, Adam
Lucas, John
Lupton, Scott
Lynch, Scott
Lyons, Michael
MacDonald, Karen
Machnig, Steve
Mackinder, Howard
Macklan, Geiffrey
Macklan, Mark
Maddock, Michael
Madge, Graham
Magus, Rick
Maher, Paul

Mahoney, Phil
Maiden, David
Maljevic, Joseph
Malone, Colin
Maltby, Nadine
Mammone, Gina
Manly, Denis
Mansfield, John
Mansfield, Susanne
Manuao, James
Marsh, David
Marsh, Jeff
Marshall, Clifford
Marshall, Daryl
Marshall, Gordon
Marshall, Greg
Marshall, Neil
Martin, John
Martin, Karen
Martin, Marion
Martin, Michael
Martin, Tony
Marting, Ross
Maslen, Heidi
McAlear, Kerri
McCabe, Brett
McCabe, Constance
McCarthy, Robyn
McCaskill, Don
McClory, Grant
McCole, Bill
McConnell, Greg
McCormack, Greg
McCurley, Dale
McDarra, Gracie
McDermott, Annette
McDermott, Michael
McDermott, Patrick
McDonald, Barry
McDonald, Malcolm
McFadden, John
McGibbon, Alison
McGlinn Christine
McGovern, Daniel
McGowan, Les
McGregor, Christine
McGregor, William
McHardie, Dean
McInnes, William
McIntosh, Anne-Marie
McIntosh, Cassandra
McIntosh, Leslie
McIntosh, Peter
McIntyre, Lynne
McKay, Denis
McKay, Lynda
McKenzie, John
McKenzie, Melissa
McKinley, Greg
McKissack, Dale
McLaughlin, Kate
McLaughlin, Matthew
McLean, David
McLean, Tiffany
McLennan, Brett

McLeod, Gregory
McLeod, Neil
McLeod, Rodney
McLeod, Steven
McMahon, Matthew
McMiles, Rodney
McMillan, Dea
McNee, Terry
McNeice, Daniel
McNeice, Michael
McNeill, William
McQuade, Phil
McRae, Peter
Micallef, Peter
Michie, Heather
Miller, Barrie
Miller, Christine
Miller, Gordon,
Miller, Iain
Miller, Melanie
Miller, Tim
Mills, Glenn
Milne, Les
Milne, Roy
Miner, Lee-Anne
Minter, Malcolm
Minturn, Peter
Mitchell, Andrew
Mitchell, Claire
Mitchell, Kirsten
Mitchell, Larry
Mitchell, Leanne
Mitchell, Stephen
Mitchell, Ted
Moar, Jill
Monk, David
Montague-Dufty, Rhette
Montesin, Lyle
Moon, Robert
Mooney, Greg
Moore, James
Moore, Peter
Moore, Russell
Moran, Leonie
Moras, Julie
Morley, Greg
Moroney, Geoff
Morton, Nigel
Moses, Jennifer
Mugridge, Barry
Muir, Keith
Mulheron, Mark
Mullavey, Marcia
Murphy, Brad
Murphy, Elaine
Murphy, Greg
Murray, Peter
Murray, William
Myles, Robert
Napthali, Ian
Nash, Peter
Nathan, Bradley
Neal, Daniel
Neilson, Bob
Neilson, Scott

Neilson, Steve
Nelson, David
Nelson, Gary
Nelson, Graeme
Neuhalls, Stephen
Newey, Kevin
Newman, Brian
Newmann, Robert
Newton, Greg
Nicholas, Kyle
Nicholson, Sue
Nicolls, Tara
Niven, David
Niven, Michelle
Noble, Ann
Noble, Robert
Nolan, Peter
Norman, Ross
Norris, Kevin
Norris, Mathew
Northbrook-Hine, Anthony
Norvill, Mick
Noyce, Les
O'Brien, Paul
O'Connor, Robert
O'Dell, Kevin
O'Donovan, Ann
O'Donovan, Elizabeth
O'Farrell, Luke
O'Keefe, Timothy
O'Laughlin, Peter
O'Neill, Bob
O'Neill, Colin
Oakley, Andrew
Odgers, Glenn
Oldfield, Roderick
Olsson, Elizabeth
Opdam, Jim
Opper, Steve
Orenda, Wendel
Owen, Grant
Owen, Lesley
Palazzi, Ken
Palmer, Robin
Parker, Ed
Parker, Marcus
Parks, Holly
Parmenter, Damien
Parsons, Brian
Parsons, Ken
Passmore, Jan
Paterson, Rob
Paton, Norm
Paton, Roger
Patterson, Leon
Patterson, Peter
Pavisic, Danny
Pearce, Steve
Pears, Gavin
Pearsall, Ken
Peart, Michael
Pearton, Gary
Peel, Terena
Pellicci, Anthony
Pendlebury, Craig

Penman, Chris
Pepperell, Roland
Perkins, Glenn
Perkins, Robert
Perry, Greg
Perry, Laurence
Perry, Troy
Peters-Smith, Nicole
Peters-Smith, Raymond
Peters-Smith, Susan
Philips, Daryl
Philips, Joe
Phillips, Eilen
Phoon, Nicholas
Piekus, Sarah
Pillidge, Jennifer
Pincus, Scott
Pines, Thirza
Pittman, Brett
Poidevin, Peter
Poile, Felicity
Poile, Gary
Pollard, Lisa
Pollock, Alan
Pollock, Brian
Pomery, Matt
Porte, Julie
Porter, Robert
Potter, Les
Prentice, Phillip
Preston, David
Preston, Gary
Preston, Jean
Price, Alyse
Pridmore, Denise
Pullin, Dale
Pullin, Jim
Pullin, Paul
Purcell, Karl
Purkis, Travis
Pye, Carlie
Quidley, Pettrina
Quinlan, Paul
Quinn, Judy
Quinn, Phillip
Quirk, Jim
Quirk, Koley
Radley, James
Ramsay, Allan
Ramsey, John
Ramsley, Stuart
Ratford, Ian
Rawson, Peter
Rayner-Sharpe, Edan
Reading, John
Reed, John
Rees, Col
Reid, Phil
Reid, Robert
Reiher, Graham
Relf, Damon
Renford, Robin
Reynolds, Michael
Rhodes, Jason
Rich, Peter

Richards, Leanne
Richards, Nick
Richardson, Kylie
Richardson, Nichole
Richardson, Pam
Riches, Kevin
Ridley, Jeff
Riedel, Graham
Riley, Len
Rimmer, Ian
Rimoldi, Peter
Ringstad, Marie
Ritchie, Francis
Ritchie, Lynn
Ritchie, Peter
Robbie, Luke
Roberson, Nole
Roberts, Bradford
Roberts, Keith
Roberts, Ken
Robertson, Alan
Robertson, Bob
Robertson, Jennifer
Robinson, Neil
Rocks, Justine
Roden, Thomas
Rogers, Malcolm
Ronan, Craig
Roots, Peter
Rosario, Keith
Rose, Chris
Rose, Ted
Rosenbaum, Mark
Roser, John
Rosier, William
Rovere, Michael
Rowan, Brett
Rowan, Haydn
Rowley, Scott
Rucska, Julius
Ruprecht, Colleen
Ruprecht, Kevin
Russ, Neil
Rutherford, Michelle
Rutledge, Kerry
Rutledge, Steven
Ryan, Michelle
Sanderson, Craig
Saunders, Dennis
Saunders, Narelle
Saunders, Tracy
Saunders, Wendy
Savage, Robert
Sawdy, Jane
Sawszak, Mark
Saxton, David
Saywell, Cheryl
Scalon, Flavio
Schirmer, Kelly
Schnepf, Jason
Schofield, David
Schultz, David
Schulz, Richard
Sciberras, Robin
Sclanders, Rhonda

Scott, Barry
Scott, Chris
Scott, Gary
Scott, Kim
Scott, Robert
Scriven, Graeme
Scriven, Jeffery
Seeto, Barry
Sellars, Mark
Semmens, Jon
Sesperez, Jorge
Seymour, Alison
Seymour, Jamie
Seymour, Norman
Seymour, Wayne
Sheehan, Alan
Shepherd, Ian
Shepherd, Kris
Shipley, Ann Marie
Shoebridge, Kate
Shoemark, Richard
Short, Warren
Shortland, Alan
Simmons, Craig
Simpson, Janet
Simpson, Mark
Simpson, Peter
Simpson, Ray
Sims, Rocklan
Skaines, Dianne
Skaines, Kath
Skinner, Jason
Skinner, Jody
Slater, Alan
Small, Robert
Smart, Steve
Smith, Bernie
Smith, Bill
Smith, Denene
Smith, Dianne
Smith, Hunter
Smith, Kevin
Smith, Lauren
Smith, Leigh
Smith, May
Smith, Norman
Smith, Robert
Smith, Russell
Smith, Steve
Smithers, Paul
Smylie, Peter
Snape, Greg
Snape, Sandra
Southwell, Malcolm
Speed, Bill
Speer, Kenneth
Speer, Terence
Spencer, Craig
Spiteri, Michael
St Quintin, Jennifer
Stabb, Michael
Stafford, Camilla
Starr, Wal
Stathakis, Nicholas
Steel, Greg

Steele, Greg
Stefanowicz, Jay
Steines, Robert
Stenhouse, Jennifer
Stephens, Rev. Len
Sterry, Paul
Stevenson, James
Still, Dianne
Stinson, Paul
Stokes, Robert
Stone, Nevenka
Stone, Rick
Storrier, Paul
Strachan, Adam
Straker, Graham
Stratford, William
Stratten, Richard
Streeter, Warren
Stuart-Smith, David
Stubbs, Michael
Suhr, Lee
Suhr, Sharon
Sulter, Chris
Sulway, Michael
Summers, Ray
Summerson, Corey
Summerson, James
Sutton, Ellen
Sutton, John
Swan, Wayne (Peter)
Symons, Joshua
Tahmindjis, George
Tate, Jenni
Taylor, David
Taylor, Greg
Taylor, Jason
Teirnan, Mark
Tekis, Sonia
Terlich, John
Thom, Stuart
Thomas, Ian
Thomas, Liz
Thomas, Michael
Thomas, Susan
Thompson, David
Thompson, Jack
Thompson, Larry
Thompson, Michelle
Thompson, Rachael
Thompson, Sallyann
Thomson, Belinda
Thomson, Glen
Thorn Richard
Thorn, Matthew
Thornton, Matthew
Thoroughgood, Mark
Thrupp, Kevin
Timmins, David
Tinkler, Evan
Toby, Keith
Todd, Rob
Todeschini, Greg
Tomek, Graham
Tomlinson, Dave
Townsend, Russell

Tozer, David
Tozer, Montez
Trevanion, Clare
Trevarthen, Janet
Triefus, Ben
Troiani, Liz
Troy, Brian
Tumulty, Connor
Turnbull, Allan
Turner, Doug
Turner, Shane Tyacke, Jean
Umback, Lois
Underwood, Timothy
Unzeitig, Anna
Urrea, Eliseo
Vale, Andrew
Van Der Linden, Fernando
Van Dyke, Mick
Van Hilst, Adam
Van-Bergen, Jerry
Vanderburg, Graham
Vanderburg, Leah
Varley, Bruce
Varnai, Jodie
Vaughan, Paul
Verdich, Sandra
Verheyden, Marcel
Verrent, Keith
Viapiana, Hector
Viapiana, Trish
Vidler, Karen
Vigurs, Dianne
Vincent, Gail
Vincent, Steve
Wademan, Barry
Walker, Jane
Walker, Rodney
Wall, Stan
Wallace, Matthew
Walters, Cherie
Wardrop, Stephen
Warman, James
Watts, Nicole
Wearne, Bruce
Webb, Neville
Webber, Richard
Weber, Jeffery
Webster, Bill
Webster, Mark
Weeding, Michael
Weekley, Paul
Weigh, Ivan
Wells, Don
Wells, Richard
Wells, Tammy
West, Trevor
Whalan, Rod
Wheatley, Phyllis
Whiley, David
White, Allan
White, Brian
White, Dennis
White, Neil
White, Peter
Whitfield, Dale

Whitfield, David
Wickham, Robert
Wiggins, Peter
Wilcox, Gary
Wilke, Gerry
Wilkinson, Greg
Willard, Rex
William, Barry
Williams, Allan
Williams, Michael
Williamson, Keith
Willis, Ian
Wilson, Brad
Wilson, Leokadia
Wilson, Matthew
Wilson, Michelle
Wilson, Tim
Wilton, Jack
Wing, Alan
Wingrove, Darren
Wiskich, Dianna
Wiskich, John
Witchard, Courtney
Witt, Peter
Woods, Frederick
Woods, Nathan
Woonton, Christopher
Wooster, Eddie
Worral, John
Worthy, Daniel
Wray, Daryl
Wray, Michael
Wrenford, Barry
Wright, Greg
Wright, Jim
Wright, Michael
Wright, Ray
Wyatt, Donna
Wyatt, Geoff
Wyithe, Kevin
Wynne, John
Yates, Barbara
Young, John
Zakulis, Eric
Zammit, Joe
Zikan, Rhonda
Zorbas, Sam
Zotos, Alex

Volunteer Rescue Association

Alexander, Neil
Allen, Bruce
Allen, Ken
Archer, Donna
Armstrong, Jim
Aspinall, David
Attard, Mick
Avery, Brenton
Belfoort, Wayne
Barber, Kevin
Battam, Tony
Black, Harvey
Bolitho, Wayne

Broad, Rick
Brown, Tony
Brumby, Michael
Buchtmann, Gerard
Buchtmann, John
Buchtmann, Mark
Camps, Maurie
Cheeseman, Mark
Chant, Rick
Clarke, Les
Colella, Mike
Collins, Geoff
Conner, Brian
Davey, Dave
Dawson, Kevin
Dawson, Rodney
Dedman, Andrew
Dickey, Dave
Driscoll, Brian
Edwards, Scott
Evenden, Matt
Fall, Alan
Farnsworth, Nathan
Fitzsimmons, Melanie
Fiumara, Pat
Fleming, Bruce
Fletcher, Trevor
Follett, Wes
Franklin, Dean
French, Anthony
Gain, Mark
Gibbons, Ken
Gibbs, Grant
Gill, David
Gill, Ray
Goldberg-Otten, Christine
Greenwood, Tony
Hams, Ian
Harris, Margot
Hatherly, Bryan
Hawkey, Trevor
Hawkins, Rob
Hegedus, Robert
Hehir, Glen
Herring, Dave
Hill, Grant
Hopkirk, Dianne
Howells, Martin
Hughes, Mike
Humphries, Alison
Humphries, James
Hutchinson, Barry
Ingal, Bill
Jackson, James
Jeffery, Clyde
Johansen, Joe
Johnston, John
Jones, David
Jones, Ed
Kesby, David
Kidman, John
King, Mike
Kisling, Mark
Lingen, Wal
Lloyd, Scott

Lockton, Brent
Loffi, Daniel
Lopez, Rocio
Lowe, Warren
Lyons, Richard
Makin, Peter
Manning, Graham
Marega, Shirley
Martin, James
Matts, Terry
McBean, Tom
McCullum, Phillip
McLean, Paul
McMurdo, Graeme
McNamara, Paul
McQuillan, Brian
Milgate, Trevor
Miller, Greg
Millington, Ben
Moore, Mary
Murphy, Paul
O'Brien, Garry
O'Connell, Peter
O'Leary, Terry
Ordonez, Fred
Otton, Warwick
Pain, Andrew
Pankhurst, Ken
Perry, Colin
Petts, Danny
Poidevin, Gordon
Pullin, Christine
Pullin, Peter
Quigg, Iain
Quigly, John
Rae, Jim
Reilly, Kevin
Renton, Warwick
Reynolds, Jack
Richardson, Wayne
Robinson, Nic
Roderick, Rod
Rooke, John
Scanes, Debra
Shalliker, Ken
Slabberkoorn, Adrian
Stark, Allen
Steenson, Robin
Stockwell, Andrew
Strachan, Ken
Summerell, Bruce
Sydney, Joe
Temple, Maria
Thewis, Ngaire
Thomas, Catherine
Thompson, Peter
Van de Weyer, Eric
Vasey, Paul
Vaughan, Brian
Venner, Ross
Walker, Paul
Warmington, Andrew
Watkins, Harry
Whale, Gwen
Whiting, Phil

Williamson, Bill
Wiseman, Alex
Woods, John
Woods, Mark
Wright, Peter
Yaynes, Yvonne

Emergency Service ACT

Apps, Craig
Backhouse, Warren
Barrett, Chris
Bekema, Claire
Block, Mindah
Blumenfield, Wally
Bodsworth, Jim
Bolitho, Andrea
Bonelli, Caroline
Boswell, Jonathon
Brandis, Leanne
Brandis, Ron
Bromham, Margie
Brown, Neil
Burkevics, Bren
Carew, Anthony
Cassidy, Carolyn
Castle, Mike
Clune, Kerrin
Davidson, Chris
Donaldson, Andrew
Dorman, Nicholle
Edson, Kate
Farthing, Kim
Galagher, Lorraine
Goodison, Tim
Goodwin, Janine
Graham, Tony
Grey, Jeff
Haines, Trevor
Hansen, Bill
Humphrey, Sy
Hunt, Clyde
Ingram, Dave
Jarrett, Wendy
Johnston, Thomas
Kelly, Scott
Koennecke, Eric
Langshaw, Brad
Lenihan, Brian
Lenihan, Chris
Leonivic, Victor
McRae, Rick
Megalli, Karen
Mikulandra, Matt
Milne, Gladdie
Niemic, Stan
O'Hara, Brendan
O'Neill, Greg
Parsons, Kaye
Pawle, Chris
Pickering, Mark
Raffaele, Vivian
Slattery, Andrew
Smith, Darren

Smooker, Nicole
Squires, Angela
Thomas, Leanne
Tunbridge, Dave
Walsh, Ron
Wiggins, Robert

Salvation Army

Aceto, Jeff
Ambachtscheer, Barbara
Archtander, Lis
Atherton, George
Barnes, Cheryl
Boate, Ken
Bromley, Garry
Bromley, Wendy
Brown, Rhonda
Burke, Barry
Burridge, Dennis
Campbell, Mark
Campbell, Tony
Carpenter, Bruce
Chapman, Bob
Cook, Heather
Cooper, Harry
Craig, Alex
Craig, Ruth
De Tomasso, Tony
Dyer, Graeme
Field, John
Glasson, Paul
Godkin, David
Goff, Allison
Goff, Glenys
Goff, John
Handcock, Donnick
Hannon, Cliff
Hills, Denis
Hynd, Jim
Ivers, Earle
Jarrott, John
Jones, Kevin
Lattouf, Oz
Laws, Peter
Lehane, Lee
Longbottom, Graham
Longbottom, James
Madsen, Janet
McDonald, Nigel
McDonald, Sandy
Midgelow, Chris
Midgelow, Craig
Newling, Keith
Newman, Keith
O'Connell, Tony
O'Connor, Peter
Ober, Graeme
Pleffer, Phillip
Plumecke, M.
Pollock, Shaun
Reed, Col
Reeves, Adrian
Roading, Joshua
Roading, Michael

Roberts, Colin
Rudland, Kevin
Shaw, Allan
Shaw, Edith
Shaw, Leanne
Shaw, Nichole
Smith, Bruce
Smith, Kathy
Strong, Bob
Sweeting, Bill
Thomas, Geoff
Thompson, Allan
Whitelaw, Christine
Wigram, Simon
Williams, Shirley
Woodland, Bernice
Woodland, Don

HMAS Albatross

Bouchaert, Tony
Burton, Martin
Coxell, Paul
Edmistone, Greg
Hancock, Steve
Hayes, Ian
Konzen, Mick
Lea, Paul
Loring, Mick

Mines Rescue Board of NSW

Douglas, Grant
Stroemer, Colin

Snowy Mountains Hydro-electric Authority

Andrews, Brian
Bennetts, Owen
Bennetts, Robert
Bonomini, Paul
Byrne, Stan
Byrne, Terry
Campbell, Paul
Cass, Adrian
Chitty, Greg
Clarke, Geoff
Clear, Murray
Crocker, Jim
Dole, Geoff
Duggan, Stan
Evans, Phil
Farmer, Brian
Foley, Tim
Freeman, Mick
Gammell, Clint
Goldspink, Grant
Goldspink, Mark
Graham, Ian
Grimstead, Jack
Harris, Allan
Healy, Greg

Hill, Bill
Hope, Bob
Hume, Dennis
Jackson, Murray
Johnson, Ron
Lister, Ken
Lodge, Dick
Mankowsky, Lucretia
McIntyre, Bill
Mortlock, Leigh
Mugridge, Barry
Mugridge, Garry
Newton, Ian
O'Donnell, Doug
Paton, Tim
Perret, Clive
Podlesak, Ludwig
Robinson, Adam
Robinson, Joe
Robson, Paul
Roche, Ron
Simmons, Keith
Smedley, Doug
Stevenson, Jim
Sutton, Tony
Swinny, Mick
Taylor, Chris
Thompson, Holly
Tobin, Greg
Werrel, Chris
Whitfield, David
Woods, Arthur

**National Parks &
Wildlife Service**

Aitkenhead, Alex
Aliendi, Bill
Allen, Dave
Allen, Will
Allnutt, Jamie
Babbage, Jack
Baker, Andrew
Barwick, Robert

Baynham, Wayne
Beattie, Bill
Bell, Peter
Bottom, Karen
Bourke, Paul
Bowden, Megan
Buggerman, Pat
Burnett, Bill
Byrne, Debbie
Cadden, Chris
Cameron, Elizabeth
Carroll, Rita
Carter, Ross
Cassidy, Mike
Cawthorn, Janice
Cholson, Dave
Collins, Dave
Corkhill, Jim
Costello, Dave
Criss, Dale
Cruse, John
Curtis, Barrie
Dagger, Bill
Darlington, Dave
Darlington, Pat
Dawson, Allan
Dickmann, Craig
Dorman, Robyn
Dunn, John
Emery, Heather
Enders, Graeme
Endt, Nicki
Everest, Nigel
Field, Karen
Fischer, Steve
Gant-Thompson, Nancy
Gaskell, David
Gillies, Cate
Green, Ken
Grinbergs, Alistair
Halstead, Nathan
Hardey, Paul
Hargreaves, Max
Harrigan, Andrew

Hayward, Brad
Healey, Richard
Healy, Des
Heath, Bernie
Hendrych, Paul
Hill, Steve
Hillman, Daryl
Hipwell, Dave
Horsell, Amy
Howard, Alistair
Hulbert, John
Hunter, Steve
Hunter, Sue
Ilsley, Joanne
Ingarfield, Joanne
Ingram, Vivienne
Ivill, Mick
Johnson, Stuart
Johnston, Gary
Jones, Steven
Judson, Vic
Kelly, Penny
Kerry, Doug
Killen, Jim
Kilpatrick, Ray
Kite, John
Knutson, Russell
Lawrence, Dave
Leary, Cameron
Lynch, John
Mackay, Geoff
Mackay, Janet
Mallard, Peter
Malone, Greg
Manns, Phillip
Manson, Gregor
Mathews, Warren
McGufficke, Raelene
Mossfield, Steve
Mylan, Peter
Nichols, Dan
O'Brien, Pam
Oliver, Lorraine
Parmenter, Terry

Pearce, Dave
Pendergast, Terry
Petersohn, Uwe
Platts, Owen
Polkington, Dave
Reedy, Ken
Ryan, Marg
Schirmer, Kevin
Schofield, Murray
Shankster, Jan
Shannon, Rory
Sharp, Prasan
Simpson, Alan
Smith, Craig
Smith, Helen
Solomon, Fiona
Spoelder, Penny
Stockden, Amanda
Stocks, Vince
Stubbs, Tony
Sturgess, Gary
Sullivan, Tony
Sutton, John
Tozer, Graeme
Treble, Rob
Tritton, Peter
Vardy, Glenn
Walsh, Damien
Walsh, Karen
Walton, Ray
Warren-Gash, David
Watts, Paul
White, Matt
White, Peter
Windle, Claire
Windle, Peter
Woods, Dave
Worthington, Dick
Wren, Liz
Wright, Genevieve
Young, Mike